P
323
.T28
Copy 1

Taggart, Jean E.

Motorboat, yacht,
or canoe--you name
it

7.50

DATE		
	~~REFERENCE~~	

© THE BAKER & TAYLOR CO.

Motorboat, Yacht or Canoe
—You Name It

from names in the mythology of 20 different countries; women of the Bible; the Saints; navigational stars; the constellations; the zodiac; famous clippers; American Western words; foreign phrases, and names from the Hawaiian, American Indian, Spanish, African, French, Japanese, Eskimo, Chinook, Latin and Arabic vocabularies

by
JEAN E. TAGGART

The Scarecrow Press, Inc.
Metuchen, N. J.   1974

Library of Congress Cataloging in Publication Data

Taggart, Jean E
    Motorboat, yacht, or canoe--you name it.

    Includes bibliographical references.
    1. Names. 2. Boat names. I. Title.
P323.T28   929   73-14607
ISBN 0-8108-0661-4

Copyright 1974 by Jean E. Taggart

I must go down to the seas again; to the lonely sea and
  the sky,
And all I ask is a tall ship and a star to steer her by,
And the wheel's kick and the wind's song and the white
  sail's shaking,
And a grey mist on the sea's face and a grey dawn
  breaking.

John Masefield
"Sea Fever"
first stanza

CONTENTS

PREFACE

Since minute details of any ship--specifications,
dimensions, tonnage, armament statistics, comparative naval
strength, pictures, illustrations, performance, conversions,
refittings, disposals, a full history--could not be included in
this book, the reader might like to know where he can find
detailed accounts. The following are excellent sources:

EMMONS, Lieut. George F., compiler.
    The Navy of the U.S. from the Commencement 1775
to 1853; With a Brief History of Each Vessel's Service and Fate as it appears on record ... to which
is added a list of private armed vessels ... a list
of revenue and coast survey vessels and principal
ocean steamers. Washington, D.C.: Printed by
Gideon & Co., 1850.

JANE, Fred T., ed.
    Jane's All the World's Fighting Ships (1898).
Reprinted New York: Arco Publishing Co., 1969.
    Pictures, dimensions, tonnages, armament details
in English, French, Italian, German. Published continuously to the present day with the last volume as
follows:

BLACKMAN, Raymond V.B., ed.
    Jane's Fighting Ships. New York: McGraw-Hill,
1972.
    Vessels in service, ships to be laid down, build-
ing, conversions, refitting, disposals, specifications
and performance dates, illustrations, photographs,
recognizable silhouettes.

NAVAL HISTORY DIVISION, U.S. Department of the Navy.
    Dictionary of American Naval Fighting Ships. 5
volumes (v. 6, in preparation, contains letters Q-Z).

Undoubtedly there are many "enshrined ships" and
"ship 'firsts' " not among the lists in this book, because of

the unavailability of sources that might have been useful, and the human element entering into a research project.

In Hawaiian, "the" is "ke" and "ka" in the singular, "na" in the plural. "Ke" is used for words beginning with "k." "Ka" precedes all the rest. "He" means the article "a" ("an"). The mid-word apostrophe found in many Hawaiian words is the glottal stop, a momentary and complete break in sound. A consonant represents the beginning of a separately pronounced syllable. Each syllable ends in a vowel. The main accent of a word falls usually on the next-to-last syllable.

Naming Boats

This book is intended as a springboard for your imagination in seeking an original and individual name for your boat. The history and trends in boat naming might be of interest and help in finding a modern name. The first American vessels from 1789 were given short, simple names of women, as Eliza and Jane. As a boat was considered feminine, masculine names were thought unlucky, nor was there a wide variety of men's names.

In pioneer days boats were built for a particular need. Fishing and trading vessels were given names for the use they were intended, as Sower, Reaper, Thrasher, Harvester. The Dutch emigrants brought their livestock to America in vessels called Cow, Horse, Pig, although one romantic Dutchman called his vessel, Bachelor's Delight. General names were also used in the early days--there were Success, Hope, Neptune. In ancient times the Greeks used the names of goddesses; Romans used gods or goddesses.

In the 1700's Roman Catholics gave the names of saints to their vessels. They picked the saint under whose protection they were placed. There was the Santa Maria, Jesus, Holy Ghost. Ships were named after historical characters, admirals and kings. If you believed in the divinity of kings you used Caesar.

In America, in the heyday of the clippers (1843-1868), names of ships stood for speed, grace, the beauty of their clouds of canvas. Birds and animals known for speed gave names to these ships--Gazelle, Swallow, Wild Pigeon, Flying Fish. Winds and windstorms were used--White Squall, Zephyr, Storm King, Trade Wind, Typhoon, Whistling Wind.

Such words as Wings, Pride, Empress, Star, Eagle, Golden, Sovereign, Monarch appeared in the name, as well as Sovereign of the Seas, Empress of China, Golden West. Names were selected for their emotional appeal, and for euphony.

Modern boat owners use humorous names. Some of these are: My Bank Account, Bonus, Tax-Refund, Patty's Pay Check, My New Sugar, Who Cares? A yacht owner in California named his craft Wicked Wahine; the Hawaiian word means "Woman." There are words and phrases in the name list useful for single or combined names. "Chinese Moon" is an Hawaiian Festival. It would be suitable for a boat used for pleasure. Combine words as "flying fiery dart," using the English and Hawaiian words: Flying Pilikiku; or, "Cocky Red Rooster": Cocky Moa Kane. Is your boat large? Then why not Bilkskiinir, Thor's palace in Asgaard which had 450 rooms. The craft owner likes his own individual name. The entire book is designed for such use, as well as for gaining information about ships.

The author is grateful to the marine museums and public librarians who provided information for the book.

Jean E. Taggart
Long Beach, California
December, 1972

I. NAMES

SYMBOLS (Abbreviations)

Mythology

MA	Assyrian	MI	Indian
MAZ	Aztec	MJ	Japanese
MB	Babylonian	MN	North
MC	Chinese	MNI	Nicaragua
MCE	Celtic	MP	Persian
MEG	Egyptian	MPH	Phoenician
MES	Eskimo	MR	Roman
MF	Finnish	MSL	Slavonic
MG	Greek	MT	Teutonic
MH	Hindu	MZ	Zuni

Words

A	African	G	German
Ar	Arabian	Gr	Greek
C	Chinese	H	Hawaiian
CH	Chinook	J	Japanese
E	English	L	Latin
ES	Eskimo	S	Spanish
F	French	W	Western (American)

In this Part I, "Names," the arrangement is by general English word, in capital letters, along the left side of the page, matched by equivalents or similar words in various other languages (and their literal meanings), with symbol for language of origin (see above).

ABODE: Home
   Casa Grande (a large house where all hands met for fun; the owner's home used in the Southwest). W
   Cocklebur Outfit (small ranch). W
   Dugout (ranch in the early days). W
   Duku (the "pure abode" where men's fates were determined by Marduk, chief of deities). MA
   Glads-heim (hall in which 12 deities occupied seats). MN
   Hacienda (ranch; western home). W

Ivavold (plain where the gods dwell). MN
Kāhimoe (a place to sleep). H
Kashima (sanctuary of the god Kami-Nari). MJ
Kalevala (house of a hero; also the national epic of
Finland). MF
K'un Lun Mountain (dwelling place of the immortals;
the ruler is Queen-Mother Wang). MC
Lotus (home of the sun during the night; the divine
lotus). ME
Mana-Heim, or Midgard (home of man). MN
Noatun (where Njörör lived; the anchorage). MN
Niblung (where King Giuki and Queen Grimhild lived).
MN
Olympus (abode of the gods). MG
Orcus (kingdom of the king of the underworld). MG
Seeland (place of Gefjon; made fast in the sea). MN

ADORABLE ONE
Kahikahiwa. H

ADVENTUROUS
Ventura. S

AFRAID-OF-HER-SHADOW
(A feminine Yuki Indian name). I

AGED
Kaikapū. H

AIR, Divinity of
Ilma. MF

AIR PLANT
Hina Hina (the silversword, heliotrope, geraniums,
artemisia; Hawaiian plants). H
Kuana'oa (the official flower of Lana'i; a yellow and
orange airplant which grows wild on barren soil).
H

ALAS FOR US!
Auwē. H

ALL HIGHEST
Hypsistos. MP

ALL RIGHT!
Pololei. H

ALLIED
    Dahkota (joined together; Omaha Indian name).   I

ALLIGATOR
    ⁹Alikekoa, or Aligetoa.   H

ALMOND
    Almendra.   S

ALONE
    A Solas.   S

AMAZONS, The
    Hippolyta (the queen of the Amazons).   MG
    Penthesilia (a later queen of the Amazons, who were
        a tribe of war-like women, said to be the daughters
        of Ares, god of battle).   MG

AMBER
    Amarillo.   S

AMERICAN HORSE
    (a chief of the Sioux Indians).   I

ANCESTOR
    Hellen (mythical ancestor of the Greeks).   MG

ANCHOR
    Heleuma.   H

ANCIENT CITY of Refuge
    Honaunau (an ancient city, Kona Coast, Hawaii).   H

ANGER
    Nemesis (personification of righteous anger of the
        gods).   MG

ANGLER, The
    El Pescador de Caña.   S

ANTELOPE
    Kwahari (an Indian name, a chief of the Comanches).
        I

ANY PLACE in the Sea Where a Footing May Be Obtained.
    Kai Hele Ku.   H

APOTHECARY
Ka'awili lā'au.   H

APPLE
Manzana.   S
Ōhi'a-ʻai (mountain apple).   H

AQUARIUM
Hale hō'ike'ike i'a.   H

ARBITRATOR
Kau Waena.   H

ARCHER
Eurytus (his son gave his father's famous bow to
     Odysseus).   MG
I (the husband of Heng-O, the moon goddess).   MC
Sagittarius (the constellation [a centaur drawing a
     bow], and ninth sign of the Zodiac).   MG

ARCHITECT
Kaha ki'i Hale.   H

ARGONAUTS
Jason was the leader of the Argonauts.   The others
     were: Admetus, Castor and Pollux (twins),
     Hercules, Hylas, Lynceus, Meleager, Orpheus,
     Peleus, Pirithous, Telamon, and Theseus, who
     went in search of the Golden Fleece.   MG

ASTROLOGER
Kahuna Kilokilo.   H

ATTENDANT
Abishad (she ministered to King David in his old
     age).   B
Fulla, or Volla (she was a sister of Frigga; her
     hair was bound by a golden circlet, representing
     the binding of the sheaf, the golden grain).   MN
Gefjon (she married a giant and was also in Frigga's
     palace).   MN

AUTHOR
Saint Gertrude, the Great (Gerthude of Helfta, who
     wrote a book about her life and revelations, is
     the same).   F

Kākau Mo'olelo. H
Teresa, Saint (she wrote books; founded convents). S

AUTUMN
La'a'ula. H

BABY or Child
Keiki. H

BAMBOO, Reed.
'Ohe. H

BAMBOO PIPES
Kā'eke'eke (these vary in length, are played by
several musicians at a time). H

BANK NOTE, The
El Billete de Banco. S

BANTAM
Moa-ha'a. H

BANYAN TREE
(has a dense network of branches and leaves and is
found in the Hawaiian Islands). H

BARBER
Kahi'umi'umi. H

BARNACLE
Unaoa. H

BARRACUDA, The
Kākū. H

BATTLE MAIDENS, The
Valkyries (they carried the slain heroes to Valhalla.
Freya and Skuld supposed to lead them to the
fray. Alvit, Gaundul, Geir-Skaugul, Gunnr, Hildr,
Skaugul, Svanhvit). MN

BATTLEGROUND
Kahua Ho'oūka. H

BEADS, Glass
    Hua aniani.   H

BEAR, The
    Otava (the great bear).   MF
    Owasse (a chief of the Menominee Indian tribe).   I

BEARER OF PEACE
    Ailina.   H
    Irene.   E

BEAUTIFUL
    Ashaki.   A
    Belle.   F
    Hermosa.   S
    Luhiehu.   H
    Pelenakeka.   H
    Sapphira (wife of Ananias).   B
    U'i.   H

BEAUTIFUL ANN
    Annabella.   E
    Anabela.   H

BEAUTIFUL WOMAN
    Wahine U'i.   H

BEAUTY, The
    Kanani.   H
    Uluwehi (growing into beauty).   H

BEAVER
    Siula (a clan of the Mohave Indian tribe).   I
    Wahas (a clan of the Yuma Indian tribe).   I

BEAVER HAT
    Pāpale Pīwa.   H

BED
    Dream Sack.   W
    Feldberg (on this summit Brynhild slept, awaited the
        coming of her liberator, Siegfried).   MT
    Prairie Feathers.   W
    Shakedown (a cowboy's bed).   W
    Star Pitch (sleep in the open).   W

BED ROLL
Velvet Couch (slang of the American cowboy for bed roll). W

BEE, The
Mehiläinen. MF
Nalo-meli Noho Hale (the drone bee). H
Meli (honey bee). H
Nalo-meli (honey bee). H

BEE, Queen
Nalo-meli Mō'ī Wahine. H

BEE, Worker
Nalo-meli Pa'ahana. H

BEEHIVE
Pahu Meli. H
Pūnana Meli. H

BEETLE, The
Anomala. H

BELONGING TO A WARRIOR
Njeri. A

BELOVED, The
Amata. S
Amy. E
Ema. H
Kealoha. H

BELT, Wide
Sichakutvaratiha (chief of the Karok Indian tribe). I

BERRIES, Red
Ohelo (red berries). H
Mokihana (lemon-green berries; the official flower of Kauai). H

BEWARE OF THE DOG
Cuidado con el perro. S

BIG
Gorda. S
Big Fly (character in a Navajo Indian myth). I
Big Foot (a Sioux Indian chief). I

BIG HOUSE
Case Grande. S

BIG ISLAND
The big island is called Hawaii. H

BIG MEDICINE
Big Medicine (a chief of the Crow Indians). I

BIG RUMBLING BELLY
Kwohitoauq (the name for a chief of the Sioux Indians).
I

BIG TREE
Adoeete (a chief of the Kiowa Indian tribe). I

BIG WHITE, The
Shahaka (an Indian chief of the Mandan tribe). I

BIRD
Āe'o (Hawaiian Stilt bird). H
'Ai Mikana (Linnet; California house bird). H
'Akapane (a bird). H
'A La E (mud hen; black wading bird). H
'Alae-kea (pond bird). H
'Alaiaha (a gray bird). H
'Amaui (Hawaiian thrush). H
'Auku'u (black crowned night heron). H
Ekelo (Mynah bird). H
'Elepaio (fly catcher). H
'Iwa (man-of-war bird). H
'Iwi (a bird with red feathers). H
Kipoka Kipoda (Bittern). H
Kīwa'a (mythical bird). H
Koa'e (white tailed tropic bird; the cliff to where the
    Koa'e dwells is Pali Ha'Akoa'E). H
Kutkilya (screetch owl; a clan name of the Mohave In-
    dians). I
Maha (small bird; name of the clan of the Mohave tribe
    of Indians). I
Mano (yellow bird with soft feathers; rare). H
Nene (Hawaiian goose; state bird of Hawaii). H
Niao (a bird). C
Nūkea (a white bird). H
Pájaro (bird). S
Palila (a bird). H
Pueo (Hawaiian owl). H

Ula (red tailed tropic bird). H
'Ūlili (wandering tatler bird). H

BIRD FEATHER
Hulumanu (plumage). H

BIRD OF PARADISE
Apus (white flowers with blue and orange flowers with
blue). H

BIRD RATTLER
Bird Rattler (an Indian chief of the Blackfeet Indians).
I

BIRDS
Stymphalides (they shot their feathers like arrows).
MG

BLACK
'Ele'ele (or dark). H

BLACK CATERPILLAR
Kala-wela. H

BLACK CORAL
This grows in the waters of Hawaii; used for jewelry.
H

BLACK DOG
Makatachinga (an Indian chief). I

BLACK HAWK
Ma-Ka-Tai-Me-She-Kia-Kiak (black sparrow hawk; the
chief of the Sac-Fox Indians). I

BLACK HOOF
Catahecassa (a Shawnee Indian chief). I

BLACK KETTLE
Black Kettle (a Cheyenne chief). I

BLACK LIZARD
Mo'o-'Alā. H

BLACK SPRING
Hah-kwah-niti. H

BLESSED, The
    Beatrice. E
    Beatriz. S
    Bran (enormous in size and strength; possessed of
        supernatural powers). MCE
    Ngozi. A
    Pōmaika'ī (also "good fortune"). H

BLOOM
    Thalia (one of the three graces). MG

BLOOMING
    'Apelila. H
    Aperila. S
    April. E

BLOSSOM, The
    Pu'ā (blossom). H
    Kapua (the blossom).

BLOWN HELTER-SKELTER
    Laumāewa. H
    Pūlunaluna. H

BLUE
    Azul. S
    Po-lū. H

BLUE ROOSTER
    A yacht that crossed the Atlantic, owned by the Dutch,
        in Colonial days. E

BLUE WHIRLWIND
    The name given a Sioux Indian squaw. I

BOAT
    Ch'uan (canoe, boat, junk). C
    Waapa. H

BOOKWORM
    Mū-'ai-puke. H

BOOM OF DISTANT SURF
    Laolao. H

BOWLEGS
    Boleck (chief of the Seminole Indians). I

Box   12   I

BOX
Un Cajón. S

BRAND
Flying Brand (one which has the letters of figures with wings). W
Lazy Brand (letter lies on one side). W
Map of Mexico (for the intricate brand of the Mexicans). W
Skillet of Snakes (intricate Mexican brand). W
Tumbling Brand (the brand leans obliquely). W

BRANDING IRON
Hao Kuni. H

BREEZE
Aheahe (light breeze). H
'Ēlau (wisp of a breeze). H
Ke Ahe Makani (gently wafting breeze). H
Kēhau. H
Kui-Lehua (a breeze blowing from the northwest of Niihau). H
Moani-'ala (a land breeze). H

BRIDGE
Bifrost (bridge of the gods). MN
Giallar (bridge over which the spirits rode). MN
Metucs (name of a Powhatan Indian chief). I
Sinvat (the bridge on which people must cross to reach the other world). MP

BRIGHT
A'ia'i (bright as moonlight; clear). H
Konane (bright as moonlight, also a game like checkers). H
La'ela'e (bright as the morning sun). H

BRIGHT FAME
Lopeka. H
Roberta. E

BRIGHT ONE
Al Na'ir. Ar

BRIGHTNESS OF HEAVEN
Alohilani. H

BROKEN ARM
Bro-Cas-Sie (a warrior of the Cree Indian tribe). I

BROKEN ARROWS
Cazazhita (chief of the Dakota Indian tribe). I

BROTHERS
Mo-Li (four brothers who guard the door of the Buddhist Temple). MC

BROWN
Castaño. S
Haeleele (brown, or blackish). H
Hauliuli. H
Hāuli (blackish, or dark). H

BUBBLING SPRING
Māpuna. H

BUILDER
Helena (a saint who built places of worship in the Holy Land and in cities where she lived). G

BUILDING
Lou (or tower). C

BULL
Taurus (a constellation, and sign of the Zodiac). MG
El Toro. S

BULL BEAR
Bull Bear (a Cheyenne Indian chief). I

BULLHEAD
Bullhead (a Sioux police chief). I

BUTTERFLY
Freya's Hen. MN
Hatimnin (chief of the Karok Indian tribe). I
Mariposa. S
Pūlelehu'a. H

BUY AT YOUR OWN RISK
Caveat Emptor. L

BUZZARD
Altair. I

Yungavish (name of the Luiseño tribe).   I

CABIN
    Camarote.   S
    Ke'ena (nook, cranny, room, office).   H

CAKE
    Meaono.   H

CALIFORNIA
    Kaleponi.   H

CALM
    La'i (contented; quiet).   H

CAMEO
    Kāmelo.   H

CANARY
    El Canario.   S
    Kenele.   H

CANDY
    Kanakē.   H
    T'ang (sugar; candy).   C

CANOE
    Kialoa (racing canoe).   H
    Kiapā (swift canoe).   H
    Ko'okāhi (carries one person).   H
    Kupe'ulu (a canoe of one piece).   H
    Mutuma (a Chimariko Indian name).   I
    Umiak (a single paddle canoe).   ES
    Wa'akau (a head fisherman's canoe).   H
    Waaloa (a long canoe).   H

CAP
    Tarnkappe (the tiny red cap that dwarfs wear to make
        them invisible).   MN

CAPTAIN
    Kapena.   H

CARDS
    Worthless as a Four-Card Flush (that is, something

beyond repair). W

CARNATION
    El Clavel. S
    Ponimō'ī. H

CAROL
    Kālola. H

CARPENTER
    Lu Pan. C

CASTAWAY
    Ōlulo. H

CAT
    El Gato. S
    'Oau. H
    Pōpoki. H

CATCH-THE-BEAR
    Catch the Bear (name of a Sioux Indian warrior). I

CATERPILLAR, The
    'Anuhe. H
    Peelua. H

CATHEDRAL
    Our Lady of Peace (cathedral in Honolulu). H

CAVE
    Avernus (the cave through which Aeneas entered Hades). MG

CELEBRATION
    Cronia (harvest fete of Cronus, god of the sky). MG

CELESTIAL WORLD
    Anshar. MA

CHAINED WOMAN
    Andromeda (a constellation). MG

CHAMELEON
    Kameleona. H

CHANT
    Oli (a chant; exultation). H
    Mele Inoa (chant and dance in honor of a chief). H

CHARIOT DRIVER
   Iolaus (driver for Heracles).   MG

CHARIOTEER
   Aku Thor.   MN
   Auriga (a constellation).   L

CHARM
   Abra.   Eg

CHERISH WITH PRIDE
   Ha'aheo (proud, haughty, prideful).   H

CHERUB
   Kelupa.   H

CHIEF
   Ali'i (highborn; ruler).   H
   Halāli'i (name of a fun loving chief).   H
   'Iele (person of distinction).   H
   Jason (was chief of the Argonauts).   MG
   Lani Ali'i (royal chief).   H
   T'ou (the first; chief).   C
   Wei-T'o (chief of 36 heavenly generals).   MC

CHIEF'S HOUSE
   Hale Ali'i (royal residence).   H

CHILD
   Kama.   H
   Thelma.   E

CHILDREN OF THE LARGE BEAKED BIRD
   Absarokee (this is what the Crow Indians call them-
      selves).   I

CHINAMAN'S HAT
   Chinaman's Hat (an island off shore Oahu that looks
      like a chinaman's hat).   H

CHINESE MOON
   Chinese Moon (a festival in Hawaii).   H

CHIROPRACTER
   Kauka Ha'Iha'i Iwi.   H

CIRCUMSTANCE
    Fortune's Wheel.   MC

CLAN, Indian
    Whistling Water (Crow clan).   I
    Shrichak, or U'u (clan name for the Diegueño Indians).
    I

CLICK BEETLE
    Kāne-Pa'ina.   H

CLIFF
    Pali Ha'Akoa'e (inaccessible cliff).   H
    Na Pali (the cliffs of Kauai, the Garden Isle).   H

CLIPPERS
    Carrier Pigeon (during the heyday of the clipper ship
        there were many colorful, romantic names given
        them.   This clipper was wrecked on the California
        coast on her first voyage).
    Electric Spark.
    Flying Cloud (one of the most admired and loved of
        American clipper ships.   Immortalized in Long-
        fellow's "Building of the Ship." Her figure-head
        was a white and gold angel blowing a trumpet.   It
        is said her crew was so fine that they worked like
        one man).
    Flying Fish (her figure-head was a replica in green
        and gold of a flying fish.   She raced the Swordfish
        around Cape Horn to San Francisco.   The Flying
        Fish came in eight days after the Swordfish.   Both
        were extreme clippers.   Flying Cloud was wrecked
        in the River Min, China).
    Hurricane (combined early and late theories produced
        in the fast ships).
    Morning Light (sold to the British and renamed Queen
        of the South).
    Nightingale (her maiden voyage was to Australia and
        the scene of the new South Wales gold discoveries.
        Her figure-head was a likeness of Jenny Lind whose
        first concert was at Castle Garden in September
        1850.   She was constructed in 1851).
    Phantom (during her lifetime this ship had the reputa-
        tion of being a very fast clipper).
    Sea Nymph (120 days out of New York she was wrecked
        in dense fog at Point Reyes, with a cargo of im-
        mense value).

Sea Witch (her figure-head had a bright gilded black
dragon on a black and shining hull. She established
records never since broken by ships of sail).
White Squall (an extreme clipper built for the China
trade).
Witchcraft (her figure-head was a crouching tiger.
There were superstitions predicting ill fortune,
but she had no more difficulties than other clippers).

CLOAK
'Ahu'ula (feather cloak, made of the feathers of the
rooster; a red feathered cloak). H
Holoku (mantle). H
Berserk (a bearskin cloak; one who wore it acquired
the strength of a bear). MN

CLOCK
Chung (clock or bell). C

CLOUD
Ao Lani (heavenly cloud). H
La Nube (cloud). S
Nānā Ao (cloud interpreter; observes omens). H
Owich (name of a Mohave Indian clan). I
Pi-Hsia-Yüan Chün (princess of the streaked clouds). C

CLOVER, Spanish
Ka-'Imi. H

CLOWN
Niki O Na 'Aka. H

COAT-HANGER, The
La Percha. S

COCK, The
El Gallo. S
Moa Kāne. H

COCOANUTS, The
Na Niu. H
Niu (the nut of the cocoanut tree). H

COFFEE-POT, The
La Cafetera. S

COIN
>   El Céntimo (a cent).   S
>   El Penique (a penny).   S

COLD
>   Frío.   S

COLLAPSE
>   Twilight of the Gods (or collapse of the universe).
>   MT

COME, ENJOY HOSPITALITY
>   E Kipa Mai.   H
>   Ho 'okipa (hospitality).   H
>   Kipa Hele (go visiting, from place to place).   H

COME HITHER
>   Icune.   ES

COME IN
>   Komo Mai (enter).   H

COMEDY
>   Sock (symbol of comedy; a light, thin-soled shoe once
>   worn by actors in Greek and Roman comedy).   MG

COMET
>   Hōkūwe'lowe'lo.   H

COMFORTABLE
>   'Olu (also "gentle").   H

COMPANION
>   Hoa.   H
>   Hoa Pili (close companion).   H
>   Kama Lua (two close companions).   H
>   Kōko'olua (companion; partner).   H
>   Pilialoha (beloved companionship).   H

CONQUERING BEAR
>   Conquering Bear (name of a Sioux Indian chief).   I

CONSTELLATIONS
>   Ariadne's Crown (constellation formed by the gift given
>   to Ariadne by Bacchus).   MG
>   Cassiopea.   MG
>   Hōkū'iwa (constellation of stars).   H

Kamāhana (the twins; Gemini). H
Kao-ea (presides over destiny of Hanalei, Kauai; a
    constellation). H
Maka'imo'imo (the Milky Way). H
Na-Hiku (the Big Dipper). H
Na-hōkū-pā (five stars form circle). H
Na-lālani-a-pili-lua. H
Northern Crown (the jewelled coronet of Ariadne). MG
Orion (the hunter). MG

COOK
    Cocinero (shortened to "Coosie" by the Westerner). S

COOK POT, The
    Taskyena (name of chief in Mohave Indian tribe). I

COOL HEIGHT CLIFF
    Nuuanu Pali (a dizzying escarpment of the Koolau
    Range). H

CORAL, Circular Ring
    Atoll (it grows upward from a sunken volcano island).
    H
    Ko'a Kohe (mushroom coral). H
    Puna Kea (white coral). H

CORMORANT
    Kakalakeke. H

CORRAL
    Pā. H

COUCH
    Hikie'e (large Hawaiian couch). H
    Pune'e (movable couch). H

COUGAR
    Koukā. H

COUNCIL OF CHIEFS
    'Aha'ula. H

COUNCILOR
    Nestor (a Grecian councilor in the Trojan War). MG

COUSINS
    Las Primas (female cousins). S

COWBOY
Pretty Cowboy (a fancy cowboy).   W
Paniolo (Hawaiian cowboy.   In the 1830's the demand
for beef led to the establishment of ranches and
then the Mexican and Spanish cowboys came to
Hawaii.   Their lasso was called Kaula'ili).   S

COYOTE
Hipa (a clan of the Cocopa Indians, as well as the
Mohave tribe).   I
Kaiote.   H
Segep (found in Indian mythology of the Yuroks).   I
Witah (fox or coyte; clan of the Kamia Indians).   I
Coyote, the Trickster (so called by the Comanche In-
dians).   I
Wahilyam (coyotes; a division of the Serrano Indians
of Southern California).   I

CRAB
'Alamichi (a small black crab; common).   H
Cancer (a constellation, and a sign of the Zodiac).
MG
El Cangrejo.   S
Tuttafcuk (name of a Virginian Indian).   I

CRADLE
Moe Luliluli.   H

CRAZY HORSE
Tashunke Witko (a chief in the tribe of the Oglala
Sioux Indians).   I

CREATION
Luonnotar (connected with the myth of creation and
is called Daughter of Nature).   MF

CREATOR
Brahma (the creator).   MI
Prajâpati (master of created things).   MI
Ptah (creator of the world).   MEG
Ra (creator of the world).   MEG
Thoth (creator of the world).   MEG

CREEPING MIST
Noe Kolo.   H

CREST OF THE WAVE
    Pū'o'aoka Nalu'alc. H

CRICKET
    'Unia. H

CROCODILE
    Sebek (a crocodile divinity). MEG

CROSSROADS
    Chimata-No-Kami (god of the crossroads). MJ

CROUCHING LION
    Crouching Lion (a rock formation in the mountain ridge
    in Oahu which resembles such a figure). H

CROUCHING TIGER
    Tecumseh (Shawnee Indian chief). I

CROWN
    Corona. S
    Kalauna. H
    Lei Ali'i (royal lei; diadem). H

CUBIC INCH, The
    La Pulgada Cúbica. S

CUPBEARER
    Ganymedes (the cupbearer of Zeus). MG
    Hebe (cupbearer of the gods). MG

CURLY BEAR
    Curly Bear (a chief in the Blackfeet Indian tribe). I

CYCLOPES, The
    Cyclopes (three divine metal workers, the sons of
        Uranus and Gaea; they were one-eyed and embodied
        the violence of the thunderstorm and the volcano).
        MG

CYPRESS, The
    Kupeleko. H

DAHLIA, The
    La Dalia (the flower). S

DAILY NEWSPAPER
Nūpepa-puka-lā. H

DANCE
Wovoka (the Ghost Dance known to the Indians from the Missouri River to the Rockies and beyond, began with a dream of the Indian Wovoka. It was a dance to give to people to show love of one another, goodness, never to fight, lie or steal. By dancing this dance all Indians would be saved. Wovoka was a Paiute). I

DANCING
Nâtarâja (king of dancing). MI

DARK
'Āhiwa (sombre, dusky). H
Kukuro (shady or dark; the clan name for the Diegueño Indians). I

DARK BLUE
Azul Oscuro. S

DARLING
Ipo (sweetheart or lover). H

DART, A
Asansck. ES

DAUGHTER
Abi (also Abijah, daughter of Zecharian). B
Ahlai (daughter of Sheshan). B
Anat (daughter of Báal. Daughter of the rain god and sister of the water god, she sprinkled the earth with dew. Also named Qadesh, as was the consort of the god of the west, Amurru). B
Amofens (an Indian maiden of the Powhatan Indian tribe). I
Antigone (daughter of Oedipus and Jocasta). MG
Athaliah (daughter of Jezebel and Ahab. The only ruling queen of Judah). B
Basmath (daughter of Solomon). B
Cozbi (a woman, princess, daughter of Zut, head of a chief house in Midian). B
Dinah (daughter of Leah and Jacob, meaning "vindicated"). B
Gerd (daughter of the frost giant, symbol of frozen

earth, melted by the sun). MN
Helen of Troy (daughter of Zeus and Leda. Eloped
with Paris and was the immediate cause of the
Trojan War). MG
Hervor (daughter of Angantyr, to whom belonged
Tyrfing, the sword which was buried with him.
She used the sword, after she cast magic spells over
his tomb, to make him rise and give it to her). MN
Ismene (daughter of Oedipus, king of Thebes). MG
Keikamahine. H
Marpessa (daughter of Evenus. She married one of
the Argonauts). MG
Noss (daughter of Freya). "delight." MN
Thrud (daughter of Thor). MN
Velamo (daughter of Ahto). MF
Vrindâ (daughter of a heavenly nymph). MI

DAUGHTERS
Danaids (the 50 daughters of Danaus, 49 of whom slew
their husbands, then were sent to Hades to pour
water into leaky jars). MG
Philomena (daughter of Pandion). MG
Procne (daughter of Pandion). MG
Kipu-Tyttö (goddess of illness and Loviatar, source of
all evil, were the daughters of the ruler of the
underworld, and were divinities of suffering). MF

DAWN
'Iao. H
Kaiao. H
Wanaao. H

DAWN LIGHT
Mali'o. H

DAY
T'ien (firmament; heaven; nature). MC

DAZZLING
Lino (shining, bright). H

DEER
Niu (clan of the Cocopa Indian tribe). I

DELICATE
Delilah (paid by the enemy to betray Samson). B

DEMON
  Ahriman (prince of demons). MP
  Kaimonio. H

DEN OF THE SHARK
  Lua Mano. H

DENTIST
  Jaw Cracker (dentist who travels over plains, to take
    care of cowboys' teeth). W

DESCENDANTS OF ROYALTY
  Pua-lani (descendant of a chief; heavenly flowers). H

DESERT
  Min (god of desert, lord of foreign lands, god of
    fertility, vegetation, protector of crops). ME

DESIRED
  Loika. H
  Lois (grandmother of Timothy). B

DESTINY
  Valkyries (the dispensers of destiny). MT

DESTROYER, The
  Siva (one of the three chief divinities). MI

DETERMINATION
  Hang and Rattle (stick to the finish). W

DEVOTION
  Saint Matilda (devout and courageous).
  Saint Susanna ('lily'; spread gospel).

DEXTEROUS
  No'eau (wise). H

DIAMOND
  Kaimana Hila (Diamond Head, extinct volcanic crater,
    Leahi on Oahu Island). H

DISAPPEARING BEACH
  White Sands (beach in Hawaii so called because of the
    heavy surf that washes sand away). H

DISCOVERER
'Imi A Loa. H

DISTINCTION
Damaris (woman of Athens, a woman of distinction).
B
Ilanohano (distinguished; honor; glory). H

DIVINATION
Daniel (versed in divination; daughter in astrology).
MPh

DIVINE
Michal (daughter of King Saul). B

DIVING BOARD, The
La Palanca. S

DIVINITY OF THE HOUSE
Domania or Domovikha (lived in the cellar of the
house while her husband, Domovoi, who was never seen, lived by the stove or threshold). MSL

DOCTOR
Kauka. H

DOCTORESS
Gula. MA

DOCTOR'S SACK
Doctor's Sack (name of a chief of the Mohave Indian
tribe). I

DOG, The
Garm (the terrible dog that howled furiously at the
border of the underworld). MT
Shonka (a chief of the Sioux Indian tribe). I

DOLPHIN
Mahimahi. H
Poseidon (Olympian ruler of the Sea Gods, who felt
that the dolphin was sacred). MG

DONALD DUCK
El Pato Pascual. S

DONKEY
'Ēkake. H

DON'T BOTHER
No se moleste. S

DOVE
Ehako (ring-necked, Hawaiian). H
Kuhukukū (turtle dove). H
La Paloma. S
Manu-nūnū. H
Sikuma (name of the clan of Yuma Indians). I

DOWNSTREAM SHARP
Pulekukwerek (in Yurok mythology). I

DRAGGING CANOE
Dragging Canoe (name of a Cherokee chief). I

DRAGON
Draco (a constellation). L
Fafnir (slain by Sigurd). MN
Kalekona. H
Ladon (guarded the golden apple tree). MG

DRAGONFLY
Pinao. H

DREAM NAME
Inoa Pō. H

DRIFT
Akauahelo (vagrant). H
Auhele (drift aimlessly). H
Kanaka 'Ae'a (wanderer). H
Lau Hala Lana (vagabound, drifter). H

DRIFTWOOD
Piha'ā. H

DRINK
Nepenthe (a magic drink that banished sorrow, given
by the Queen of Egypt to Helen of Troy after the
Trojan War). MG

DRIPPING WATER
Iniwach (a clan of the Karok Indians). I

DROOPING WITH AGE
    Kāluheu'a.   H

DRUID
    Keluika.   H

DRUM
    Ahqwohhooc (name of a Virginia Indian).   I

DRY, Barren
    Arida.   S

DRY BLACK OAK
    Mam-K'ima (the chief of the Katos, a tribe of the
        Huchnom Indians).   I

DUCK
    El Pato (the duck).   S
    Koloa (Hawaiian wild duck).   H
    Manu Kakā (tame duck).   H

DULL KNIFE
    Dull Knife (a Cheyenne Indian chief).   I

DUSTY FLAT
    Onp'Otilkei (a place name of the Yuki Indians).   I

DWARF
    Andvari (he had the power to turn himself into a fish
        and live in water).   MT
    Lit (slain by Thor).   MN
    Megwomets (a bearded dwarf who distributed vegetal
        abundance, carried acorns on his back--a myth
        of the Yurok Indian tribe).   I

DWELL
    Chu (live, dwell).   C
    Valaskialf (dwelling of Vali who was destined to survive
        the last battle, and the twilight of the gods, to
        reign with Vidar over the regenerated earth).   MN
    Wahi Pa'a (dwelling place).   H

EAGLE
    'Aeko (the eagle).   H
    'Aeko-kula (the golden eagle).   H

Aquila (constellation containing the bright star Altair).
S
El Aguila. S
Eagle (emblem of Zeus). MG

EAGLE OF DELIGHT
Hayne Hudj'Hini (wife of Shaumonekusse, of the Kiowa
Indian tribe). I

EAGLE RIBS
Pe Toh Pee Kiss (mystery man; medicine man; name
of a brave of the Blackfoot tribe of Indians). I

EAR OF CORN, The
Spica (the brightest star of Virgo, the virgin). L

EARTH
Bau (mother earth). MA
Ga-Tum-Dug. MA
Gê (the earth, sister of Uranus). MP
Gula. MA
Innini. MA
Jörd (daughter of Nott; also Erda). MN
Kish. MA
Ninkhursag. MA
Prithivi. MI
Ti (the ground, locality, peace). C
Ti-Kuan (agent of earth). MC

EARTH DIVINITY
Anunnaki (on earth and the underworld). MA

EAST
El Este. S
Hikina. H

EATING MAT
Papa 'Aina (also dining table). H

EBB
El Reflujo. S
Kai Emi. H

EEL
La Anguila. S
Puhi. H

EIGHT
      'Awalu. H
      Wa'lu. H
      Ocho. S

ELBOW
      Mirfak (elbow of the Pleiades; a second magnitude
          star). Ar

ELECTRIC VEHICLE
      Ka'a Uila. H

ELEVATED PLACE
      Ka'anu'a (sleeping place in a grass house). H

ELF LIGHT
      Will of the Wisp. MN

ELK'S HEAD
      Hah-Ha-Ra-Pah (a Sioux Indian chief name). I

ELYSIAN FIELDS
      Elysian Fields (the abode of the blessed in Hades;
          home of the blessed in after life). MG

EMBLEM
      Brisinga-Men (emblem of the stars; fruitfulness of the
          earth, a necklace of precious jewels longed for by
          Freya). MN
      Elde (emblem of the phosphorescence of the sea; noted
          for quickness; Aegir's servant). MN
      Gambantein (emblem of office, of the god Hermod).
          MN

EMERALD
      Pōkahu 'ōma'oma'o (a green stone). H
      Verde Esmeralda (emerald green). S

EMPEROR
      Kuan-Ti (god of war; governor and protector of the
          people; predicts the future). MC

EMPRESS
      T'ien Hou (empress of heaven). MC

ENCHANT
      Circe (enchantress encountered by Odysseus). MG

Encanto (enchantment). H
Medea (wife of Jason and an enchantress). MG

ENCLOSURE
    Corral. S

ENCORE
    Hana Hou. H

END
    Pau (finished). H

END OF THE RIVER
    Acamar (navigational star; part of the constellation
        Eridanus, the river). Ar

ENJOY IN COMFORT
    Nanea. H

ENJOY TODAY
    Carpe Diem. L

EVENING
    Aurora of the Evening. MSL
    Fitima (dusk). A

EVERYTHING IS ALL RIGHT
    No Pilikia. H

EXALTED ONE
    Ka-lani-ana-'ole plus name. H

EXPERT
    Akamai (wise, clever). H

EXPRESSES GRATITUDE
    Ālohaloha (expresses affection, compassion, friend-
        ship). H

EXTRAORDINARY THING
    Rara Avis (extraordinary person or thing). L

EYE OF THE DAY
    Makalika (flower--daisy). H
    Na'ena'e-Puakea (daisy; a large round flower with
        purple florets on each head). H
    Na'ena'e Ula (daisy; orange color). H
    La Margarita. S

FAIR
>Lōkālima (fair as a rose; Rosalie). H
>Lokelima (fair, pretty rose; Rosalind). H

FAIR HAVEN
>Honolulu. H

FAITH
>Clytie (water nymph who was turned into a sunflower
>for her faithfulness in watching Apollo as he
>travelled through the sky). MG
>Fidus Achates (faithful friend). L
>Sigyn (the faithful wife). MN
>Vör (faithful attendant to Frigga. She knew all that
>was to happen in the world). MN

FALCON
>Palekona. H
>Falcon Plumes (enable Freya to flit through the air
>like a bird). MN

FALLING EAGLE, or Vulture
>Vega (brightest star north of the celestial equator and
>third brightest in the sky). Ar

FAMOUS
>Famoso. S
>Kaulana (fame). H
>Loke (famous; Rose). H
>Ndunga (famous). A

FAR, Afar
>Lejos. S

FARMER
>Dogieman (a nester or small farmer). W
>Sunpecked Jay (a rural resident). W

FATE
>Ummei. J

FATES
>Atropos (cut the thread of life and is represented by
>the shears). MG
>Clotho (spun thread of life and is represented by the
>spindle). MG

Lachesis (twisted the thread of life and is represented
by the scroll, globe). MG
Norns (three sisters who lived near the fountain Urdar,
who weaved the web of fate and kept the sacred
tree Yggdrasil fresh and green. Their names
were Urd [past], Verdandi [present], Skuld [fu-
ture]). MN
Wyrd (goddess of fate, mother of the Norns). MN

FATHERLAND
'Āina Makua. H
'Āina Kūpona (land free from all rent and taxes). H

FAVORITE
Hiwahiwa (also 'precious'). H

FEARLESS
Verdandi (one of the Norns; active, young, looked
straight before her). MN
Wiwo'ole. H

FEAST
Luau (heavenly feast). H
Lugnasad (one of the feasts of the Celtic year). MCE

FEBRUARY
Pepeluali. H

FEEBLE ONE
Alphecca (brightest star of Corona Borealis, the
northern crown). Ar

FELICITY
Amitabha. MC

FELLOW
Ka'aka (person). H

FEMALE WARRIOR
Bellatrix (west of the belt of Orion; the hunter; in a
box). L

FERN
'Ākōlea (native fern). H
'Ēkaha (deep sea plant rarely seen). H
Haili-o-pua (native fern; small). H
Hihiawai (swamp fern). H

'Iwa'iwa (maiden hair fern). H
Kikawaiō (native fern). H
Neke (tropical fern). H

FERRIS WHEEL
Huila Pōniuniu. H
Ka'a Pōniuniu. H

FERRYBOAT
Wa'apā. H

FERRYMAN
Charon (ferryman over the river Styx). MG
Harbard ("grey beard"; Odin's disguise). MT
Nessus (a Centaur). MG

FESTIVAL
Lupercalia (festival in honor of Faunus, the Roman
Pan). MG
Mahahiki (festival of thanks for bountiful crops). H
Matronalia (festival in honor of Hera). MG
Narassus (festival in Hawaii in January). H
Panathenaia (festival held in honor of Athene at
Athens). MG

FICKLE
Lolelua (unstable; inconstant). H

FIDDLE
Pila (any musical instrument). H

FIERY DART
Brigida (mighty; strong). S
Bridget. CE
Pilikika. H

FIG TREE JOHN
Fig Tree John (lived near the Salton Sea; most famous
of the Cahuilla tribe of Indians). I

FILM-FAN
El Aficionado al Cine. S

FINE WEATHER
Buen Tiempo. S

FIRE
>   Chin-Cha-Pee (Assinneboin Indian chief; "the fire bug
>   that creeps"). I
>   Ka'a Kinai Ahi (fire engine). H
>   Ka'a Pauahi (fire engine). H
>   Ke Ahi O Kā-Maile (famous firebrands thrown over the
>   cliffs at Kā-Maile). H
>   Loki (he was both destructive and helpful). MN
>   Svarovich (god of fire). MSL

FIRST
>   Ask and Embla (two trees whom the gods decided to
>   make mortals. Odin gave them breath; Hoenir
>   gave a soul and reasoning; Lodur gave warmth and
>   the colors of life. From these came the entire
>   race of man). MT
>   Eve ("life"). B
>   Pandora (first woman; created in heaven. She brought
>   evil into the world). MG

FIRST BORN
>   Hiapo. H

FISH
>   'Aha-mele (yellow spotted needlefish). H
>   Āhole (a fish found in both fresh and salt water). H
>   Akule (scad fish). H
>   'Ama'Ama (mullet fish). H
>   'Anini (dwarf fish). H
>   A'u (swordfish, marlin, spearfish). H
>   Huwai (shellfish). H
>   I'a (marine animal). H
>   I'a-iki (little fish). H
>   'Iao (silversides; fish in shallow water). H
>   I'a-'ula-'ula Uli (carp). H
>   Kaha-uli (striped dark fish, small). H
>   Kamanu (sea salmon). H
>   La Carpa (the carp). S
>   Mahaha (sturgeon fish). H
>   Mahimahi (dolphin). H
>   Mālolo (flying fish). H
>   Nākea (fresh water fish). H
>   Nala (fish, kind of). H
>   'Ōlepe (oysters). H
>   'Ōpae (shrimp). H
>   Pāpa 'I (crab). H

Pisces (the fishes, a constellation and a sign of the
Zodiac). MG
Uhu (parrot fishes). H
'Ula 'Ula (red snapper). H
Wana (sea urchin). H
Yü (fish; rain). C

FISH-BONE, The
La Espina. S

FISH EATERS
Pagaits (name of a Paiute Indian). I

FISH SCALE
La Escama. S

FISHERMAN
Dictys (befriended Perseus and later made a king).
MG
El Pescador. S

FISHERMAN'S HUT
Pāpa 'I Lawai'a. H

FISHING BOAT, The
El Barco Pesquero. S

FISHING FESTIVAL
Hukilau. H

FIVE
Alima. H
Cinco. S

FLAGSHIP, The
El Buque Almirante. S

FLAT
Maitra (name of an Chimariko Indian; also means
"river bench"). I

FLAT BOAT
Lancha Plana. S

FLEDGLING
Pūnua. H

FLEET OF SHIPS
    'Au Moku. H

FLINT MAKER
    Taharatan (name of a Karok Indian). I

FLOAT
    'Ālewalewa (floating, buoyant). H
    Ālewa (floating like a cloud). H
    Pūlana (floating object). H

FLOWER
    Asphodel (flower that grows in Hades). MG
    Ayanna (beautiful flower). A
    Balderblom (little white flower that grows in the
        Scandinavian mountains). MN
    Hinahina (silvery gray geraniums; the official flower
        Kahoolawe). H
    Hua (flower; blossoms). H
    'Iima (chrome yellow, official flower, of Oahu). H
    Pua Kukui (candlenut; official flower of Molokai;
        creamy-white). H
    Lau'awa (pagoda; scarlet; the Pagoda flower, clusters
        of scarlet flowers). H
    Lehua (native flower sacred to the gods, to Pele,
        goddess; flower of island of Hawaii, red, salmon,
        yellow, pink, white hibiscus). H
    Lehua-Kahiki (clover). H
    Lok (official flower of Maui). H
    Mikilana (Chinese rice flower). H
    Moonvine (flower and vine of Hawaii). E
    Pua (flower). H
    Pua'ala (fragrant flower). H
    Pua Niu (coconut flower). H
    Pualani (heavenly flower). H
    Pupu (white flower of Niihau). H
    Torch Ginger (a brilliant red Hawaiian flower). H
    Viola (water of life; violet). E
    Waiola (water of life; Viola; violet). H

FLY, The
    Fei. C
    La Mosca (fishing fly). S
    Nalo (the common house fly). H
    Nalo-nahu (biting fly). H
    Nalo-pilau (bluebottle fly). H

FLYING CLAN
Dasvak (name of chief of Huron clan). I

FLYING CLOUDS
Paytakootha (a warrior of the Shawnee Indian tribe). I

FLYING EAGLE
Altair (flying vulture; star). Ar

FLYING PIGEON
Rant-Che-Wai-Me (a Kiowa Indian woman's name). I

FOAM
Jamul (place of the Diegueño Indians). I

FOG
Tucktodo (fog). ES

FOLLOWER
Aldebaran or Tauri (follower of the Pleiades, in Taurus, the bull group of stars). Ar; L

FOOD OF GODS
Ambrosia. MG

FOOT
Rigel (the left foot of Orion; brilliant bluish star in corner of a box surrounding the belt of Orion). Ar

FOOT OF THE CENTAUR
Kapua'i Akua. H
Rigel Kentaurus (first magnitude star near the Southern Cross). Ar

FOOTSTOOL
Ke'ehana Wāwae. H

FOR FUN
De Burla. S

FORBIDDEN ISLAND
Niihau (the forbidden island in the Hawaiian Islands). H

FORD OF THE COW, The
Bosphorus. MG

FOREIGNER TO ISLANDS
 Haole (white person, a stranger to Hawaiian Islands).
  H

FOREST
 Lin (forest or grove). C
 Mother of Metsola. MF
 Nahele (forest grove or wilderness). H

FORGET-ME-NOT
 El Nomeolvides. S

FORTRESS
 Pā Kaua. H

FORTUNE
 Ventura. S

FORWARD
 Adelante. S

FOUNDER
 Saint Bertha (founder of convent in France, the
  Convent of Blangy). G

FOUNTAIN
 Hvergelmir (fountain which spread the waters of 12
  rivers, near the tree Yggdrasil under which Odin's
  steed browsed). MT
 Mirmir (in which dwelt all wisdom). MT
 Quickborn (a magic fountain owned by Hilda). MN
 Urd (fountain of the Norns. From it they sprinkled
  the ash tree, Yggdrasil). MT

FOUR
 'Ahā. H
 Cuatro. S

FOUR BEARS
 Mah-To-Toh-Pa (a Mandan Indian name). I

FOUR CLAWS
 Four Claws (a Sioux Indian name). I

FOUR O'CLOCK, The
 Nani-ahiahi (herb; red-yellow; white; striped. Opens
  in the late afternoon). H

FOUR WATERS, The
     Na Wai'ehā. H

FOUR WOLVES
     Chah-Ee-Chopes (Crow Indian chief). I

FOX
     Chaparral Fox (a sly tricky one). W
     Kewewish (clan name of the Luiseña Indians). I
     El Zorro. S

FRAGRANT
     Anuhea (cool and fragrant like a mountain breeze; soft
          fragrance as of the upland forests; sweetness;
          coolness). H
     Kō-Ba-Shi-I (fragrant). J
     Māpu (a rising fragrance; wafted). H
     Onaona (inviting, attractive fragrance, soft and sweet).
          H

FREE
     Aditi (free from bonds; one of the tryad, Mitra and
          Varuna; the sky, the air, all gods; the past and
          future; good leader). MI
     Makana (present; prize; reward). H

FREIGHT CONVEYANCE
     Ka'a Hali Ukana. H

FRESH
     Chloe. E
     Moani-'ala (fresh sweetness brought by the wind). H
     Phyllis. E
     Piliki. H
     Versch (fresh water river). D

FRIDAY
     Pō'alima. H

FRIEND
     Aikāne. H
     Kaupili (beloved friend). H
     Molokai (friendly island; one of the Hawaiian Islands).
          H
     P'eng (companion). C

FRUIT
    Java Plum. E
    Poha (small, yellow, like a cherry). H
    Lotus (fruit of the lotus brings enchantment, forgetful-
        ness). MG

FULL GROWN LAMB
    Hamal (brightest star of the constellation Aries, the
        ram). Ar

GADABOUT
    Kamapuka. H

GALE
    Kaila (Gale [Gail], a girl's name). H
    Kelawini (a wind). H
    El Temporal (a gale). S

GARDEN
    Garden of the Gods (a wilderness of ravines, buttes,
        red dirt, green grass). H
    Hesperides (garden where the golden apples grew,
        guarded by Hesperides). MG
    Un Jardin. S
    Yüan (a garden; orchard; teahouse). C

GARDENIA
    Nānū. H

GARLAND
    Lei of Stars (necklace or garland of stars). H
    Leilani (garland of heaven; royal child). H

GATE
    Gate of Horn (through this gate come the true dreams,
        from the cave of Hypnos, the god of sleep). MG
    Gate of Ivory (the deceitful gate of dreams). MG

GATHERING
    'Ākoakoa (assembled). H
    Ho'olaule'a (large party gathered for a celebration).
        H
    Keopulani (queen; gathering of the clouds). H
    Oahu (the gathering place; "an island"). H

Wees-Kon-San ("Gathering of the Waters": an Indian chief of the Chippewa tribe). I

GAZELLE
Dorcas (a woman of good deeds). B
Kapika (Tabitha). H
Tabitha. B

GENERAL
Heng-Ha-Erth-Chiang (sniffing general and puffing general are found as door gods on or in Buddhist Temples; Sniffer: his mouth is shut; Puffer: his mouth is open). C
Kenelala. H

GENII
Gudiri-Mumi (mother of thunder). MF
Korka-Murt (man of the house, or spirit of the house). MF
Muzem-Mumi (earth mother). MF
Shundi-Mumi (mother of the sun). MF

GENTLE
Lāhela (gentle, innocent; Rachel). H
Rachel. E
Raquel (gentle innocence). S
Sala. A

GERONIMO
Goyathlay ("one who yawns"; Geronimo is known to the Indians as Goyathlay, to the whites as Geronimo; an Apache Indian chief). I

GHOST
Lā'pū (ghost, apparition, haunted). H

GIANTESS
Bestla (daughter of Ymir). MT
Fiorgyn (mother of Frigga and Jörd). MN
Grid (Odin fell in love with her). MN
Hyrrokin (put her shoulder to the stern of Balder's ship, Ringhorn, and shoved it out into the water). MN
Skadi (personification of cold mountain). MN

GIFT
Dora ("gift of God"). G

Kola. H
Makana (gift; prize). H
Makana Aloha (gift of friendship). H

GILDED
    El Dorado ("gilded or gold one"). S
    Jeunesse Doree ("gilded youth"). F

GINGER
    'Awapuhi (wild ginger). H
    'Awapuhi-Melemele (yellow ginger). H
    'Awapuhi-'ula'ula (red ginger). H

GIRAFFE
    Kilape. H

GIRL
    Georgia ("girl of the fields"). H
    Kamali'i Wāhine (girls; a group). H
    Keokia ("Georgia"). H

GLOBE
    Poepoe (to gather in a circle). H

GO
    Hele Aku (go away). H
    Hele Me Ka Hau'oli (go with joy). H
    Hele Pēlā (go away! get out!). H
    Ku A Hele! (go!). H

GOAT
    Capricornus (a constellation and a sign of the Zodiac; also Capricorn, "goat-horned"). MG
    Heidrun (a goat that browsed in the branches of the ash tree). MT
    Kao Keiki (young goat). H

GOD
    Achelous (river god with whom Heracles wrestled to win Deianira). MG
    Aegir (god of the deep sea). MN
    Aeolus (god of the winds). MG
    Ahto or Ahti (chief water god, who lived in a cliff). MF
    Akua (god, goddess, ghost, devil). H
    Akua Pahulu (god of nightmares who carried persons to distant places in their sleep). H

Alpheus (river god). MG
Anu (sky god who reigned over the heavens, the
    supreme god). MA
Asopus (river god). MG
Aulanerk (god who causes waves). MES
Bishamonten (god of happiness and war). MJ
Cephisus (river god; father of Narcissus). MG
Ciaga (water god). MNI
Fukurokuju (god of wisdom). MJ
Glaucus (sea god). MG
Hermes ("the hastener"; god of wind; Roman: Mercury).
    MG
Hermod ("the valiant in combat"; messenger of the
    gods; rapid motion). MN
Icelus (god of dreams). MG
Kane (god of light and life). MH
Kawa-No-Kami (god of Kawa River). MJ
Khons (god of moon, called the navigator; also:
    Khensu). ME
Ku (major god; wife was Hina). H
Kukailimoku (war god of Kamehameha). H
Kunado (god of the place not to be visited). MJ
Kura-Okami (rain god who dwells in valleys; also:
    snow flake god). MJ
Lei-Kung (god of thunder). MC
Lono (ancient Hawaiian god of peace). H
Melicertes (sea god; Melicertes was a mortal who
    became a sea god, Palaemon). MG
Mimir (god of the primeval ocean). MN
Minato-No-Kami (mouth of the river god). MJ
Morpheus (god of dreams). MG
Naka-Yama-Tsu-Mi (god of the mountain slopes). MJ
Neptune (god of the sea; Greek is Poseidon). MR
Nereus (personification of the calm aspect of the sea;
    sea god). MG
Njord (god of the wind). MN
Oceanus (lord of the ocean that encircles the earth).
    MG
O-Wata-Tsu-Mi (greatest sea god, also called old man
    of the tide, Shio-Zuchi). MJ
O-Yama-Tsu-Mi (chief god and lord of the mountains).
    MJ
Palaemon (sea god. He had been Melicertes, spirit
    of which became patron of sailors. Protected
    seafarers). MG
Peneus (river god). MG
Phantastus (god of dreams). MG

Phorcys (sea god). MG
Pontus (deep sea god). MG
Portunus (god of the harbors). MR
Shigi-Yama-Tsu-Mi (god of the mountain foot). MJ
Shina-Tsu-Hiko (god of wind). MJ
Stribog (god of winds). MSL
Susanoo (ruled the plain of the seas). MJ
T'Ak-Shan (god of the mountain who helps look after
     mankind). MC
Take-Mikazuchi (god of thunder; god of rolling thunder
     is Kami-Nari). MJ
Tatsuta-Hiko (wind god; his wife: Tatsuta-Hime;
     goddess of wind). MJ
Terah or Etrah (god of the moon). MPH
Tezcatlipoca (god of the night; god of the wind). MAZ
Thaumas (sea god). MG
Thor (Thrud-Vang or Thrud-Heim was the realm of
     Thor, god of thunder and lightning. He is called
     Old Thor in Norway. He wore a crown on the
     point of which was a glittering star or a burning
     flame). MN
Tonatiuh (sun god). MAZ
Tsuki-Yomi (god of the moon). MJ
Vanas, the (sea and wind gods). MN
Varpulis (god of wind and thunder). MSL
Xiuhtecutli (god of fire). MAZ
Xochipilli (god of merriment and dancing). MAZ
Yaso-Maga-Tsu-Bi (god who puts things right). MJ
Zephyr (the sky god; the warm gentle west wind;
     Boreas was the stormy north wind). MG

GOD IS MY OATH
Bessie. E
Laika ("Eliza"). H
Pakake ("Bessie"). H

GOD-DAUGHTER
La Ahijada. S

GODDESS
Aegina (daughter of the river god). MG
Akua Wahine (a goddess). H
Amaterasu (goddess of the sun). MJ
Amphitrite (goddess of the sea). MG
Anta (goddess of arms with shield). MEG
Anuket (goddess of the river). MEG

Aphrodite (also Venus [Roman]) (goddess of love and
beauty; "dove and seagull"; born from the sea).
(Also Anadyomene, "she who came out of the
sea, " Astarte [Phoenician], and Pelagia). MG
Arianrod (in the constellation Corona Borealis). MCE
Artemis (goddess of the moon and hunt. Twin sister
of Apollo. First moon goddess was Phoebe,
grandmother of Artemis. Symbols are silver
chariot, silver bow and arrows). MG
Asherat of the Sea (mother of 70 gods). MPH
Astarte (goddess of beauty). MPH
Athene (also Pallas Athene, Minerva [Roman]) (goddess
of wisdom, household arts; symbols: owl, olive,
Gorgon's head). MG
Aurora (goddess of the dawn. She opens the gates of
heaven for the chariot of the sun). MR
Ba'alat (chief goddess in Phoenician Mythology). MPH
Bast (the goddess of pleasure; the cat goddess. One
of the great divinities. Her other names are:
Pekhet, Beni Hasan, Speos Artemidos. MEG
Bau (goddess of earth: daughter of Anu). MA
Benzaiten (goddess of love and happiness). MJ
Brechta (goddess of spring. Also called White Lady.
Dutch called her Vrou-Elde, and the Milky Way is
known to the Dutch as Vrou-Elden-Straat). MN
Brigid, Saint ("bride"; called a triple goddess of
plenty--learning, culture, skills). MCE
Charybdis (goddess of the sea who lived under a stone
on the straits. The water she spewed made a
whirlpool which mariners feared). MG
Chloris (goddess of flowers and spring; the Roman
is Flora). MG
Coyolxauhqui (goddess of the moon). MAZ
Danu (goddess of plenty). MCE
Devana (goddess of the hunt). MSL
Devi (goddess of the Hindus). MH
Fortuna (goddess of fortune). MR
Freyja (goddess of beauty and love. She rode in a
chariot pulled by white cats). MN
Frigga (goddess of the clouds. Queen of the gods.
She wore snow-white or dark garments. Patroness
of the housewife). MN
Furies (these were Alecto, Tisiphone, Megaera--three
sisters, goddesses of vengeance). MG
Gefjon (goddess of fertility; called "the river"). MT
Gorgons (the sea goddesses who lived in a cave, far
at sea. Medusa was the mortal one, Euryale and

Stheno could not die.
Graces, the (goddess of charm in nature and humanity:
    Aglaia, "brilliance, splendor"; Euphrosyne, "joy,
    mirth"; Thalia, "bloom"--three sisters). MG
Gullveig (a sorceress goddess). MT
Halcyone (she was changed into a bird). MG
Harpies (sea goddesses; Podarge and Celaeno). MG
Hathor (sky goddess). MEG
Hebe (goddess of youth; daughter of Zeus). MG
Hecate (goddess of the dark of the moon; of witch-
    craft). MG
Hestia (goddess of fire and family hearth; the Roman
    is Vesta). MG
Hiiaka (sisters of Pele and legendary goddesses; there
    were 12). H
Hina (a goddess). H
Hulda or Frau Holle (goddess of the weather. When
    snowflakes fell, she was shaking her bed; when
    it rained, she was washing her clothes; the white
    clouds were her linen put out to dry. Long
    strips of grey clouds meant she was weaving.
    She was diligent). MN
Hypermnestra (one of the 50 Danaides and the one who
    did not murder her husband on her wedding night).
    MG
Idum (goddess and keeper of apples that kept the gods
    young). MN
Idun (goddess of immortal youth). MN
Ino (goddess of the sea). MG
Iris (goddess of the rainbow; a fleet footed messenger
    of Hera (Juno) whose name was "rainbow, " and
    whose path through the clouds was marked by the
    many colored mantle of colors as she sped on her
    way). MG
Isis (goddess of protection; Aset is Egyptian). MG
Istar (chief Babylonian goddess). MB
Laka (goddess of the hula). H
Lea (goddess of canoe builders; "star"). H
Leucothea (a Theban princess leaped into the sea and
    became a sea goddess; she is protector of sea-
    farers). MG
Maan-Eno (goddess of fertility; wife of the god of
    thunder, Ukko). MF
Maat (goddess of truth and justice). MEG
Matuta or Mater Matuta (goddess of sea travel and
    the dawn). MR

Morrigan (goddess who appeared in battle in disguises; battle goddess). MCE
Naiads (water nymphs who dwelt in the streams and springs). MG
Nephthys (mistress of the palace). MEG
Nereid (one of the 50 daughters of the King of the sea, Nereus; goddesses and sea nymphs). MG
Nike (goddess of victory). MG
Nina (goddess of the deep). MB
Nut (goddess of the sky, the heavens). MEG
Pele (goddess of fire whose home was once the extinct volcano, Diamond Head). H
Podarge ("fleet foot"; had the body, wings, and claws of a bird, face of girl; sea goddess. See Harpies). MG
Poli'ahu (goddess of storm; goddess of now, said to live on Mauna-Kea, Hawaii). H
Ran (goddess of the sea; she lurked near dangerous rocks, enticed mariners). MN
Renpet (goddess of springtime and youth). MEG
Saranyu (goddess of the clouds). MI
Sarasvatî (goddess of music, wisdom and knowledge; might have been a goddess of the water earlier). MI
Sati or Satet (guardian goddess of the cataracts). MEG
Scylla (a sea goddess). MG
Sedna (goddess of the sea and sea animals). MES
Sengen-Sama (goddess who lives on the peak of the volcano Fujiyama). MJ
Seshat (goddess of writing, history; "mistress of the house of books"). MEG
Sif (goddess of household; the goldenhaired). MN
Sirens (the goddesses of the sea; they are Parthenope, Ligeia, Leucosta). MG
Sri (goddess of beauty). MH
Tailtiu (mother goddess). MCE
Tsukiyomi (goddess of the moon; gave the kingdom of night). MJ
Tyche (goddess of chance). MG
Urania (goddess of astronomy). MG
Ushas (dawn goddess). MI

GODS

Men-Shen (the door gods found on the outer doors of Chinese houses. One has a red or black face, the other white. They keep away evil spirits. They are Ch'in Shu-Pao and Yu-Ch Ih Ching-Te). MC

GOLD NUGGET
    Pu'upu'u Kula. H

GOLDEN
    De Oro (the golden). S

GOOD
    Agatha ("good"). G
    Agueda ("good, kind"). S
    Akaka ("Agatha"). H
    Maika'i ("beautiful, good to look at"). H
    Vohu-Mano ("spirit of good"). MP

GOOD LUCK
    Buenaventura ("good fortune"). S
    Pōmaik'i ("prosperous"). H
    Pōmhika'i ("good luck"). H

GOOD VIEW
    Buena Vista. S

GOOD BYE
    Adiós. S

GOOSE, The
    El Ganso. S

GOPHER, The
    Kopahela. H

GORILLA, The
    Kolila. H

GRACE
    Ane ("Anna"). H
    Aneka ("Anna"). H
    Anita ("little Ann"). S
    Anna (first woman to acclaim Christ). B

GRACIOUS GIFT
    Juana. S
    Wanika (Juanita). H

GRANDDAUGHTER
    La Nieta. S

GRANNY
    Kūkū. H

GRASSHOPPER
    'Ūhini. H

GRAY
    'Ahiehie (silvery, faded gray). H
    Gris. S
    Ma'oha (grayish). H
    Ualehu (ash gray). H

GREAT CHIEF
    Hongs-Kay-De (chief of Mandan Indians). I

GREAT MEDICINE
    Mah Hossah Leash Kit. I

GREAT SPRING
    Mishawum (name of an Indian). I

GREAT WALKER
    Moanahonga (great chief of the Iowa Indians). I

GREEN
    Mama'o (green, light). H
    Ma'o. H
    'Ōma'oma'o. H
    Verde. S

GREETING
    Aloha (greetings, farewell, welcome). H
    Aloha Kakou! (greetings everybody). H
    Saludos. S

GREY EAGLE
    Grey Eagle (a Sioux Indian chief). I

GRIZZLY BEAR
    Caleb or Cale (trappers name for the bear in the
       Rocky Mountains). B
    Yosemite (a place of the Miwok tribe of Indians). I

GUARDIAN
    Alberich (a dwarf; guardian of the treasure of the
       Nibelung king). MT
    'Aumakua (a spirit guardian). H

Cerberus (guardian dog to the entrance of Hades). MG
Daemon (spirit of a person; guardian). MG
Fylgie (guardian spirit assigned to the human being,
    attending him throughout life in the form of a hu-
    man being or an animal). MN
Gunlod (guardian of inspiration). MN
Heimdall (guardian of the rainbow; white-clad, she
    watched it day and night. Also: Heim-Dellinger,
    "herald of the day"; mostly known as "god of
    heaven," "warder of the rainbow," "of the fruitful
    rains and dews"). MN
Hesperides (guardian of the golden apples; they were
    three beautiful nymphs). MG
Iolana ("Yolanda"). H
Kahu ("keeper"; "one with a pet"). H
Kia'i'kai (sea guard). H
Kia'i'kino (bodyguard). H
Kia'i Ma Ka Lae (guardian of the cape). H
Pholus (guarded the wine of the centaurs). MG
Shedu (guardian spirit that acted as a good genii). MA
Winifred ("guard"). GR
Winipeleke ("Winifred"). H
Yolanda ("guard"). E

GUEST HOUSE
La Casa de Huéspedes. S
La Fonda. S
Hale Kipa (lodging house; inn; guest house). H

GUIDE
Kekako'i (Pele's guide on forest trails). H

GUITAR
'Ukulele (miniature guitar; leaping flea; musical instru-
    ment). H

GULL
Coihgwus (a Virginia Indian tribal name). I

HAMMOCK
'Ahamaka (a hammock in general). H
Maka'aha. H

HANDLE-COMES-OFF
Handle-Comes-Off (Yuki Indian chief). I

HANGING LAMP
>   Hale Ipukukui (lighthouse). H
>   Ipukukui (hanging lamp). H
>   Ipukukui Hele Pō (lantern). H

HAPPY
>   Fu-Hsing (god of happiness). MC
>   Hau'oli Mahiki Hou (Happy New Year). H
>   Mag Mell (the field of happiness). MCE
>   Runako (happiness; feminine name). A
>   Shou-Hsing (god of long life). MC

HARE, The
>   La Liebre. S

HARMONICA, The
>   Pilapuhipuhi. H

HAT
>   Mao (hat; cap). C
>   Pahu Pāpale (hat box). H
>   Petasus (the winged cap of Hermes). MG

HAWK
>   Gavilán. S
>   'Io (sacred hawk of Hawaiian legend). H

HE WHO GOES ALONE
>   Yuki Taikomor (this creator made men and earth). MI

HEAD OF THE DRAGON
>   Eltanin (brightest star in the constellation Draco, the
>   dragon). Ar

HEAD OF THE SERPENT CHARMER
>   Rasalhaque (forms triangle with Altair and Vega). Ar

HEADMAN
>   Tye-Yea. CH

HEART'S DESIRE
>   Makakēhau. H

HEAVEN
>   Ahulani (heavenly shrine). H
>   Gimlé (high heaven). MN
>   'Iulani (highest point of heaven). H

Kaiulani (exalted place; princess of the peacocks). H
Kanoe Lani (heavenly mist; mist is the sign of the gods
     travelling). H
Mauna Lani (heavenly mountain). H
Na Lani (the heavens). H
Oka Lani (of the heavens). H
Pililani (close to heaven). H
Pua-Lani (heavenly flowers). H
Pukalani (heaven's door). H

HELPER
     Joan, Saint (followed the disciples, found a place for
          them to sleep, food to eat). F
     Ran (helped Aegir rule the sea). MN

HERE LIES ...
     Alibamo ("here we rest"; Muscogee Indian name). I
     Hic Jacet. L

HERO
     Adapa (he was given the wisdom and prudence, but not
          immortality). MA
     Cú Chulainn (Celtic hero figure). MCE
     Etana. MA
     Gilgamesh (most famous of Assyrian heroes; a king of
          the land of Sumer, partly imaginary and partly
          fact). MA
     Kā'e'a'e'a (hero expert). H
     Väinämöinen (chief hero of the Kalevala, the national
          epic of Finland). MF

HERON, The
     'Auku'u (night heron, black crowned). H

HIGH
     Hai-lo-keaka (high low jack and the game). H
     Ikū Lani (highest officer; president). H
     Kahakea (high; inaccessible). H

HILL
     Adchu (an Algongquin Indian name). I
     Chananagi (a Creek Indian name). I
     Matta ("great" hill). I
     Shan (hill or mountain). C
     Wachuset (Indian name). I

HOLDER
Atlas (holder of heaven). MG

HOLIDAY
Lā Maka Kanaka (holiday; festive days). H

HOLY
Oleka ("Olga"). H

HONEYCOMB
Waihona Meli. H

HONEY-SUCKLE, The
La Madreselva. S

HOPE
Absit Omen ("hope this is no bad luck"). L
Esperanza. S
Mana'olana (hope; confidence). H

HORIZON
'Alihilani (horizon). H
El Horizonte (the horizon). S

HORNET
Kopena (hornet; wasp; scorpion). H
Nalo-'aki (hornet; gnat). H

HORSE
Pegasus (symbol of poetic inspiration; the winged
horse). MG

HORSESHOE
Kapua'ihao. H
La Herradura. S

HOURS, The
Horae (they stand at the cloud gate of Olympus through
which the gods pass when they descend to earth;
they regulate days and seasons). MG

HOUSE
Fang (house; room). C
Hale 'ilio (dog house). L
Hale Ipukukui (lighthouse). H
Hale Lana (house that floats). H

Hale Lanalana (house built on a double canoe; as for
    chiefs). H
Halele'a (house of joy). H
Ka'a Hale (trailer). H
Ka Mua O Ka Hale ("the first house"). H

HOW BEAUTIFUL!
!Que Hermosa! S

HUNT
Atalanta (huntress). MG
Callisto (huntress; a nymph; she was changed into the
    Great Bear, her son into the Little Bear). MG
Canis Venatici (the hunting dogs; a constellation). L
El Cazador (the hunter). S
La Trompa De Caza (the hunting horn). S
Ninurta (the hunter). MA
Orion (the hunter, who became a constellation, was
    the son of the sea god, Poseidon). MG

HURRY
Wikiwiki (hurry, hurry; be quick). H

HYACINTH, The
El Jacinto. S

ICE
Nootaikok (spirit of icebergs). MES
Vasud (personification of the icy wind). MN

ILLUSTRIOUS
Kalea ("Claire"). H

IMMORTAL
Phoenix (the immortal bird of great beauty fabled to
    live 500 years in the Arabian wilderness, to burn,
    rise from the ashes into youth, live through another
    cycle of years). L

IN A CLASS BY ITSELF
Sui Generis. L

INCOMPARABLE
Ka-Lani-Ana-'Ole (incomparably exalted one). H

INDEPENDENT
      Kūha'o. H

INDISPENSIBLE
      Sine Qua Non. L

INDUSTRIOUS
      Emalia ("Emily"). H
      Emele ("Emily"). H
      Emilia ("Emily"). S
      Kapule ("Deborah"; also, prayer). H

INK
      Mo (black). C

INSURANCE POLICY
      Palapala 'Inikua. H

INTELLECT
      Ea (vast intellect). MA

INTERPRETER
      Cockenoe (an Algonquin Indian chief). I

IRIS
      Mau'u-Lā'ili (yellow iris). H

IRON
      Iarn-Greiper (iron gauntlet; Thor used as a hammer,
         generally red hot). MN
      Iarnsaxa (the giantess who married Thor). MN
      In-Ne-O-Cose (Iron Horn; Indian chief of the Blackfeet
         Indians). I

ISLAND
      Aeaea (Circe's island). MG
      Aegina (named after Aegina who bore Zeus' son). MG
      Aeolia (island of the winds). MG
      Aeolus (place of the winds). MG
      Bigeh (island of Hapi who resided in his cavern on
         this island). MEG
      Buyan (island on which the three winds lived). MSL
      Cythera (off which the south wind steered Aphrodite).
         MG
      Cyzicus (on which Heracles left the expedition of the
         Argonauts). MG
      Delos (floating island in the Aegean Sea). MG

Fyn (Odin's favorite island). MN
Lessoe (here the sea ruler, Aegir, lived). MN
Moku (ship; floating island). H
Nisyrus (formed by Poseidon hurling a rock into the
    sea). MG
Ogygia (belonged to the nymph Calypso). MG
Philae (where Isis worshipped). MEG
Polynesia ("many islands"). H
Seheii (island of the goddess of cataracts). MEG

IT IS SUN UP
    Ee-Dah-How (Shoshone Indian name). I

JACKAL
    Iākala. H

JACKASS
    Kēkake (jackass or donkey). H

JADE
    Yü-Ti (the ancient one of the Jade; ruler of the
        Chinese heaven; a father-god). MC

JAGUAR
    Iākua. H

JANUARY
    Iānuaili. H

JAVELIN
    Ihe (dart; spear). H

JEWEL
    La Joya. S

JOKER
    Pepa Ki'i. H

JOURNEY
    Lu (road; journey). C

JOY
    Apikalia ("Abigail"). H
    Ayo. A
    El Gozo. S

Hau'oli (happiness). H
Hō'oli (joy giver). H
'Oli (joy). H
Yarilo (god of joy). MSL

JUDGE
Samavurti (impartial judge). MI
Tholus (judged music contest). MG

JUNE
Iune (month). H

JULY
Iuali (month). H

KANGAROO
Kanakalū. H

KEEPER OF SEALS
Proteus (changed his shape at will; skilled in prophecy).
MG

KICKING BEAR
Kicking Bear (a Sioux Indian warrior at Custer's Last
Stand with Sitting Bull, Rain-In-The-Face, Crazy
Horse). I

KICKING BIRD
Kicking Bird (chief of the Kiowa Indians). I

KING FISHER, The
Tei Da Ga Yi (Indian name given by the Biloxi and
Ofo Indians). I

KINGDOM
Aupuni (people under a ruler; kingdom). H
Epirus (within the city of Dodona). MG

KNIGHT
Naika. H

KNITTING NEEDLE
Kui Ulana. H

KNOW-HOW
   Savoir Faire. F

LADY IN WAITING
   Fulla (to Frigg; she carried a goblet). MN
   Gna (to Frigg who rode a horse faster than the wind).
      MN
   Lin (to Frigg). MN
   Ninkhursag (lady of the great mountain). MAS
   Ninki ("lady of the earth"; companion to Ea). MAS
   Pele ("lady with the restless feet"; goddess of vol-
      canoes). H

LAKES
   Oluksâk (divinity of lakes). MES

LAMENT
   Uwē. H

LAND
   Accomac (Indian tribe of the Virginia Confederacy;
      "land beyond"). I
   'Āina Kūpono (land free from all rent and taxes). H
   'Āpa'a (land one has lived on for a long time). H
   Dodona (in the land of oak trees). MG
   Nana'e (a small piece of land). H
   On'Chil-Ka (place name of the Yuki Indians; "land
      gap"). I
   On'Pu (place name of the Yuki Indians; "land floats").
      I

LANGUID
   Leah (sister of Rachel). B

LARGE
   Chuvava (large cook pot on supports; Mohave Indian
      name). I
   Ka'apeha (large mass of clouds). H
   Ka'iālana (large travelling company). H

LARK, The
   La Alondra. S

LAUGHTER
   'Aka'aka (laughter; merriment). H

E Ha Wee (laughing maid; feminine name of the Dakota
    or Sioux Indians). I
Hsiao (laugh; smile). C
La Risa (laughter). S

LAW
    Asha (the universal law). MP
    Misharu. MA

LAZY
    Kūhana 'Ole (do nothing). H

LEADER
    Alaka'i (guide; director). H
    Alkaid (leader of the daughters of the bier; second
        brightest star in the big dipper group). Ar
    Titus Tatius (led the Sabines against Rome). MG

LEAF
    Yeh (night; leaf). C

LEAP YEAR
    Makahiki Lā Keu (extra day year). H

LEFT HAND
    Left Hand (an Arapaho Indian name). I

LEG OF THE CENTAUR
    Hadar (first magnitude star). B

LEGEND
    Ka'ao (legend; tale; fiction). H
    Menehunes (legendary tribe of dwarfs of Hawaii; they
        performed marvelous feats of construction in a
        night; they were thought to be the original inhabi-
        tants of the islands). H

LEI
    Ilima (the yellow lei of Oahu). H
    Kukui (the white candlenut blooms for leis of Molokai).
        H
    Lehua (from the Ohia tree; fiery-red; on the island of
        Hawaii). H
    Lokelani (the leis of Maui). H
    Mokihana (berries used in leis on the island of Kauai
        [lemon-green]). H

Pupu (shells are white and used in leis of island of
    Niihau). H

LEMON
    Kukane (the fruit). H
    Limón (the fruit). S

LET 'ER RIP
    Wela Kah Ao! (strike while the iron is hot). H

LET'S GO!
    E Hele Kaua. H

LIAR
    Lana (lie at anchor; floating). H
    Pecos Bill (mythical character of the west; a liar). W

LIBERTY
    El Buey Suelto Bien Se Lame (liberty is a blessing).
        S

LIBRARY
    Kahu Puke (Buke), also Mea Mālama Puke (a librarian).
        H
    Waihona Puke. H

LICKING DEER
    Licking Deer (the name of a Maidu Indian). I

LIFE
    Eva ("Eve"; "life with vitality"). S
    Eve (the first woman). B
    Evita ("Eve"). S
    Ha'awina or Ho'omau (life pension). H
    Iwa ("Eve"). H
    Lif (maiden who survived the destruction of Ragnarokk
        [destiny of the gods]). MN
    Maka Maka Ola (a friend who extends hospitality). H
    Maka-O Kona Ola 'Ana (all the days of his life). H
    Mōlama Ola (means of livelihood). H
    Ola (life; health). H
    El Salvavidas (the lifebelt). H

LIGHT
    Claro Y Oscuro (M) or Clara Y Oscura (F) (light and
        dark). S

Kukui ("light"; oily nuts of this tree [candlelight] were used as miniature torches by early Hawaiians). H
Lios-Beri (the Norwegian month of Vali, "the light-bringing"). MN

LIGHTNING
Kantoki No Ki. J
Tien Mu (flashes of lightning). MC

LILY
Kukana ("Susan"; "lily"). H
Kuke ("lily"; "Susie"). H
Susana ("white"; "lily"). S

LILY OF THE VALLEY
El Lirio De Mayo. S

LION
Leo (sign of the Zodiac and a constellation). G
Liona ("lion"). H
Liona Kai ("sea lion"). H
Nemean Lion (killed by Heracles). MG
Nolina ("Noreen"; "lioness"). H
Noma ("Norma"; "lioness"). H

LITERATURE
Wen Ch'ang (god of literature). MC

LITTLE
Alioth (brightest star in the big dipper group). Ar
Ari-Sonac ("little springs"; name of a brave in the Papago Indian tribe). I
Arizuma ("Little Creek"; name of a Pima Indian chief). I
Cantillo ("little song"). L
Capella (navagational star; north of the belt of Orion). L
Chetan-Wakan-Mani (name of a Sioux Indian chief). I
Chico ("little"). S
Kaina ("little brother, Cain"). H
Little Bear (an Arapaho Indian brave). I
Little Big Man (name of a Sioux Indian brave). I
Little Grass Shack (song composed by William O. Cogswell). H
Little Raven (name of an Arapaho Indian chief). I
Mah-To-Chee-Ga ("Little Bear"; name of a Sioux Indian chief). I

Menehune (legendary dwarfs having magical powers to
    perform incredible tasks of engineering, as con-
    struction of fish ponds, water courses, overnight).
    H
Michikinikwa (Miami Indian chief; "Little Turtle"). I
Nāmū (legendary little people; "the silent ones"). H
Paola ("Pauline"). S
Poleke ("Paulette"). H
Polina ("Pauline"). H
Poni ("little good person"). H
Procyon ("before the dog, rising before the dog star,
    Sirius"). L
Tsan Usdi (a Cherokee Indian chief; "Little John";
    John Ross). I
Ursola ("little bear"). H
Ursula ("little bear"; "strong as a bear"). S
Vulpecula ("little fox"; a constellation). L

LIVELY
    Wiwiana ("Vivian"). H

LOG CABIN
    Hale Kua. H

LONELY ONE
    Kamehameha, King, the First ("the lonely one"; a
        wise and loved king was King Kamehameha III;
        Kamehameha IV was "the sad king"). H

LONG, Tall
    Okafalaya (long or tall people; a chief of the Choctaw
        Indians). I

LONG HAIR
    Long Hair (chief of the Crow Indians; had the longest
        hair of any man in the nation). I

LONG LIFE
    Ola Loa. H

LOOKING GLASS, The
    He Aniani. H
    Too-Hul-Sul-Suit ("Looking Glass"; a chief of the Nez
        Perce Indians). I

LOONS
    Maak (name for a chief of the Potawatomi Indians). I

LOVELY
Linda Rose ("lovely rose"). S
Linda Vista ("lovely view"). S
Muduva ("the loved"). A
Olopua (heart broken; love-lorn). H
Pamela ("loved one"). S
Pamila ("loved one"; "Pamela"). H

LURE
'Onihilehua (said to catch fish without fail). H

MAGIC
Brihaspati (master of magical power). MI
Megin-Giörd (owned by Thor, the magic hammer which
always returned to his hand). MN
Miölnir (magic belt owned by Thor). MN
Orenda (Iroquis Indian name for chief; "magical power";
"mystery"). I

MAGNOLIA
La Magnolia (the flower). S

MAIDEN
Anromeda (when chained to a rock, she was rescued
from a sea monster by Perseus). MG
Camilla (a maiden warrior). MG
Coronis (a maiden loved by Apollo). MG
Dryope (a mortal girl transformed into a Dryad). MG
Gefjon (visited the King of Sweden, begged for land
she might call her own; she was given all she
could plow in one day and a night; she wrenched
out the land, took it down into the sea where she
made it fast and called it Seeland). MN
Kiliwia (maiden of the forest; "Sylvia"). H

MAKE HASTE SLOWLY
Festina Lente. S

MAKE YOURSELF AT HOME
Está Usted en su Casa. S

MAN
Kane ("husband, male"). H

Mientras Que en mi Casa Estoy Rey Soy ("a man's house is his castle"). S

MARCH
Malaki (month). H

MARIGOLD
Melekule. H

MARINE SPONGE, The
Niörd's Glove. MN

MASTER
E Ku'u Haku (my master [a chief so addressed]). H
Haku (lord, master, ruler). H

MASTERPIECE
Opus Summo Artificio Factum. L

MAZE
Labyrinth (the Minotaur was kept in this maze). MG

MEADOW
Kele ("Shirley"). H

MEDICINE
Kahuna Lapa-au ("medical doctor"). H
Medicine Crow (a Crow Indian chief). I
O-Kuni-Nushi (god of medicine connected with sorcery). MJ
The House of Life ("sanctuary"). MEG

MEETING
Huina (a meeting point; crossroads). H

MERCHANT
Sadko (a rich merchant who sailed the sea for 12 years and for 12 years sailed on the Volga River). MSL

MERCY
Merced ("Mercy"). S

MERMAIDS
Sirens (lived on a rocky island; lured mariners to death by seductive music). MG
Wahine Hi'u I'a (mermaid). H

MERRY
    Mapela ("Mabel"). II

MESSENGER
    Anakela (messenger; angel). H
    'Ānela ("angel"). H
    'Ānela Kia'I ("guardian angel"). H
    'Elele (messenger; delegate). II
    Hermes (messenger of Zeus; Roman: Mercury). MG
    Takami-Musubi (messenger of Amaterasu). MJ
    Triton (messenger and trumpeter of Poseidon). MG
    Zaqar (messenger of Sin). MA

METEOR
    Hōkū-lele. H
    Hōkū-lewa (moving star). H
    Lele (jump; leap; fly, as a meteor). H

MICKEY MOUSE
    El Ratoncito Mickey. S

MIDGET
    Peke. H

MIDNIGHT
    'Aumoe. H

MIGHTY
    Hileka ("Hilda"; "mighty in battle"). H

MILD
    Svasud (mild and lovely). MN

MILLSTONE
    Grotti (ground out gold, peace and prosperity by two
        giantesses). MN

MIMOSA
    Mimoka. H

MIRACLE, A
    Hana Mana. H

MIRAGE
    Waili'ulā. H

MIRROR
    Ching. C

MIRTH
    Euphrosyne (one of three graces; gave happiness to
        those they favor). MG

MIST
    La Bruma. S
    Hŏ'ohu (form mist). H
    'Ohu (mist; light cloud on a mountain). H
    Shina-To-Be (goddess to blow away the mist). MJ

MONDAY
    Pō Akāhi. H

MONSTER
    Echidna (half woman, half snake). MG
    Griffins (half eagle, half lion). MG
    Sphinx (half woman, half lioness; she asked riddles of
        every passerby). MG

MONTH OF THE SOUTHERN FISH
    Fomalhaut (first magnitude star). Ar

MOON
    Aah. MEG
    Ch'ang-o or Heng-o (the moon goddess). MC
    Hoalya (Mohave clan name). I
    Koali-pahu (moon flower). H
    Kuu. MF
    Mah. MP
    Mahealani ("night of full moon"). H
    Mahina ("moon"). H
    Mahina Hapa (half moon). H
    Mahina Hou ("new moon"). H
    Mahina Meh ("honeymoon"). H
    Mahina Piha ("full moon"). H
    Moon Hawk (a Pomo Indian name). I
    Myesyats ("the old, or bald uncle"; the moon). MSL
    Ojai. S
    Thoth. MEG
    Varuna (the god that presides over air, sky, water;
        stars are his eyes and the wind his breath;
        "moon"). MI

MORNING
Aurora of the Morning. MSL
Ishtar (goddess of morning and evening). MA
Kakahiaka ("morning"). H
Koali and Koali-'awa ("morning glory"). H
Kukui-Wana'ao ("morning star"). H
Wa Ba Nang ("morning star"; the name of a Chippewa Indian chief). I

MOSQUITO
Makika. H

MOTHER OF PELE
Haumea (Pele's legendary mother). H

MOUNTAIN
Adchu (Algonquin Indian name). I
La Cabra Montés (the mountain goat). S
Chabin (Assiniboin Indian name). I
Eryx ("mountain where there is a shrine to Aphrodite"). MG
Gerania, Mt. MG
Helicon, Mt. (where the winged horse lived; also: Mount Parnassus). MG
Hindarfiall (a tall mountain on which Brunhild was placed, surrounded by a ring of flames to wait for her future husband). MN
Ida. MG
Jokul (highest mountain peak). MN
Kuaola (verdant mountain). H
Mauna-loa (mountain on Hawaii; "long mountain"). H
Oeta, Mt. (where Heracles died). MG
Ossa, Mt. (the Giants placed it on Mount Olympus, on top of which they piled Mt. Pelion in order to reach and attack the gods). MG
Othrys, Mt. (place where the ark rested after the flood was caused by Zeus). MG
Parnassus, Mt. (here Apollo built a house at Delphi, on top of the mountain). MG
Pillars of Heracles (also: Gates). MG

MOUSE, The
'Iole ("mouse"). H
'Iole Li'ili'i (little rat). H

MOVE QUIETLY
Halolani (to move gently, as a soaring bird). H

MUCH IN LITTLE
Multum in Parvo. L

MUSES, The
Calliope ("of epic poetry"). MG
Clio ("of history"). MG
Erato ("of lyric poetry"). MG
Euterpe ("of music"). MG
Melpomene ("of tragedy"). MG
Polyhymnia ("of sacred song and oratory"). MG
Terpsichore ("of the dance"). MG
Thalia ("of comedy"). MG
Urania ("of astronomy"). MG
The nine muses were called the Pierides. MG

MUSIC
Arion (poet and harpist, was carried to land by a
dolphin). MG
Gusli (a stringed musical instrument). MSL
Lyre (invented by Hermes when he took a tortoise
shell, stringing strings across the empty shell;
he gave it to Apollo). MG
Marsyas (a Satyr, who entered a musical contest with
Apollo). MG
'Ulī'ulī (gourd rattle musical instrument). H

MUSKRAT
Muskwessu (Indian name of the Abnaki tribe). I

MY SON
Ugnera. ES

MYSTERIOUS
Kapolakā. H

NAME
Ming (name; fame; intelligent). C

NASTURTIUM
Pohe Haole. H

NATIONAL ANTHEM
Mele Aupuni. H

NAUTILUS
  Naukilo. H

NAVIGATOR
  Hilo ("to twist"; a famous Polynesian navigator). H

NECKLACE
  Brisinga-Men (Freya's golden necklace). MN
  Lei Palaoa (ivory pendant; necklace worn by royalty).
  H

NEEDLE, A
  Kileting ("Needle Rock"; an Indian name). I
  Panygmah. ES

NEREIDS
  Arethusa (turned into a spring). MG
  Galatea (brought to life by Pygmalion). MG
  Thetis (chief of the Nereids, who were nymphs of the
    Mediterranean Ocean). MG

NEST
  El Nido ("the nest"; abode; home). S
  Pūnana. H

NEVER
  Jamás. S
  Nunca. S

NIGHT
  Jūgoya (night of the full moon). J
  Kia 'I Pō (night watchman). H
  Māka 'I Pō (night watchman). H
  Moe'ino (nightmare). H
  Oasis (night club in Oahu). H
  Pahulu (nightmare). H
  Po. H
  Pō Mahina (moonlight night). H
  Pōpolo (black nightshade). H
  Tukma or Tokuma (created sea animals; world,
    plants). MJ

NIMBLE
  'Akakē ("spry; light; nimble"). H

NINE
'Aīwa. H
Nueve. S

NO-NAME
K'Amun Hoyowash (a Yokut Indian name). I

NO TRESPASSING
Kapu (keep off; forbidden). H

NOBLE
Akela ("Adele"; noble maid). H
Aleka ("Alice"; cheerful; noble). H
Alicia ("Alice"). S
Aukele ("Audrey"; noble helper). H
Ekela ("Ethel"; noble). H

NOISY
Kakani. H

NON-INTERFERENCE
Laissez Faire. F

NORTH
'Ākua. H
Ho'olua (north wind is strong). H
Kio-pa-a (North Star). H
El Norte. S
Pei. C
Wēlau-'ākau (North Pole). H

NOSE
Enif ("nose of the horse"; a star). Ar
Menkar ("nose of the whale"; a star; in the constella-
tion Cetus, the Whale). Ar

NOVEMBER
Nowemapa. H

NURSE
Alice, Saint (she nursed the sick). G
Emalaina ("Emmeline"; "nurse"). H

NUT
Agoza. H
Akoka. H
Nuez. S

NYMPHS
Arethusa (pursued by the river god and changed into a stream that flowed underground). MG
Charybdis (sea nymph; she guarded the narrow passage of the sea). MG
Egeria (she gave her name to a fountain). M
Juturna (Roman goddess of springs). MR
Pleiades (seven daughters of Atlas who were constantly running away from Orion and who were finally turned into stars). MG
Sabrina (river nymph; invented by Milton). E
Salmacis (river nymph). MG

OBJECT
Kia Hō 'Ailona (any large object with a sign). H

OCEAN
Apsu (sweet water). MA
Del Mar (of the sea). S
Kau-maka-nui (ocean sunfish). H
Mimar's Well (god of the ocean; the ocean). MN
Moana (open sea; ocean). H
Oceanos (the river, was also called father of all things). MG
Yang (ocean; vast; foreign). C

OCTOBER
Okakopa. H

OCTOPUS
He'e (the squid). H
El Pulpo. S

ODIN
Vegtam (took this name when he wished the prophetess to know who he was). MN

OGRESS
Angerboda. MN
Hydrokkin (shriveled by fire). MN
Ran (ransacked sunken ships). MN

OH, SEE THIS!
Enanal. H

OLD
> Elle (old woman, who was Old Age, with whom Thor
> wrestled). MN
> Kālona (slowpoke; old plug). H
> Kama'āina (old timer). H
> Mah-To-He-Ha ("the old bear"; a Mandan Indian name).
> I
> Old Chuckle Head (a Modoc chief's name). I

OLEANDER
> Noho-malie. H

OLIVE
> Aceituna (fruit). S
> Verde Olive (color). S

OMEGA
> 'Omeka. H

ON THE TOP OF
> Onondago (an Iroquois Indian name). I

ONE
> 'Akā Hi. H
> Elnath ("one butting with horns"; one of the principal
> stars in the constellation Taurus, the bull). Ar
> Goyathlay (one who yawns; see Geronimo). I
> Iolani-Palau (one above all others). H
> One Eyed Moose (a Modoc chief's name). I
> Uno or Una ("one"). S

ORANGE
> 'Alani (orange, the fruit). H
> El Azahar (orange blossom). S

ORCHID
> Hawaii (Orchid Island). H
> La Orquidea. S
> 'Okika. H

ORION'S BELT
> Hula'Ch-Um (Indian name of the Luiseño tribe). I

ORNAMENT
> Adah ("Ada"; first woman after Eve to be mentioned in
> the Bible). B
> Aka ("Ada"). H

OSPREY
    Okepela. H

OVERSEER
    Luna (high; supervisor; overseer). H

OWL
    Pehe ("owl snare"). H

PACIFIC RIM OF FIRE
    Rim of Fire (a volcanic mountain range that circles
        the Pacific Ocean). H

PAINT
    Meng T'ien (he invented the paint brush). C
    Pintado ("painted, mottled"). S

PALACE
    Bilskirnir (palace of Thor in Asgard; it has 450
        rooms). MT
    Folkvang (Freya's palace). MN
    Glitnir (it was so radiant it could be seen from a
        distance). MN
    Himinbiorg (palace of the guardian of the rainbow
        bridge; it was found at the highest point of the
        bridge). MN
    'Io-lani ("one above all others"; former royal palace
        in Hawaii). H
    Pensalir (the hall of mists, or sea; the palace of
        Frigga). MN
    Valhalla (a palace with 540 doors). MN
    Vana Heim (dwelling of the sea and wind gods). MN

PAPYRUS
    Kaluhā. H

PARADISE
    Palekaiko. H
    Paradise Park (in Manoa valley on Oahu). H
    Paraíso. S

PARROT
    Gyazru (name for the parrot clan of the Hopi
        Indians). I
    El Loro (parrot). S

Manu-Aloha (parrot). H

PARTICULAR NEMESIS
Bete Noire. F

PARTRIDGE
Manu-Aihue. H
La Perdiz. S

PASSENGER CONVEYANCE
Ka'a Hali 'Ohua. H

PASSPORT
Golden Bough (the passport to Hades). MG
El Pasaporte. S

PASTIME
Hana Punahele (hobby; favorite pastime). H

PASTURE
Pony Pasture (a small pasture for horses). W

PATH
Ala (road; trail). H
Ala A Ka Manu (a bird's trail). H

PATRICIAN
Pakelekia ("Patricia"). H

PATRON
Frey or Fro (German for gladness). MN
Melicertes (spirit, patron of sailors; also the name
given Palaemon when he became a sea god). MG

PATRONESS
Agatha, Saint ("good"; "Agatha"; patroness of nurses). G
Agnes, Saint ("chaste"; patroness of young girls). G
Anne, Saint ("grace"; patroness of housewives). E
Catherine, Saint ("pure one"; patroness of philosophers
and scholars). G
Clare, Saint ("clear; bright"; patroness of embroidery
workers and laundresses; founder of the order of
Clarisses). F
Dorothea, Saint ("gift of God"; "a martyr"; patroness
of gardeners and florists). E
Elizabeth, Saint ("god is my oath"; patroness of chari-
ties for the poor). E

Irene, Saint ("peace"; patroness of young girls; also,
"the peaceful one"). G
Martha, Saint ("sorrowful"; patroness of housewives,
innkeepers and laundresses). E
Monica, Saint ("alone"; patroness of mothers). L
Ursula, Saint ("little bear"; patroness of teachers and
young people). L
Veronica, Saint ("image of truth"; patroness of linen
weavers). G

PEACE
Calumet (peace pipe and war pipe). I
Ku'Ikāhi ("peace, unity, agreement to make peace"). H
Laule'a ("peace, happiness, friendship"). H
Oliwa ("Olive"; "peace sign"). H
Oliwia ("Olivia"; "peace sign"). H
Pax ("peace"). L
Salome ("peaceful"). B
Vjofn ("peace keeper"). MN

PEACH
Melocotón. S

PEACOCK
El Pavo Real ("the peacock"). S
Pīkake ("peacock, also Arabian jasmine--a shrub"). H
Pīkake-hōkū ("star jasmine"). H

PEARL
Makaleka ("Margaret"; "pearl"). H
Makoli ("Marjorie"). H
Margaret, Saint ("believer"). L
Momi. H

PELE
Pele's Hair (the threads of volcanic glass which may
be carried by the wind from a bubbling lava
fountain). H
Waimaka O Pele (Pele's tears). H

PELICAN
Pele Kana, also Pelikana. H

PENGUIN
Manu-hele-ku. H

PENNY
    Kenali. H

PEOPLE
    Hehlkoan ("people of the foam"; a Tlingit Indian name).
    I
    Pomo (place of the Pomo Indians). I

PEPPER AND SALT
    Nioi and Pa'akai. H

PERCH
    Haka (a hen roost; perch). H
    Halakau ("perch high as a bird"). H

PERFECTION
    Haurvatat ("perfection"). MP

PERIWINKLE
    Pipipi-kolea. H

PERSON
    Persona Grata ("a favorite person"). L

PERSONIFICATION
    Gerda ("the flashing Northern Lights"; Frey ["master"]
       proffered golden apples to Gerda to induce her to
       marry him; she was fleet footed and hard to win).
       MN
    Rinda ("of hard-frozen rind of earth"). MN
    Vali ("of lengthening days"; also Ali, Bous, Beav). MN
    Valkyr's Steeds ("the clouds"). MN
    Vidar ("of the primeval forest"; symbol of resurrection
       and renewal). MN

PHANTOM
    Kāhoaka. H

PHEASANT, The
    El Faisán. S
    Kolo-Hala (Chinese pheasant). H

PHYSICIAN
    Eira (also Eyra; "skilled physician"; taught women
       her science). MN

PIERCED NOSE
Hinmaton-Yalatkit ("thunder coming up over the land from the water"; a famous chief of the Nez Pierce, meaning "pierced nose"; he became famous as Chief Joseph). I

PILGRIMAGE
Bridget, Saint ("pilgrimage to the Holy Land"; real name was Brigitta). E

PILLOW
Uluna. H

PINE-NUT-EATER
Pine-Nut-Eater (name of an Indian maiden of the Maidu tribe). I

PINEAPPLE
Hala-Kahiki ("the pineapple"; the king of fruits). H
Piña. S

PINK
'Ākala ("pink"). H
'Ōhelohelo ("pink, rosy"). H
Rosado O Rosa. S

PIRATE
El Pirata. S

PLACE
Aeaea (Circe's Island). MG
Arcadia or Arcady (central district of the Greek peninsula). MG
Asphodel (place of shadowy plains). MG
Ch'u ("place, point"). C
Elysian Fields or Elysium (also called the blessed isles; paradise in which live souls in endless happiness). MG
Enna (Vale in Sicily). MG
Fountain of Wisdom. MN
Heliopolis (temple of the sun). MG
Hlidskialf (lofty throne of Odin). MD
Kahua O Mali'o (place of happiness; Mali'O was a mythical woman who entertained with music). H
Kula Manu (place of birds). H
Landvidi (the wide land). MN
Leahi ("place of fire; giant crater of Oahu"). H

Lethe (pool of forgetfulness). MG
Mt. Haleakala (world's largest extinct volcano). H
Mt. Halemaumau (a fire pit of molten lava in the
    center of Kilauea crater, where the fire goddess,
    Pele, lived). H
Muspellsheim (land of fire). MT
Niflheim (world of cloud and shadows). MT
Noatum (favorite residence of Njord on the seashore).
    MT
Nuuanu Pali (1200 foot cliff where Kamehame-ha I
    won his last battle on Oahu). H
Punchbowl (extinct volcanic crater now a national
    cemetary on Oahu). H
Rainbow Falls (on Hawaii). H
Tempe (lovely vale in Thessaly through which flow
    the Peneus river). MG
Tir Fo Thuinn (the land under the waves). MCE
Tir Na Noc (land of youth, land of bliss). MCE
Upshukina (the hall where the gods met to determine
    man's destiny). MA
Water Hole (place where cattle are watered or a bar).
    W

PLANET
    Ka'ā-wela (might be Jupiter or Venus). H

PLAY
    Hoa Pili ("close friend"; "playmate"). H
    Kahua Le'a, Kahua Le'ale'a (playground). H
    Wan ("to play; enjoy"). C

PLEASANT
    Naomi ("pleasant to behold"). B

PLEIADES
    Chehay-Am (name given by the Luiseño Indians; "the
        Pleiades"). I
    Doto Doto (name of a Maidu Indian). I
    Electra ("a pleiad"). MG
    Na-Huihui (the Pleiades). H

PLENTY WOLF
    Plenty Wolf (a Sioux Indian chief). I

PLOVER
    Kōlea (golden plover). H

PLUM
>Ciruela (plum; fruit). S
>Palama. H

PLUMBAGO
>'Ilie'e (wild plumbago). H

POCKET
>Bolsa (a shut in place; enclosed on three sides). S

POLARIS
>Polaris ("the pole star"; Polaris was used to determine
>latitude by the time of Columbus). L

POLICEMAN
>Kaiko. H

POPPY
>La Amapola (the flower). S

PORPOISE
>Nai'a. H

POWDER FACE
>Powder Face (an Arapaho Indian woman's name). I

POWERFUL, The
>Anu ("the powerful born"; a great god). MA
>Ikaika ("strong; energetic; powerful"). H

PRAISE
>Māhalo ("praise; thanks"). H

PREACHER
>Sky-Pilot (Westerner's name for a preacher). W

PRECIOUS
>Makamae ("much desired"). H

PRESERVER, The
>Vishnu (third of the trinity; the others are: Brahma,
>the creator; Siva, the destroyer). MI

PRETTY
>Bonito (m) or Bonita (f). S
>Chula Vista ("pretty view"; "graceful"). S

PRIEST
>Kahunapule. H

Triptolemus (a priest who travelled around the world teaching men the art of planting). MG

PRIESTESS
Hera (she held aloft a beacon to light Leander, as he swam across the Hellespont to see her in the tower where she tended the sacred swans and sparrows). MG
Pythoness (Pythia gave out mysterious oracles supposed to have come from the god Apollo; the place of the oracle was possessed by Python until Apollo killed him). MG
Vestal Virgins (they were of the temple of Vesta at Rome). MG

PRIME MINISTER
Kuhina Nui. H

PRIMROSE WILLOW
Kāmole. H

PRINCE
Keiki Ali'i. H
Paris (he eloped with Helen of Troy). MG
Regulus ("the prince"; brightest star in the constellation of Leo, forms the southern end of the handle of the sickle). L

PRINCESS
Aethra (daughter of King of Troezen). MG
Agave (daughter of King of Thebes). MG
Antigone (daughter of Oedipus, King of Thebes). MG
Creusa (a Trojan princess). MG
Europea (Zeus who took the form of a bull carried her to Crete). MG
Gudrun (dark flower of the wood). MN
Helle (daughter of King Athamas; was drowned in the Hellespont). MG
Hiordia (daughter of the King of the Islands, Eglimi). MN
Kala ("high born; princess"; "Sarah"). H
Kamāli'i Wahine ("Sarah"). H
Kawelu (princess of the Lowlands; she lived in the lowlands in the legend of Hawaii, "The Arrow and the Swing"). H
Kinau (daughter of Kamehameha I). H
Laodamia (daughter of Bellerophon). MG

Poomaikalani (Princess of Maui). H
Rina (daughter of King of Ruthenes, who was wooed
by Odin in the disguises of a smith, an old gen-
eral and a dashing warrior; their son was called
Vali, personification of the lengthening days). MN
Sara ("Sarah"). S
Sarah (wife of Abraham; also: Sarai; "high-born"). B
Thora (daughter of King Hakon, became the wife of
Elf). MN

PRIVATE
Privado. S

PRIZE
Briseis (prize of war, a young woman, captive maiden
of Achilles). MG

PROMENADE
Enlil's Way (a place in the heavens reserved for Enlil).
MA

PROMISSORY NOTE
He Palapala Hooia E Uku Aku. H

PROPHET
Elkswatawa (name of a Shawnee Indian; brother of
Tecumseh, possibly his twin). I
Kahuna Kāula (prophet). H
Kāula (seer; prophet). H
Melampus (soothsayer). MG
Tiresias (blind soothsayer). MG

PROPHETESS
Cassandra (princess whom no one believed). MG
Deborah (a prophetess; also a judge). B
Sibyls (prophetesses of the ancient world). MG
Vala (these were the Norns, who when called Vala had
the power of divination; they were: Idises, Dises,
Veleda; "protectors"). MN
Volva (prophetess). MN

PROTECTOR
Kompira (protector of sailors; also Kuvera). MJ
Malu-Lani (under heaven's protection; celestial shade).
H
Ptah (protector of artisans and artists). MEG

PROTECTORESS
Buto (protectoress of Lower Egypt). MEG
Neith or Neit (protectoress of marriage; "wears red
crown, skilled in home arts"; also "sky goddess").
MEG

PROUD-COYOTE
Proud-Coyote (m) (an Indian brave of the Mohave
Indians). I

PUBLISHER
Luna Ho'opuka (publisher). H

PURPLE
Morado. S
Poni. II

PURE
Kakaline ("Kathleen"). H
Keke ("Kate"). H
Lilia ("Lily"; "Purity"). H
Liliana ("Lillian"; "sign of purity"). H
Pua Lilia ("Lily"). H

QUAIL
Manu-kapalulu (the California quail and Japanese quail
are found on the Hawaiian islands). H

QUANAH PARKER
Quanah Parker (an Indian name of the Comanche that
meant terror on the Texas frontier). I

QUEEN
Amphitrite (Queen of Sea Gods). MG
Antiope (Queen of the Amazons; mother of twins). MG
Dido (Queen of Carthage; founder). MG
Ereshkigal (Queen of the underworld). MA
Grimhild (she was Queen at Niblung and versed in
magic lore). MN
Hecuba (Queen of Troy). MG
Hera (Queen of Heaven; Juno in Roman; "the peacock";
"goddess of atmosphere and marriage"). MG
Hermione, also Harmonia (Queen of Thebes). MG
Jerusha (Queen mother). B
Jocasta (Queen of Thebes). MG

Ka Ahu Pahau (the Queen Shark of the Waters in the
    legend of the "Blond Shark"). H
Kaahumanu ("Queen"; also "feather cloak, " worn by
    the royal family). H
Kuini ("King"). H
Liliuokalani (last Queen of the Islands). H
Medb (warrior queen). MCE
Penthesilia (a queen of the Amazons), MG
Persephone or Cora. MG
Sparta (Queen of Laconia). MG
Taltiu (an earth goddess who married Eochaid Mac
    Eire, King of the Fir Bolg). MCE
Tethys (wife of Oceanus; Queen of the Ocean). MG
Titania (Queen of the fairies). MN
Wang (Queen mother). MC

QUICK
    Alamimo ("nimble"). H

QUIET
    Miaplacidus ("quiet of still waters"; a second magnitude
        star, nearest of the 57 navigational stars to the
        south celestial pole). L

QUILT
    Kapa 'Āpana. H

RABBIT, The
    El Conejo. S

RAGING
    Midgard Snake (the raging sea; the snake Thor and
        Hymir encountered in the sea). MN

RAIN
    Ao Kuang, Ao Jun, Ao Shun, Ao Ch'In (all dragon
        kings living in the Crystal Palace; they bring the
        rain). MC
    Ka'au (a fine rain in Kohala). H
    Kā'ele-loli (rain in Makiki, Oahu). H
    La Lluvia (the rain). S
    Ōpua Lani ("heavenly clouds; or heavenly rain clouds").
        H
    Parjanya (the rain). MI
    Quiateot (rain god). MN

Rain-In-The-Face (a Sioux Indian chief, leader against Custer). I
Taka-Okami (lives on the mountains; a rain god). MJ
Ua ("rain"). H
Ua-'Apuakea (name of a famous rain so named for a beautiful woman changed to rain by the goddess Hi'I-Aka). H
Ua A Kalīpoa (fine cold rain). H
Ua Limua (period of constant rain). H
Ua Loa (long period of rain). H
Uwanami (rain makers). MZ
Yü-Tzu (master of the rain). MC

RAINBOW
Ānuenue (rainbow; a hill in Hawaii). H
Ao akua (rainbow; godly cloud). H
El Arco Iris (the rainbow). S
Asabru. MN
Bifröst (the rainbow bridge; it extended from heaven to earth). MN

RAINCOAT
Kukaweke. H

RAM
Aries (a constellation and sign of the Zodiac). G

RASCAL
Kupu'eu. H

RASPBERRY
Frambuesa ("fruit"). S

RAVEN
El Cuervo. S
Memory (flew over the world every morning to bring back what had been seen by him, to Odin). MN
Thought (flew over the world every morning to bring back what he had seen to Odin). MN

REAPER
Keleka ("Theresa"; "reaper"). H
Teresa (also: Teresita). S

REBELLION
Miliama ("Miriam"). H
Miriam ("Miriam"; "rebellion"). B

Molly (dim. of Molly is Polly or Pole). H

RECOGNITION
 Laura. S
 Lola ("Laura"; "receive recognition"). H

RED
 Colorado O Rojo. S
 Duhk-Pits-A-Ho-Shee (a Crow warrior; "Red Bear"). I
 Hung ("red; good luck"). C
 Kūnono (bright red). H
 Mahpiua Luta (from a meteor that turned the sky
  scarlet at the time of Red Cloud's birth; he was
  an Ogalala Sioux). I
 Mesquakie ("red earth people"; the Indians of Iowa
  called themselves this name). I
 Red Eagle (a Creek Indian chief). I
 Red Iron (a Sioux Indian chief). I
 Red Tomahawk (a Sioux policeman). I
 Rojo ("red"). S
 'Ula ("scarlet"; short for Koa'e-'ula--red-tailed tropic
  bird). H
 'Ula Wel (dark red). H
 'Ula Wena (glowing red). H
 Waimea (canyon of Kauai with reddish water). H

REFUGE
 Refugio. S

REST
 Descanso ("rest"). S
 Hana ("rest"; ancient seat of Hawaiian culture nestles
  in valley on east of Haleakala; beautiful with water-
  falls and steep cliffs). H
 Haulani ("restless; constantly on move"; also "plunge,
  as a canoe"). H
 Requiescat in Pace ("rest in peace"). L

RICH
 Soyini ("richly endowed"). A

RIDDLE
 Nane ("riddle"). H
 Nane Huna ("conumdrum"). H

RIGHT WING OF THE RAVEN
 Gienah (brightest star in the constellation Corvus, the
  crow). Ar

RING
>Andvaranaut (ring of Andvari). MN
>Draupnir (ring of Odin; emblem of fruitfulness). MN

RIVAL OF MARS
>Antares (also Scorpii; brightest star in the constella-
>tion Scorpio, the scorpion). G

RIVER
>Acheron (river in Hades; river of woe). MG
>Cebe ("river"; Indian name of the Dakotas). I
>Cocytus (river in Hades; river of lamentation). MG
>Eridanus (river in which Phaethon fell when Zeus
>struck him with a thunderbolt to stop the runaway
>horses of Apollo). MG
>Ifing (river that surrounded Idavold; the plain where the
>gods dwelled). MG
>Lethe (river in Hades; the river of forgetfulness). MG
>Maeander (now called Menderes; located in central
>Asia Minor; flows aimlessly; famous for its
>swans). MG
>Pactolus (river in which Midas washed, and which be-
>came rich with gold). MG
>Phlegethon (river of fire). MG
>Scamander (sometimes called Zanthus). MG
>Tuoni (the infernal river). MF

ROAD RUNNER
>Met'a (name of a Yuma Indian tribe). I

ROAR
>Haluku ("bang; rattle"). H
>Hālulu ("sea urchin"). H
>Halulu ("thunder"; make racket; loud noise). H

ROBIN
>Chaypoin (an Indian name of the Powhatan tribe). I
>Lopin ("robin"). H

ROCK
>Gioll (a rock). MN
>Guyapipe ("rock lie on"; a place of the Diegueño
>Indians). I
>Myoto-Ga-Seki (the wedded rocks). MJ
>Pōhaku. H
>Rock Swallows (a character in the mythology of the
>Navajo Indians). I

Symplegades (the clashing rocks passed by the
   Argonauts). MG
Tarpeian Rock (rock from which criminals were cast
   to their destruction in the city of Rome). MG

ROCKET
   El Cohete. S

ROCKING CHAIR
   Noho Paipai. H

ROGUISH
   Lei'āpiki (name given to the ilima lei because it was
   believed to attract mischievous spirits; some
   didn't wear this lei but others considered it lucky;
   "crafty; mischievous; garland of flowers"). H

ROLL
   Ka'a'owē (to roll along with a rustling sound). H
   Roll Your Wheels (a term to express start your wagon
   rolling; start the team). W

ROOSTER
   Moa Kāne. H

ROSE
   El Capullo ("rosebud"). S
   Loka ("Rhoda"; "Rose"). H
   Loke Hihi ("climbing rose"). H
   Loke Lani ("heavenly rose"; official flower of Maui;
      a small red rose; also, Roselani; "a red cottage
      rose"). H
   Loke-lau (green rose). H
   Lokemele ("Rosemary"; rose of the sea). H
   'Ohi'a-loke (rose apple tree). H
   Rhoda ("Rose"; maidservent in the house of Mary). B
   La Rosa ("the flower"). S
   Rose, Saint ("Rose"; a simple, devout life). H

ROYAL SCRIBE
   Kākau Ali'I. H

RUNS
   Ma'Ikiviripuni ("runs down from up the hill"; Indian
   name of the Karok tribe). I

RURAL
> Ainahau (rural home of the Princess Kaiulani, where an idyllic life was led). H

RUSH
> Kalukalu ("rush or grass"). H

SACK
> Poke (sack in which the cowboy carries his belongings). W

SACRED
> La'a ("the dedicated one"). H

SADDLE
> Cheyenne Roll. W
> Markab ("saddle of Pegasus"). Ar
> La Montura. S

SAFE
> Awa ("harbor; port; safe harbor"). H
> Awa Pae ("landing place"). H

SAFFRON
> Keloko. H

SAGE
> Ds'ah ("sagebrush"; name of an Indian chief of the Navajo tribe). I
> Fu (a sage). C

SAILOR
> Acetes (befriended by Dionysus). MG
> 'Aumoana ("to travel on the open sea"). H
> Holo A I'a ("to sail like a fish"). H
> Kelamoku ("sailor"). H
> Luina ("sailor"). H

SANDALS
> Talaria (winged sandals of Hermes). MG

SANDPIPER
> Upupā. H

SAPPHIRE
Kapeilo. H

SATURDAY
Pō'aōno. H

SATYR
Silenus (Pan's son: half goat, half man). MC

SCALES
Kau Paona (the scales; balance). H
Libra (sign of the Zodiac; a constellation). G

SCHOOL TEACHER
Angela, Saint ("Angel"). G

SCHOONER, The
He Kialua (Kia Lua is a brig, two masted schooner).
H
La Goleta. S

SCORPION
El Alacrán. S
El Escorpión. S
Scorpio (constellation; sign of Zodiac). G

SCULPTOR
Kahuna Kālai. H

SEA
Ākai ("by the sea"). H
'Akihi-ke'ehi-'ale (small black sea bird). H
Alani (brown seaweeds; moss). H
Aob ("the sea"). ES
'Aukai ("to travel; seafaring; sailor"). H
Hāhālua (sea devil; manta ray). H
Hai ("the sea"). C
Haukau (sea like choppiness). H
Hler ("sea ruler"). MN
Honoka'a (sea cave). H
Hune Kai ("sea spray; foam"). H
I'kai ("direction of the sea"). H
'Ilio 'Aukai ("sea dog"; experienced sailor). H
'Iwa (man of war bird; "the heavenly seabird"). H
Kai Huli (the sea that dashes and recedes). H
Kai Lū He'E (the deep sea). H
Kai Pupule ("crazy, restless sea"). H

Kaiolohia ("calm, tranquil sea"; peace of mind). H
Kaupau (seaweed [brown]). H
Kimau (a seaweed). H
Ko Ākai (those by the sea). H
Kualakai (sea creature). H
Lī'ō (sea bird; same as 'A'o). H
Līpoa, Nano'o ("seaweed"). H
Maka-hālili (the seashell). H
Makai (seaward; Mauka: inland, at the mountains). H
Makakai (sea washed). H
Mar, El, or La (the sea, ocean). S
Maris ("of the sea"). L
Miniole (sea creature). H
Miramar ("sea-view"). S
Nano'o ("purple seaweed"). H
Nēnē-'au-kai ("sea gull"). H
Ōhelo-huihui. H
'Okole Emiemi ("sea anemone"). H
Sea Otter (a feminine name of an Indian tribe). I
Tiamat (personification of the sea). MA

SEAL CAVES
    Agloolik (spirit of the seal caves lives under the ice).
    ES

SEATTLE
    Suquamish (the greatest Indian friend the white settlers
        ever had; he devoted his life to promoting peace;
        he saw Vancouver arrive in the "Discovery"). I

SECOND
    Sabik ("second winner or conqueror"; a star). Ar

SEPTEMBER
    Kepakemapa. H

SERPENT
    Iörmungandr (Odin threw Loki's offspring into the sea
        where it stretched itself, grew until it encircled
        the earth and could bite its own tail). MN
    Lakhmu and Lakhamu (the first two to be born were
        these gods). MA
    Lernean Hydra (a water serpent with nine heads, which
        killed Heracles). MG
    Nidhöog (the cunning serpent). MT

SERVANT
>Hapi (the god who offers river products to the other gods). MEG
>Kauwā ("servant"). H
>Roskva (Thor's servant). MN

SEVEN
>'Ahiku. H
>Siete. S

SHADOW
>Ying ("shadow; image"). C

SHARK GOD
>Hi'u. H

SHELL
>Ka-pes-ka-day (a brave of the Sioux Indians). I

SHELTER COVE
>Tangating (a place name of the Athabascan Indians). I

SHEPHERD
>Daphnes (invented song and story). MG
>Endymion (Artemis visited him each night in his immortal sleep). MG

SHIELD
>Pale Kaua. H
>Randgrior (a Valkyrie). MN

SHINE
>Alohi ("shining; brilliant; glitter"). H
>Chao ("to shine"). C

SHIP
>Argo (ship of the Argonauts). MG
>Mannigfual (a colossal ship of the giants; the captain paced the deck on horseback). MN
>Nagelfar (a ship made of nails). MN
>Ringhorn (Balder's ship). MN
>Skidbladnir (a magic ship that was made of wood slats; it was so elastic it could contain all the gods, their steeds, weapons, equipment, or be folded up into the smallest compass and thrust into Frey's pockets, to whom it belonged; it sailed over land or sea, by favorable winds; it represented a sum-

mer cloud; the dwarf, Dvalin, made it for Loki, to pacify Frey). MN

SHOE
Kāma'a (boot). H

SHOOTS SWIFTLY
Akuni-hashki (Indian name for a brave in the Karok tribe). I

SHORE DWELLER
Ko A Kai. H

SHOULDER
Menkent ("shoulder of the Centaur"; a star of the 2nd magnitude and with Antares and Rigel Kentaurus forms a large triangle).

SHOWER
Danae (Zeus visited her as a shower of gold). MG

SHUT IN
Cupheag (an Algonquian Indian chief). I

SICKLE
Pahi Keke'e. H

SILENT
Hāmau. H
Vidar ("the silent"; personification of the primeval forest). MN

SILVER
De Plata, Plateado, or Plateada (f). S
The Silver Sword (grows on mountain slopes with flat leaves pointed like daggers which gleam like silver; grows in desolate places). H

SINGER
Lan Ts Asi-ho (street singer; one of the eight immortals). C

SIRENS
Aglaophonos ("of the brilliant voice"). MG
Circe (she had the power to charm by song so that sailors were impelled to cast themselves into the sea). MG

Molpe ("song"). MG
Peisinoe ("the persuasive"). MG
Thelxepia ("of the words which enchant"). MG

SISTER
Aino (sister of Joukahainen). MF
Danaids (fifty daughters, ordered to kill their husbands;
    one who did not was Hypermnestra). MG
Gordons (sea goddesses who were sisters; Medusa was
    slain by Perseus and afterwards worn on the shield
    of Athena). MG
Graeae (three sisters who had only one eye between
    them; old women of the ocean). MG
Heliades (sisters of Phaethon). MG
Hesperides (sisters who guarded the golden apples).
    MG
Philomena and Procne (daughters of Pandion). MG
Pleiades (seven sisters who were nymphs). MG

SITTING BULL
Tatanka Iyotake (most famous chief of the Teton or
    Western Sioux; his father was Jumping Bull; Slow
    was his boyhood name, changed formally to Sitting
    Bull). I

SIX
Aōno. H
Seis. S

SKILLED
Lug (of the long armed and the skilled). MCE

SKY
Aoūli ("blue vault of heaven"). H
El Cielo Está Nublado. S
Igigi (sky people; divinities of sky). MA
Lani ("sky"). H
Lani Loa ("vast sky"). H
Uranus (first ruler of the universe, sky). MG

SKYROCKET
Kao Lele ("javelin"). H

SMALL
Half-Pint Size. W
Pygmies (attacked Heracles, who wrapped them in his
    lion's skin). MG

Wish-Book (women who did their wishful window-
    shopping in the mail order catalog). W

SMITH
    Govannan ("a smith"). MCE
    Ilmarinen (forged a mysterious talisman). MF
    Ivashtar ("forged the thunderbolt of Indra"). MI

SNAIL
    Abalone ("great sea-snail"). S
    Homeka ("snail"). H
    Pipipi ("sea snail"; "small mollusks"). H

SNAKE
    Hayah (Indian name of the Pecos for the snake clan).
        I
    Naheka Wela (fiery snake). H

SNAP
    Mikonoh ("snapping turtle"; a Chippewa Indian chief
        name). I
    Nani-o-ola'a (snapdragon family; blue; an annual). H

SNARE
    Lopeka ("Rebecca"). H
    Rebeca ("to bind; snare"). S
    Rebekah ("Rebecca"). B

SNOW
    Hau Kea ("white snow"). H
    Lau Kalakoa ("the snow bush"; mottled green and
        white). H
    Yallo Bally ("snow peak"; Indian place name). I

SOARING
    'Iolana ("Yolanda"; "fairest"; "soaring hawk"). H

SOFT
    Julia ("the soft-haired"). S
    Kulia ("Julia"). H
    Malihina Mele ("soft green seas"). H

SOLITUDE
    Soledad. S

SOME OTHER TIME
    Kekāhi Manawa. H

SON
> Kama Kāne. H
> Keiki Kane ("son or boy"). H

SONG
> Aloha Oe ("song"). H
> Dithyramb (wild song sung by the Bacchanals). MG
> Manu-mele (songbird). H
> Mele ("song; chant; poem"). H
> Oli ("chanted song"). H

SORROWFUL
> Martha. B
> Milena ("Myrna"). H
> Niobe (changed into a stone from which her tears
> flow continuously). MG

SOULS
> Las Animas ("the souls"). S
> Psyche ("the soul; also, butterfly"; personification of
> the human soul). MG

SOUTH
> El Sur ("South"). S
> Hema. H
> Ka Lee ("south point, a high bluff in Hawaii"). H
> Kaus Australis ("southern part of the bow"). L
> Zubenelgenubi ("southern claw"; of the Scorpion; it is
> the southern or western basket of Libra, the
> balance). Ar

SPARROW
> El Gorrión. S
> Manu-li'ili'i. H

SPEAR
> 'Ēlau ("spear point; bayonet; top; tip"). H
> Gugnir (spear of Odin). MN
> Pololu (spear signifying peace). H

SPIDER
> Arachne (a maiden who was turned into a spider by
> Athena). MG
> Nananana. H

Pūnāwelewele. H

SPINNING WHEEL
Frigga's Spinning Wheel (the constellation as it was
called in the north). MN
Orion's Girdle (so called in the South). MN

SPINSTER
Chih-Nii (a divinity and daughter of Jade; she spins
robes). MC

SPIRIT
'Aumakua (family god; spirit). H
Daemon (protective spirit; in Roman [Genius]). MG
Kyoi (creator; Indian name). I
Lemures or Larvae (the evil spirits of the dead). MR
Mana (spiritual strength). H
Manes (the good spirits of the dead). MR
Näkki (water divinities; genie of the water). MF
Vu-Nuna (water-uncle; good spirit). MF

SPLENDOR
Aglaia (one of the three graces). MG

SPOTTED
Kiko Kiki ("spotted; dotted; speckled; discolored"). H

SPOTTED TAIL
Spotted Tail (a Sioux Indian chief). I

SPREADING WATER
Ni-Ubthatka (Omaha Indian chief). I

SPRING
Aganippe (spring on Mt. Helicon, home of the Muses).
MG
Aleyin (spirit of springs).
Castalia (near Delphi; those who drank or bathed in
this spring were touched by poetic inspiration). .
MG
Hāpuna ("spring; pool"). H
Hippocrene (spring on Mt. Helicon). MG
Kupulau (spring season). H
Papa Lele Kawa ("spring board for diving"). H
Tooan Tuh (dústú) ("spring frog"; name of a Cherokee
chief). I

SPUR
    Kēpā. H

SQUALL
    Kīkīao. H

SQUIRREL
    Kengish (clan name of the Luiseña Indians for a ground
        squirrel). I
    Kiulela. H
    Ratatosk (a squirrel who spreads gossip in Yggdrasil,
        the world tree). MN

STAFF
    Caduceus (golden wings at the top, intertwined with
        serpents, symbol of his authority as messenger of
        the gods; "golden staff"). MG
    Thyrsus (a staff tipped with a pine cone carried by
        Dionysus or Bacchus). MG

STAGE
    Chan (stage of a journey; station; stop). C

STANDING ELK
    Standing Elk (a Sioux Indian chief). I

STAR
    Acrux (brightest star in the Southern Cross).
    'Ae-ae-a-hiwa (star name). H
    Ai-kanaka (star name). H
    Ala pō'ali (orbit of stars; circular road). H
    Ali'i-o-Kona-i-ka-lews (name of star that guided
        navigators). H
    Alphard ("solitary star of the serpent"; brightest star
        in the constellation Hydra, the water monster). Ar
    Amatsu-mika-boshi (August star in heavens). MJ
    Anahita (identified with Venus). MP
    Aniani-i-ka-lani (name of star said to be in Milky
        Way). H
    Ankaa (brightest star in Phoenix). Ar
    Ao-hōpū (name of a star; possibly Jupiter). H
    Arcturas ("the bear's guard"; star of first magnitude). G
    Ashtart (of the sky of Ba'Al, was most beautiful of all
        heavenly bodies ... Venus). MPH
    Atria (navigational star).
    Avior (navigational star; star of the constellation Vella,
        the sails, or false Southern Cross).

Canopus (a bright star, on the edge of the Milky Way). G
Diphda (the second frog; part of the constellation
    Cetus, the Whale). Ar
Dubbe ("the bear's back"; a star that forms the outer
    rim of the bowl of the big dipper). Ar
Ekekela ("Esther"). H
Ester ("star"; "Esther"). S
Esther ("star"). H
Estrella ("star"). S
Gacrux (northernmost star of the Southern Cross).
Ha'ilona (name of a star). H
Haku-pō-kano ("Lord of the dark night"). H
Hale Kilo Hoku ("star observatory"). H
Hesperus or Hesper (the evening star; Roman: Vesper).
    MG
Hoku ("night of full moon").
Hōkū ("star"). H
Hōkū 'ae 'a ("wandering star"). H
Hōkū-'ai-'āina (navigator star). H
Hōkū-ala (rising star). H
Hōkū-ho'okele-wa'a (canoe guiding star). H
Hōkū-ke'a (Southern Cross). H
Hōkū-lele (shooting star). H
Hōkū-lewa (moving star; planet). H
Hōkū li'ili'i (small star; asteroid). H
Hōkū-noho-aupuni (Milky Way; lit. "ruling star"). H
Hōkū Ukali (satellite star). H
Hsing ("star"). C
'Iao (name of Jupiter when it is the morning star). H
Ihu-ku (any guiding star [Ku: above the bow; Ihu: of a
    canoe]). H
Ihu-moe (a star). H
I'Kawao-lani (name of a star). H
Ka'a'ei (a star appearing in the Māhoe nights of the
    moon). H
Ka'a-lolo (Tutelary star of Niihau). H
Kaha-i-kaha'I (star in the Milky Way). H
Ka-'ili-'ula (Tutelary star of Ka'Ō, Hawaii). H
Kaho-ea ("star"). H
Kahu'a ("star"). H
Kahuli-ali'I ("star"). H
Kāka'e ("star"). H
Kalua-o-ka-ohe ("star"). H
Kama'I'O ("star"). H
Kani-ha'alilo ("star"). H
Kaoma 'aiku ("follower of the Pleiades"; or Aldebaran;
    in the horns of the constellation Alpha Tauri). H

Kape-a ("crux star"). H
Kau-ano-meha ("placed in holy stillness"; possibly
    Sirius). H
Kawao-nui-a-ola ("star"; "great forests of life"). H
Kawelo-ali'i ("royal family"). H
Keahi-lele (the firebrand; a star). H
Keala-ka'a (star; rolling pathway). H
Kealohi-lani (star; "the brightness"). H
Keawe (Southern Cross). H
Kekai-hili (Southern Star). H
Kekela ("Stella"; star). H
Keola (patron star of Lanai). H
Kikī-'ula (star). H
Kilo hōkū (star gazer). H
Kio-pa'a (North Star). H
Kochab (shortened form of "North Star"; forms the
    outer rim of bowl of the little dipper). Ar
Kupua-lalo-o-kalani (demigod beneath the heavens). H
Lehua-kona (star in the Milky Way). H
Lena (name of a star). H
Lipo (star in the Southern skies). H
Maiao (star in navigation). H
Maka-'alohilohi ("bright eyes"; star). H
Malu-lani (a star). H
Mana-wahine ("female power; a star"). H
Na-au-ake-'ai-haku (lit. "heart eager to rule as a
    lord"). H
Nānā-mua (the star, Castor). H
Nāpēhā (star). H
Naua-a-keau-haku (a Milky Way star). H
Nui (star). H
Nu'u-anu ("cool heights; a star"). H
Pā-ao (star; one of large group resembling a double
    canoe). H
Pae-loa-hiki (star in the Milky Way). H
Peacock (brightest star in the constellation Peacock).
Phosphor (the morning star). MG
Procyon ("before the dog"; bright star east of Orion,
    the Hunter). G
Puana-kau (Tutelary star of West Maui). H
Sirius (dog star; "the scorching one"; brightest star in
    the heavens in the constellation Canis Major, the
    "large dog, " of Orion the Hunter). G
Suhail (star of second magnitude, along the Milky Way). G
Tishtriya (the dog star). MP
Vashti ("star"; wife of King of Persia). B
Waileia (star in the morning). H

Wai-Loa (near the Pleiades). H
Wai-Naku (patron star of Hilo). H
Zvezda Dennitsa (morning star). MSL
Zvezda Vechernyaya (evening star; twin of above). MSL

STEED
Grane or Greyfell (descendant of the eight-footed horse
of Odin, Sleipnir). MN
Gullfaxi [golden-maned] (raced with Thor's steed). MN

STEEP WIND, The
Tah-Teck-A-Da-Hair (a Sioux Indian chief). I

STEER
Wrinkle-Horn (an old steer whose horns have become
wrinkled and scaly). W

STEP-DAUGHTER, The
La Hijastra. S

STINGY MOUNTAIN LION
Stingy Mountain Lion (name of a brave in the Huchnom
Indian tribe). I

STOREHOUSE
Hale Ahu Waiwai (a heap of goods). H

STORM
'Akē'akē (Hawaiian stormy petrel; also: Lupe 'Akeke).
H
Guantauva (goddess of storms). MNI
Kona-lea (storm; cold of Kona). H
Thiassi (storm giant). MN
Thor's Hat (storm clouds; in Sweden he wore a broad
brimmed hat). MN
La Tormenta (the storm). S

STORY TELLER
Kākā'olelo. H
Peddler of Loads (a teller of tales). W

STRANGE
Ch'i (uncommon; rare). C
Malihini (newcomer; stranger; guest). H

STRAWFLOWER
Nani-mau-loa (white or yellow; everlasting beauty;
Nani: "splendor"). H

STREAK
Kaula Ulla (streak of lightning). H

STRENGTH
Odysseus and Ulysses (Roman) (great physical strength;
greatness of mind; example of heroic success).
MG

STRIKE UP THE MUSIC
Ho'okani Pila ("play music"). H

STUNTED
Kakanali'i (small). H

SUGAR CANE
Kō. H

SULKY
Kanūha (sulky one). H

SUMACH
Neleau (Hawaiian sumach). H

SUMMIT
Cima. S

SUN
Aka'ula (red sunset; lit. "red shadow"). H
Aten (as a solar disk). MEG
Atum (the setting sun). MEG
Dazhbog (the sun). MSL
El (the sun god). MPH
Harakhtes (the sun in its course across the heavens).
MEG
Horos (the solar god; "sun"). MG
Hvare-Khshaeta (dazzling sun). MP
Kahikū (sun rising). H
Kaula'i Lā (sun bath). H
Lā (sun). H
Marmakhis (symbol of rising sun). MEG
Mitra (the sun). MI
Päivä (sun). MF
Pale Lā (sun protection). H

Ra or Re or Phra (the sun sovereign lord of the sky).
    MEG
Shai ("to sun; to dry in the sun"). C
Shamash (sun god; his coachman was Bunene which
    means vigor, courage). MA
Sol (the sun driver). MN

SUNDAY
    Lāpule. H

SUNFLOWER
    Clytie (the maiden who, heart broken when Apollo
        deserted her, was changed into a sunflower, the
        symbol of faithfulness). MG
    Nānā-lā (sunflower). H
    Pua-nānā'lā (sunflower). H

SUPERIOR
    Lua 'Ole ("matchless; superior"). H
    'Oi ("superior; sharp"). H

SURGEON
    Kauka Kaha. H

SURVIVOR
    Pyrrha (only female survivor of the Deluge). MG

SWALLOW, The
    La Golondrina. S
    Manu-'io'io. H

SWAMP FOX
    Osceola (a Creek Indian chief). I

SWAN
    Brunhild ("swan maiden"). MN
    Nokekula ("swan"). H
    Valkyrs ("the swan maidens"). MN

SWEET
    Hua-pala (the sweetheart vine; orange trumpet). H
    Poni-mō'ī-li'ili'i (Sweet William). H
    Pshan-Shaw ("sweet scented grass"; the name of a
        Mandan Indian chief). I
    Sweet-Acorn (f) (the Indian name of a Yuki Indian
        woman). I
    Sweet Leilana (song; Harry Owens, composer). H

Weshcubb ("the sweet"; name of an Indian chief of the Chippewa tribe). I

SWIFT

Berrendo ("antelope"). S
Gna (Frigga's swift messenger who mounted Hofvarpnir). MN
Gull-Top (bore Heimdall over the rainbow bridge; a swift golden-maned steed). MN
Kūkini (swift messenger; runner). H
Māmā (speedy). H
Māmā I Ka Holo (fast in running). H
Swift Bear (a Sioux Indian chief). I

SWORD

Kusanagi (sword of the ruler of the seas). MJ
Tyrfing (mythical sword which cut through ice and stone given to Angantyr; it fought of its own accord). MN

TABU

Deneb ("tail of the hen"; brightest star in the constellation Cygnus, the Swan). Ar
Denebola ("tail of the lion"; second magnitude star). Ar
Kapu ("forbidden"). H

TAKES HIMSELF

Takes Himself (a Crow Indian chief). I

TALK

T'an ("to chat; talk; converse"). C

TANGLES

Witches' Bridle (the tangles of a horse's mane). W

TARANTULA

Kalanakula. H

TEAKETTLE

Kikila Kī. H
La Tetera ("the tea-pot"). S

TELESCOPE

'Ōhe-nānā. H

TEMPEST
Erisvorsh ("god of the holy tempest"). MSL
La Tempestad. S

TEMPLE
Heiau ("temple of the gods"). H

TEN
Diez. S
'Umi. H

TENDERFOOT
Mail-Order Cowboy ("without experience"). W

TERN
Manu-o-ku. H

THICKET
Alba (Choctaw Indian name). I

THISTLE
Tumbleweed ("a man with roving tendencies is called
a tumbleweed"). W

THOROUGHBRED, The
El Caballo De Pura Sangre. S

THOUGHT
Hugi (a swift runner). MN
Pansy ("thoughtful").
El Pensamiento. S

THREAD, A
Pignagogah. ES

THREE
'Akolu. H
Tres. S

THRONE
Noho Ali'i. H

THUNDER
Adad (god of lightning and the tempest). MA
Hinmaton-Yalakrit ("thunder coming from the water up
over the land"; Chief Joseph). I
Hino (the thunder spirit). I

Kahekili ("the thunderer"; the most famous native
   rulers; ruled Maui, Lanai, Molokai, Oahu at time
   of death). H
El Rayo (the thunderbolt). S
La Rayo (the thunderstorm). S
Manuhekili (thunder cloud). H

THURSDAY
   Pō'aha (Thursday). H

TIDE
   Kai A Pele (tidal wave; Sea of Pele). H
   El Marea (the tide). S

TIGER
   Kika. H

TIME
   Mei ("May"; time of blessing). H
   Tempas Fugit ("time flies"). L
   Shih ("time; season; hour; the age"). C

TINY
   Li'i (small, tiny, diminutive; affectionate name for
      youngest child in the family). H

TITANS, The
   Children of Uranus, the sky and Gaea, the earth. MG
   Cronus (the harvester). MG
   Hyperion (the wanderer on high; the sun). MG
   Iapetus (the hurler). MG
   Mnemosyne (memory). MG
   Oceanus (the river of the ocean). MG
   Phoebe (the bright one). MG
   Rhea (the earth). MG
   Tethys (the nourisher). MG
   Thea (the divine one). MG
   Themis (justice or law). MG

TO BE ASTONISHED AT NOTHING
   Nil Admirari. L

TOMORROW
   Āpōpō. H
   Mañana (denotes leisurely postponement). S
   Mañana Será Otro Dia (tomorrow is another day). S

TOP MOST
Ting. C

TORNADO
Kaipuni ("typhoon"). H
Makani Ka'A Wiliwili. H

TOWER
'Ale'o (tower; high lookout). H
Na Pale 'Ale'o (towering cliffs). H

TRADE
Kālepa (trader; merchant). H
Mālua-kele (trade wind). H
Moa'e (trade wind). H

TRANSFORMATION
Metamorphosis. MG

TRAVELLER
Chang-Kuo Lao (a man who rode a donkey which
    travelled thousands of leagues each day; one of
    the eight immortals). MC
Kahuna Pule Ka'ahele (travelling preacher). H
Kama Hele (traveler). H
Kemhisem (roamer; traveller; Indian name for a Karok
    brave). I
Nagaicho (great traveller; Indian name). I

TREE
Kikala. H
Koa (tree used for bowls and trays). H
Monkeypod (wide spreading shade tree). H
Niu-kahiki (date palm). H
Poinciana (has an umbrella of orange to red showy
    flowers). H
Yggdrasil (ash tree; it grew in the center of the earth,
    and had an indestructible trunk). MT

TRIAD
Anu, Enlil, Ea (the great gods). MA
Sin, Shamash, Ishtar (the astral gods). MA

TROLLS
Maras (the female trolls, or nightmares). MN

TROUBLED WATER
   Missouri (most Indian Nations called the Missouri
      river, troubled water). I

TRUMPETER
   Triton (trumpeter and messenger of the seas; he had
      a dolphin's tail instead of legs). MG

TUESDAY
   Pō'alua. H

TUGBOAT
   Kolomoku. H

TULIP
   El Tulipán. S

TURKEY FOOT
   Turkey Foot (name of a Miami Indian chief). I

TURTLE
   Commotins (chief of a clan of the Powhatan Indians). I
   Etaa (turtle clan name in the Zuni Indian tribe). I
   Honu (turtle; general name for tortoise and turtle). H
   Honu-kahiki ("a tortoise"). H
   La Tórtola (the turtle dove). S
   Tortuga ("turtle, tortoise"). S

TUTOR
   Chiron (a gentle and learned Centaur, tutor of heroes).
      MG

TWENTY DOLLARS
   Iwakalua Kālā. H

TWINS
   Gemini (constellation and sign of Zodiac). MG
   Heavenly Twins (were Castor and Polydeuces). MG
   Iphicles (twin of Heracles). MG
   Māhoe ("twins"). H
   Pollux (twin son of Zeus; the brighter of the twins of
      Gemini). MG
   Shu (twin of Tefnut). MEG
   T'ien Wang (heavenly twins; the door gods in Buddhist
      Temples). MC

TWO
> Dos. S
> Lua. H

TWO CROWS
> Pa-Ris-Ka-Roo-Pa (orator and councillor; name of a
> Crow Indian chief). I

TWO MOONS
> Two Moons (a Cheyenne Indian chief). I

TWO STRIKE
> Two Strike (a Sioux Indian chief). I

UMBRELLA
> Ho'omānalu ("parasol"). H
> Māmalu ("shaded"). H

UNDERWORLD
> Hel and Niflheim. MN
> Mana, Manala, Tuonela (Tuoni was the ruler; Wife,
> Tuonetar). MF
> Pwyll (Lord of the underworld when he changed places
> for a year and a day with Arawn, British prince
> of Hades). MEC
> Yomi-Tsu-Kuni (land of darkness). MJ

UNDISTURBED IN MIND
> Aequo Animo. L

UNITED STATES
> Moku'Āina-Hui-'Ia. H

UNIVERSE
> New World (the universe that came into existence after
> destruction of the world on the day of Ragnarokk).
> MN

UPLAND DWELLER
> Ko A Uka. H

VALLEY
> Kela ("Della"). H

Maui ("valley island"). H
Waipo ("valley"; a place name in Hawaii). H

VEHICLE
Ka'a Ōhua (vehicle carrying passengers for hire). H

VEILED
Skuld (third Norn who was closely veiled who held a
book or scroll not yet opened). MN

VERANDA
Hale Kia ("porch"). H
Lānai ("porch"; "balcony"). H

VICTORY
Pelenike ("Bernice"). H
Wikola ("victory"; "Victoria"). H

VINE
'Auko'i (a yellow vine; yellow flowers and seeded pods).
H
Ma'alewa (aerial vine). H

VIOLET
Nani-Wai-'Ale'Ale ("Violet"). H
La Violete (flower). S
Waioleka ("Violet"). H

VIRGIN
Adhara ("the virgins"; one of a group of three stars). Ar
Virgo, the Virgin (a constellation and sign of the
Zodiac). L

VISION
Hihi'o (vision or dream). H

WAGON
Chuck Wagon (the mess wagon of cow country). W
Holligan Wagon (one used for short trips and which
carried water and fuel). W
Trial Wagon (one hitched to another wagon when moving
camp). W

WALKS DOWN HILL SLOWLY
Anifakich (a Karok Indian name). I

WALRUS
   Pala'o. H

WAR
   Camilla (feminine warrior). MG
   Hildr (one of the Valkyries; a warrior). MN
   Ka'a Kaua (war chariot). H
   Kukailimoku (war god; personal god of King Kamehame-
      ha I, Hawaii's first king). H
   Luika ("Louise"). H
   Luisa ("Louise"). S
   Solymi (a race of warriors). MG

WASHTUB
   Kapu Holoi. H

WATCH
   Cerberus (watchdog). MG
   Eggther (harpist; warrior who kept watch on the king-
      doms of gods and men alike). MT
   Hale Kia'i (watch tower). H

WATER
   'Ae Kai (place where sea and land meet; water's
      edge). H
   Aka ("water"; name for a brave in the Chimariko
      tribe of Indians). I
   Apa (the waters). MI
   Apo (the water). MP
   Aquarius (a constellation and a sign of the Zodiac;"the
      water bearer"). G
   Ea ("house of the water"). MA
   Elf or Elb ("a water sprite or divinity). MN
   Hler ("water"). MN
   Kawaihae ("water of wrath"; a bay in Hawaii). H
   Kul (the water spirit that haunted deep waters and
      lakes). MF
   Lorelei, the (a siren maiden who sits on the Lorelei
      Rock near St. Goar, on the Rhine, and whose
      song lures the mariner to death; daughter of Old
      Father Rhine). MN
   Mii-No-Kama (causes water to flow from earth). MJ
   Mimme ("great"; Dakota Indian name). I
   Nârâs, The Waters. MI
   Pipi Pākē (water buffalo). H
   Rusalka (a water divinity, resembled moonlight, sang
      songs, sometimes bewitched). MSL

Shui ("water; river"). C
Shui-Kuan ("agent of water who averts evil"; one of
   the triad of water, earth, heaven). MC
Sisseton ("water people"; a Dakota Indian name). I
Undines (female water divinities; "gentle, lovable
   beings"). MN
Viz-Anya (water mother; a water spirit). MF
Vizi-Ember (water spirit living in lakes and rivers).
   MF
Vizi-Leany (maiden of the water; water spirit). MF
Vodyanoi (water spirit that haunts the mill pond in
   different guises, and doesn't like humans). MSL
Wai-'ale'ale ("rippling water"). H
Wai Kīkī ("rapid water"). H
Wai Lani ("heavenly water"). H
Waina ("place of water"). H
Waina Lani ("beautiful water"). H
Waioli ("singing water"). H
Wai Puhia ("wind blown water"). H
Waipu'Ilani ("water spout"). H
Wassermann ("water man"; also nixie women who sat
   on the river banks combing their long golden
   hair). MT

WAVE
Hydra ("water monster"; constellation). MG
Hydrus ("water snake"; constellation). L
Las Olas ("the waves"). S
Mummu ("tumult of the waves"; born from the mingled
   waters of sea and ocean). MA
Nalu ("surf"). H
Wave Maidens (nine giantesses who played around the
   Viking ships whom they favored; also called the
   billow maidens; they were: Atla, Augeia, Aurgiafa,
   Egia, Gialp (who caused storms), Greip, Iarnsaxa,
   Sindur, Ulfrun). MN

WE ARE SCHOLARS
He Poe Haumana Kakou. H

WEALTH
Kubera (god of wealth). MI
Ts'Ai-Shen ("wealth"). MC

WEATHER
Blue Whistler ("a norther"). W
Chinook (warm wind from the Japanese current). W

Cow Skinner (severe winter storm). W
Fence Lifter ("a hard rain"). W
Hell Wind ("a tornado"). W
Idaho Brain Storm ("a twister"). W
Kâla ("weather"). MI
Silver Thaw ("rain that freezes as it hits"). W

WEDNESDAY
Pō'akola. H

WELCOMER
Bragi, also Heimdall (shared the honor of welcoming
the heroes to Valhalla). MN

WEST
El Oeste ("west"). S
Komohama ("west"). H

WHALE
Ballena ("whale"). S
Kohalā ("whale"). H
Moku O Kohola ("whaleship"). H

WHEELBARROW
Kaapalala. H

WHERE?
'Auhea ("where"). H
'Auhea Ho'I ("where indeed?" implies indifference). H
¿Donde? ("where?"). S
¿A Dońde? ("where to?"). S

WHIRLPOOL
Charybdis (sea monster representing a whirlpool;
name for the whirlpool under a rock on the Scilian
side of the Straits of Messina). MG

WHIRLWIND
Haya-Ji (whirlwind god). MJ
Puahiohio ("whirlwind"). H

WHISKBROOM
Pūlumi. H

WHISTLE
Kōkio ("musical pipe; small gourd whistle"). H

WHITE
Aliali ("crystal clear"). H
Azucena, La ("white lily"). S
Blanco (m) Blanca (f) ("white"). S
Casa Blanca ("white house"). S
Chat ("white owl"; clan name of the tribe of Luiseña
Indians). I
Kaipolequa ("white nosed fox"; name of a Sauk Indian
brave). I
Kai'ūpoho ("white caps; breakers"). I
Kea ("shining white"). H
Lā Kea ("white fin"). H
Mahaskah ("White Cloud"; Iowa Indian name). I
Nakai ("white stranger"). H
Santana or Satanta ("White Bear"; a Kiowa sub-chief).
I
Wabishkeepenas ("white pigeon"; a Chippewa Indian
name). I
Waubeshik ("White Cloud"; A Winnebago Indian name).
I
White Antelope (a Cheyenne Indian brave). I
White Bird (a Nez Perces chief). I
White Horse (a Cheyenne Indian chief). I
Wun-Nes-Ton ("White buffalo"; a Blackfoot chief looked
on as the Sir Oracle of the nation). I

WHITHER?
I Hea ("whither?; to what place?; where?"). H

WICKER CHAIR
Noho'ie. H

WIDOWER
Wohpekumeu ("widower across the ocean"; "the one
who makes things as they are; a tricky, un-
reliable benefactor of man"; a Yurok Indian
name). I

WIGWAM
Wikiwama. H

WILD
El Jabali ("the wild boar"). S
Logi ("wild fire"). MN

WILD CAT
Kainchush (name of a Chicksaw Indian clan). I

Nimi (name of a Cocopa Indian clan). I
Tukum ("wild cats"; division of the Serrano Indian
tribe of Southern California). I

WILL YOU HAVE THIS?
Maconmeg. ES

WILLOW
Kahabi ("Willow clan"; Hope Indian tribe). I
Kai (Willow clan of the Navaho Indian tribe). I
Pachlu (Indian brave in the Chimariko tribe). I
Wīlou ("willow"). H

WILLY NILLY
Nolens, Volens. L

WIND
'Aiko'o (name of a wind at Nu'Alolo). H
'Āpa'Apa'a (name of a strong wind). H
Auster (Roman south wind; Notus [Greek]). MR
Boreas (stormy, north wind). MG
Dogoda (west wind). MSL
Ecalchot (wind god). MNI
Eka ("wind good for sailing"). H
'Ehu-kai (wind of Molokai). H
Enlik ("lord of winds"). MA
Eurus ("east wind"). MG
Feng-Po ("Earl of Wind"; later in this mythology Earl
of Wind was changed to Feng-Po Po, or Mrs.
Wind). MC
Hihio ("soft whistling sound, draft of wind"). H
Hippotades and Aeolus (Kings of Winds). MG
Kili'o'opu ("wind"). H
Kiu Inu Wai ("mountain wind"). H
Kono ("wind"; "warm, humid"). H
Konāhau ("strong and damp"). H
Kūpapaūla ("exposed to the wind"). H
Makani Hau None ("ice cold wind"). H
Mat-Hachva ("wind"; a name of a Mohave Indian clan).
I
Pahele-hala ("a wind"). H
Quetzalcoatl ("wind god"). MAZ
Vâta or Vâyu ("the wind"). MI
Zephyr ("the warm gentle west wind"). MG
Zephyrus, Boreas, Notus, Eurus (were the four winds,
and brothers; Aeolia was the island on which the
king of winds lived). MG

WINDS
>Fresh Breeze, Half a Gale, Trade Wind, Tempest
Blizzard, Whirlwind, Blast, Squall, Flurry, Flaw,
Capful of Wind, Chinook, Monsoon, Simoon, Sirocco,
Gale, Hurricane, Storm, Gust, Twister (kinds of winds
to use in a compound name).

WINE
>'Ea'ula ("wine colored"). H
I-Ti ("winemaker"). MC
Kaomi ("wine press"). H
Kī Aha Inu Waina ("wine glass"). H

WISDOM
>Kopia ("Sophia"). H

WITCH
>Grimhild (wife of Guiki, the Nibelung king; a wise
witch). MN
Gullveig ("from Vanaheim"). MN
Valpurgisnacht ("the witches' dance"). MN

WIVES
>Abiah (wife of Hezron). B
Alcestis (wife of Admetus). MG
Alcmene (beloved by Zeus, wife of Amphitryon). MG
Amata (wife of Latinus who fought Aeneas). MG
Anah (wife of Esau). B
Andromache (wife of Hector in the Trojan War). MG
Asenath (wife of Joseph; daughter of a priest of the
great national temple of the sun at Heliopolis). B
Bath-sheba (wife of David). B
Clytemnestra (wife of Agamemnon who was leader of
the Greeks in the Trojan War). MG
Drusilia (wife of the Roman procurator at Caesarea).
B
Eglah (one of David's wives). B
Elisheba (wife of Aaron; "god is an oath"). B
Eriphyle (wife of Amphiaraus of the Seven against
Thebes). MG
Eurydice (wife of Creon who killed herself in grief).
MG
Evadne (wife of Capaneus). MG
Frigga (wife of Odin, Woden, Wuotan, who was the
highest and holiest god of the northern races; she
sat in the watchtower, Hlidskialf, where she could
look over all the world). MN

Gerda (wife of Frey). MT
Grid (wife of Odin). MN
Haggith (wife of David). B
Helah (one of Ashur's wives). B
Hodesh (wife of Shaharaim). B
Iounn (wife of Bragi). MN
Jael (wife of a Canaanite chieftan). B
Jedidah (wife of Amon). B
Jehosheba (wife of the high priest of the lord,
    Johoiada). B
Jerioth (wife of Caleb). B
Judith ("praise"; wife of Esau). B
Keturah (wife of Abraham). B
Medea (wife of Jason; a powerful enchantress who
    assisted Jason in obtaining the Golden Fleece). MG
Megara (first wife of Heracles). MG
Mehetabel ("god makes happy"; wife of Hadar). B
Merope (loved by Orion and wife of Sisyphus). MG
Nanna (wife of Balder). MN
Peninnah (wife of Elkanah). B
Phaedra (wife of Theseus). MG
Rhea (wife of Chronus). MG
Sid (wife of Thor). MT
Side (wife of Orion). MG
Sigyn (wife of Loki). MN
Skaoi (wife of Njöror). MN

WIZARD
    Ashipu. MA

WOLF
    Ha-Na-Tah-Nu-Mauh ("wolf chief"; a chief of the
        Mandan Indians). I
    Lupo ("wolf"). H
    Moah ("wolf"; name of a chief of the Potawatomi clan).
        I
    Wolf ("the creator"; so called by the Comanche
        Indians). I
    Wolf Plume (chief of one of the Blackfeet). I

WOMEN
    Ah-Kay-Ee-Pix-En ("woman who strikes many"; a
        Blackfeet Indian name). I
    Calico (western name taken from the dress material
        women wore in the early days). W
    Calico Queen (a woman of the honkytonks). W

Catalog Woman (wife secured through a matchmaking bureau). W
Cookie Pusher (a waitress). W
Cucheneppo ("woman"; a Powhatan Indian name). I
Dulce (Spanish for sweet; a sweetheart, his girl, his lady friend). W
Hadassah (Hebrew for Esther (star), who saved her own people). B
Hagar (an Egyptian, handmaiden of Sarah). B
Hamutal (wife of Josiah). B
Heart and Hand Woman (woman or wife obtained through a matrimonial bureau). W
Heph-Zibah (wife of King Hezekiah). B
Huldah ("prophesied"). B
Jemima ("daylight"). B
Keren-Happuch("horn of antimony"). B
Kezia ("fragrance of a flower"). B
Laie ("woman of the twilight"; the beautiful; she was the Princess of the Rainbow). H
Live Dictionary (a school teacher). W
Lo-Ruhamah ("she will not be shown compassion"). B
Long-Haired Partner (a cowboy calls his wife). W
Noadiah (false prophetess; she tried to prevent the rebuilding of the walls of Jerusalem in 445 B.C.). B
Orpah (sister-in-law of Ruth). B
Runnin' Mate (used by cowboy to express his wife or pal). W
Sage Hen (nickname). W
Sherah ("a builder"). B
Syntyche ("one of first teachers of early church"). B
Wahine ("woman; female"). H
Zillah ("shadow of darkness"; wife of Lamech, the poet). B

WOOD
Nawkaw (chief in the Winnebago tribe of Indians; "wood"). I
Wooden Horse (device invented by Odysseus to bring victory to the Greeks in the Trojan War). MG

WOODPECKER
Emblem of Zeus. MG

WORKSHOP
Hale Hana ("workshop"). H

WORLD
    Alf Heim (world of the elves). MN
    Darkalf Heim (world of the gnomes). MN
    Ho'Olpoakamalanai (world of the soft gentle trade
        winds). H
    Jotun Heim (world of the giants and trolls). MN
    Midgard (world of the earth). MN
    Muspel Heim (world of fire). MN
    Niflheim (world of fog; home of the dragon, Nidhogg).
        MN
    Vana Heim (world of the Vanir gods). MN

WRITING
    Nabu (along with his wife, Tashmetum, invented
        writing; presided over belles-lettres; chisel, en-
        graving tablet, serpent-headed dragon his attribute).
        MA
    Pahu Palapa'a ("writing desk"). H
    Ts'ang Chieh (invented writing). MC

YELLOW
    Amarillo. S
    Huang. C
    Lena ("yellow"). H
    Melemele ("yellow"). H
    Ousamequin (also Massasoit; "yellow feather"; great
        chief of the Wampanoags). I
    Pualena ("yellow color"). H

YES
    'Ae ("yes, assent"). H

YONDER
    Awennye. ES
    Young Man Afraid of His Horses (chief of a clan of
        Sioux Indians). I
    Yucca Flower (a woman's Indian name). I

ZODIAC
    Kokiaka. H

II. SHIP "FIRSTS"

ADMIRAL, first U.S. Navy

David Glasgow Farragut was the first admiral in the U.S. Navy, a rank created for him by Congress. Farragut became a national hero in April 1862 when he took a fleet of eight steam sloops-of-war and 15 gun-boats carrying an army, and ran the gauntlet of the Confederate defenses at New Orleans, capturing that city. He continued on up the river to Vicksburg, for he knew the strategic importance of controlling the Mississippi. Thus Louisiana, Arkansas and Texas were cut off from the rest of the Confederacy.

The chief defenses of the South were the Forts Jackson and St. Philip below New Orleans. The Confederates strung a heavy chain cable between the two forts, supporting it on floating rafts. Beyond the cable they fortified still further by stationing armored rams and loading fire rafts with pine knots. It took Farragut's men some days to cut the chain, as they continuously fired on the forts. The naval squadron then passed them during the night without serious damage to the fleet. Then Farragut on his flagship, the Hartford, sailed up to New Orleans, the emporium of the Mississippi Valley, and second largest port in the United States, took the city on the 1st of May 1862, battling its 3000 Confederate defense troops.

During this battle it is recorded that mortar firing was the main factor in achieving the Confederate surrender. The heavy guns that threw shells at a high angle of fire had been built for the New Orleans campaign.

Farragut was considered the outstanding naval officer of the war. He was raised to the newly created rank of rear admiral after the Battle of New Orleans in July 1862. Up to this time captain, or commodore, was a courtesy title for a captain in charge of more than one ship.

Another naval triumph brought Farragut further honors. Mobile Bay harbor was closed by Confederate submerged torpedoes or mines. The Union fleet of 14 wooden vessels and four monitors sought to reach the Bay through a narrow passage. The Confederates had protected the Bay by three small wooden gun-boats, their wonder ship, an ironclad ram called the Tennessee, and the guns of Fort Morgan. Farragut climbed the main mast of the Hartford to view the battle more clearly, above the smoke of enemy gunfire. One of his men strapped him safely to the mast while Farragut directed the movements of his fleet. The Brooklyn led the main column. Then the Tecumseh, a monitor, struck a mine, sank. The Brooklyn stopped to warn Farragut of the mines. In so doing the ships that followed her closed in, giving the Confederates an opportunity for heavy cross fire. Farragut steamed ahead, took the lead, saying, "Damn the torpedoes." His skill in battle and his bravery carried him through to victory after a terrible battle in which the Union Squadron with its powerful guns forced the Tennessee to surrender on the 5th of August 1864. Fort Morgan surrendered on the 23rd of August, and the city of Mobile was completely blockaded.

After the battle of Mobile Bay, Congress made Farragut a vice-admiral on 23 December 1864. On the 26th of July 1866, he was commissioned admiral for life. The following year he was appointed commander of the European Squadron.

During these two battles Farragut ordered mud smeared on the hulks and visible parts of his ships, which might be the forerunner of ship camouflage.

The Hartford, a wooden-screw, steam sloop-of-war (named for Hartford, Conn.), was 226 feet by 43 feet, weighed 2790 tons, and launched at Charlestown Navy Yard, Boston, 22 November 1858. There were 22 nine-inch smooth-bore guns in the broadside; two 20-pounder Parrott rifles. The flagship was brought to Washington in 1939, restored, and became the nucleus of the Naval Museum. See also Part IV under HARTFORD.

AFRICAN STAR, S.S.
The first commercial radar installation, the "Mariner," went into operation on this American South African liner on 1 May 1946, after being installed on 27 April 1946 by the General Electric Co. Her maiden voyage was from New York City to a South African port.

AL-KI (Steamboat)
This vessel was the first steamboat to set off for the Klondike. It was jammed with supplies, horses, cattle and passengers, until there was no room left. It was built in 1884 by the Pacific Coast Co., and was made of wood, a propeller type.

ALARCÓN, HERNANDO DE
It is recorded that this man was the first European to
see the land that is now the state of California. As he
ascended the Colorado River he went ashore several
times.

ALBATROSS (Ship)
Thomas W. Doak, a skilled carpenter, thought to be
from Boston, came on this vessel to the West Coast in
1816. He is the first American to settle in California,
settling in the Monterey and Santa Cruz area. After
baptism he changed his name to Felipe Santiago.

ALERT (Brig)
The first North American merchant man to enter the
River Platte. This 120-ton vessel was built at Salem,
Mass. in 1798 and owned by Robert Stone, leading owner, Dudley L. Pickman and others, all business men.
    While commanded by Captain Robert Gray of "Colum-
bia" fame, a French privateer captured her late in 1798.
The vessel was taken into Montevideo, Uruguay, late in
1798. Gray was released. He returned to command the
James in 1801. The Spanish then fitted out the vessel as
a privateer. It was not until a century later than the
heirs of the brig recovered compensation.

ALERT (Clipper)
First State of Maine clipper. This vessel was launched
at Damariocotta, Maine, by Metcalf & Norris, November
1850. It arrived in New York to load for San Francisco. With Captain Francis Bursley commanding, the
vessel sailed for San Francisco 29 December 1850 and
was found to be too small (764 tons) for Cape Horn use
and the California trade; and disappointingly slow, making the passage in 150 days. After its second voyage to
the Pacific Coast it was sold in 1857 at Calcutta. The
following year, October 1858, the vessel was lost in the
China sea taking half the crew with it.

ALERT (Ship)
The first British vessel to be taken during the War of
1812 as it searched for the U.S.S. Hornet in the Atlantic Ocean. Her guns were thrown overboard, the
vessel sent to St. John's with the prisoners aboard,
under Lieutenant Wilmer.

ALEXANDER   (Ship)
    The first Yankee trick in the history of San Diego was
    perpetrated by the captain of this vessel. Captain John
    Brown arrived in the harbor from Boston on 26 Febru-
    ary 1803 with a long tale of woe. His sailors were
    sick with scurvy. Could he get permission to land and
    take care of the sick men. So they were allowed to land,
    but were forbidden to carry on trade, and were ordered
    to keep away from the fort.
    The Alexander stood in the harbor eight days. During
    this time the captain and his men were busy buying all
    the otter skins they could get from the Indians and the
    soldiers. On the fifth evening of the vessel's stay in
    port, officials of the port found 491 otter skins which
    they removed from the vessel. The captain was then
    asked to leave San Diego without his valuable skins.

ALEXANDER LA VALLEY   (Craneboat)
    The first steamboat (self-propelled) to pass through the
    Panama Canal, on 7 January 1914. The following
    August, commercial traffic was inaugurated.

ALFRED   (Man-of-war)
    First American man-of-war and the first naval ship com-
    missioned by the Continental Congress. The vessel was
    formerly the Black Prince, an Indiaman and old mer-
    chant ship, converted to a flagship for Commodore Esek
    Hopkin's Squadron, America's first make-shift navy; and
    renamed after Alfred, the Great.
    For the first time the American flag was raised on a
    commissioned naval vessel, 3 December 1775; and hoisted
    by First Lieutenant John Paul Jones in the Delaware
    River at Philadelphia. The flag was known as the "Grand
    Union" flag, which had the old British Union Flag, or
    Jack, placed in the canton, with a field of 13 red and
    white stripes.
    This vessel made the first strike of the U.S. Navy,
    18 February 1776, on Nassau, with the seven other ships
    of the Squadron, where they seized 71 cannon and 15
    mortars, although the British were able to ship off a big
    powder supply.

ALLIANCE   (Frigate)
    The first ship, so named to commemorate the alliance
    between the United States and France, was built at
    Salisbury, Mass. in 1778 by William and John Hackett.
    She was noted for her speed and beauty. On her first

voyage she conveyed Lafayette to France.
When peace with Britain was declared 11 April 1783,
the Navy was disbanded. The Alliance was converted
into an Indiaman, and in 1787 sailed in the China and
India trade.

AMADOR (Side-Wheeler)
One of the first very large river craft ever built, being
221 feet long, 985 tons, constructed in 1869. A calliope
and huge golden eagles decorated its paddle boxes. It
became a ferry boat in the San Francisco Bay, then the
property of the University of California. It was anchored on the east side of the Oakland Estuary until it
was dismantled in 1905.

AMAZON (Brig)
The first whaler said to have made the voyage across
the equinoctial line to the Brazil Banks. This Nantucket
brig left for the Banks in 1774, returned 19 April 1775
with a full ship of bone and hogsheads of whale oil. Its
Captain, Uriah Bunker, returned with the news that the
South Atlantic whaling grounds between the Platte River,
Argentina and the Falklands were open.

AMELIA (British Whaler)
The mate of this vessel, Archilaus Hammond of Nan-
tucket, it is alleged, was the first European to harpoon
a whale in the Pacific Ocean, when Captain James
Shields took this ship on a pioneering voyage around
Cape Horn.

AMERICA (Privateer)
This vessel is said to have been the most successful in
operating as a Massachusetts privateer. She made a
record day's run of over 240 miles, which was considered highly successful. The vessel was the fastest
of the period. It was built in 1809 by Retire Becket;
473 tonnage.

AMERICA (Schooner)
The first American yacht to win the America's Cup
which was given by the Royal Yacht Squadron for the
Race around the Isle of Wight, Cowes, England in 1851.
It defended the cup in 1870. This two-masted schooner
was built in 1850 expressly for the race and to represent
the New York Yacht Club. George Steers, naval architect, designed it.

The America had unusual sailing ability and was
called the "fastest small sailing vessel in the world."
It made the historic crossing of the Atlantic in 21 days;
defeating 14 English yachts. Donald McKay, famous
American clipper ship-builder, used the entrance and
run lines features when he built the clipper, Lightning.
Later the yacht became a Confederate despatch boat.
When it was captured, it served as a practice ship at
the Naval Academy. In 1921 she was permanently docked
at the Naval Academy.

AMERICA (Ship)
This vessel was the first ship-of-the-line to be built in
America for the U.S. Navy, at Portsmouth, N.H., 5
November 1782. It was one of Joseph Finkham Woods'
"continent" ships. It had at least 74 guns mounted on
three decks. By unanimous vote of the Continental Congress, it was commanded by John Paul Jones. Later it
was given to our French allies.

ANCON (Merchant Ship)
This vessel was the first regular merchant vessel to go
through the Panama Canal in commercial service, which
was on the 15 August 1914.

ANN McKIM (Clipper)
The first Yankee clipper ship was built in 1832-33.
Isaac McKim, wealthy Baltimore merchant, ordered
Kennard and Williamson of Fell's Point, Baltimore to
construct a vessel that closely followed the superior
sailing qualities of the clipper brigs and schooners of
the day, without regard for cost. Eventually the vessel
was to cost $50,000.
So the builder constructed long easy water lines, low
freeboard, a raking stem, three tall light masts. The
decks were brasswork; the fittings Spanish mahogany,
and the sheathing imported red copper. The result was
a handsome, fast and most unusual vessel. But it
stowed so little cargo that it was looked upon as unprof-
itable; and for several years longer, the full-bodied brigs
and schooners were used. The ship was 143 feet long,
31 feet wide and of 493 tons register. She was named
after the owner's wife, and with John Martin in command, her first captain, she sailed in the China sea
trade for a number of years. In 1837 she was sold at
Valparaiso, ending her career under the flag of Chile.
This vessel is said to have influenced progressive

builders. Howland and Aspinwall, who owned her for a
while, later ordered the first extremely sharp clipper of
the era, the Rainbow. Others claim she did not directly
influence ship builders, as no other ship was built like
her. Eventually it was discovered that the clipper
strained less in a heavy sea, crossed calm belts better
than the low-riggers. It was soon seen that the clipper
was ideal for the China tea trade, for since tea lost its
flavor quickly in the hold of a ship, the faster delivery
of that product by the clippers was advantageous.

By 1843 these long narrow wooden sailing vessels
with their lofty canvas gave the shipping world its greatest development in speed and beauty. From 1843 to
1868 the clippers were the queens of the oceans.

ANTELOPE   (Side-Wheeler)

This steamer, a former Long Island excursion boat
built in 1847 on the East Coast, carried the first mail
to San Francisco, 15 April 1860. The hot and tired
Pony Express rider with his dusty mail bags, making a
coast to coast mail trip, probably stepped aboard the
vessel gratefully. The vessel took him and other passengers down the Sacramento River, leaving the city of
Sacramento, 15 April 1860.

This vessel had come West to answer the siren of the
Gold Rush on the River. She carried gold dust and bul-
lion for Wells Fargo Express Company, so was given the
name, The Gold Boat. She kept a tight, regular schedule,
making her a favorite among the miners. In the summer
of 1857 she usually alternated with, or sometimes was a
running mate of the New World.

ARCHANGEL   (English Ship)

The first accurate surveying, chart-making expedition was
made on this 60-ton vessel, of the Maine Coast by Captain George Weymouth, whose original intention had been
to look for a northwest passage to China and the Indies.
After being icebound between Baffin Island and Greenland,
he returned to England late in 1604. He left Dartmouth,
England, again on 31 March 1605 to return and explore
the Atlantic coast. On the 14th of May the vessel had
sighted Nantucket and sailed north on its surveying expedition. Carefully Weymouth surveyed and explored
this area, entering the Kennebec River (Sagadahoc). He
wrote glowingly of the great source for forest products,
suitable for ship building; told of the abundant fish and
game; of the deep river that the natives used for com-

merce. He took back the first accurate knowledge of
the coast of Maine, resulting in the English concentrat-
ing on colonization at the mouth of the Kennebec during
1605-1608.
   The written account of James Rosier, who chronicled
the story, is admittedly falsified as to the geographical
location, latitudes, true positions and landmarks, because the writer felt that the true information might get
into the hands of a foreign nation, and that others might
gain knowledge of the place and take advantage of the
fruitfulness of the country. The verbal account was accurate, and resulted in King James I giving a grant to
the Plymouth Company to plant colonies in northern Virginia. To the London Company he gave the right to colonize southern Virginia.

ARCHITECT (Clipper)
   The first clipper to make the run from the East Coast
to the California coast, leaving 16 January 1849 and arriving at San Francisco 28 June 1849, a run of 160 days.
This vessel of 520 tons was built by L. B. Culley, Baltimore in August 1848 for Adams Gray of Baltimore.
In 1853 she won the tea race from China to London,
making the run in three to eight days better time than
six of the best of the world's best clippers. She was
sold to the British in Hong Kong for $23,000 in June
1854.

ARIZONIAN (Ship)
   The first merchant vessel to use the Panama Canal on
a voyage between ports beyond the canal terminals. This
occurred on 15 and 16 August 1914.

ASTREA I (Ship)
   The first tidings of the 1783 peace were brought on this
vessel to the United States by Benjamin Franklin when
he arrived from France. Captain John Derby, Master,
had carried to England the news of the beginning of the
American Revolution.

ASTREA II (Ship)
   This vessel is claimed as the first American vessel to
visit Manila flying the Stars and Stripes in Manila Bay
for the first time where it opened trade 3 October 1796.
This Salem-Philippine trade in sugar, indigo, hemp continued as long as Salem men owned vessels.
   The vessel was built at Bradford, Massachusetts, in

1795 for Elias H. Derby of Salem. Its first commander
was Captain Henry Prince, Master. On it Nathaniel
Bowditch sailed as supercargo. Mathematics was a pas-
sion with him. He taught 12 members of the crew to
take and work lunars, the only method of getting longi-
tude without a chronometer, which no Salem vessel could
afford. In 1801, Bowditch issued the Practical Navigator,
which became a standard American treatise on navigation.

ASTROLABE (Ship)
This vessel, with the Boussole, was the first foreign
ship to anchor in Monterey Bay, arriving 15 September
1786. They were French vessels voyaging around the
globe in a scientific expedition.

ATLANTA (Ship)
One of the first steel vessels for the U.S. Navy was
authorized by Congress 3 March 1833. The others were:
Dolphin (dispatch boat), Boston, and Chicago.

ATLANTIC (Ship)
This Salem owned ship, launched in 1785 and commanded
by Elias Hasket Derby, Jr., was the first, in 1788, to
hoist the American flag in the ports of Calcutta and
Bombay, India. The powerful East India Company monopolized the trade; but Derby began to carry cotton and
blackwood from these ports to Canton, challenging their
monopoly.

ATLANTUS (Ship)
The first concrete ship launched: 4 December 1918.

ATREVIDA (Ship)
This vessel brought a John Groem, or Groom, or
Graham, supposedly from Boston, who is said to be the
first European-American man to reach Alta California.
He landed at Monterey with Alejandro Malaspina's Expedition of discovery on 13 September 1791. He was
buried there on the day of his arrival.
    Malaspina commanded the Atrevida and the Des-
cubierta. He had left Spain in 1789 to make scientific
explorations in various territories of the Pacific Ocean.
He looked for the Strait of Anián, a mythical strait,
supposed to connect the Atlantic and Pacific Oceans.

AUNT SALLY   (Motor Boat)
    It is thought that Samuel Morey created the world's first
    motor boat in 1820.   This small mechanical boat was
    launched in a pond.   It was thought that Morey applied
    an internal combustion engine to it.   For some reason
    he filled the boat with rocks and sank her.
    Morey, a New Hampshire inventor, who has been
    called the second greatest American inventor of steam-
    boats, built his first boat in a shed behind his house on
    the Connecticut River at Orford.   He moved it against
    the current, upstream, with a single paddle wheel in the
    stern, which pulled the boat, instead of driving it.
    Morey developed and made tests with stern wheel steam-
    ers on the East River and Long Island Sound.   This ex-
    perimental craft had boilers and engines that worked
    well.   They attained a speed of five miles an hour.
    Stevens and Livingston, in 1796, approached Morey.
    It is said Morey laid the foundation for Livingston and
    Fulton to produce steamboats that made money.

BADEN-BADEN   (Ship)
    This vessel was the first rotor ship to enter an Ameri-
    can port, which occurred on 9 May 1926 in New York
    Harbor.   It was in command of Captain Peter Callsen.
    It had come from Hamburg, Germany, by way of the
    Canary Islands.   Anton Flettner invented this vessel with
    its two 45-foot towers nine feet in diameter.   These ro-
    tated at a speed of 120 revolutions a minute.   The Baden-
    Baden attained a speed of 9 1/2 knots.

BALAENA   (Whaler)
    This vessel was one of the first two American craft to
    be sent to the Hawaiian Islands.   The other was the
    Equator.   Captain Edmund Gardner commanded this New
    Bedford, Massachusetts whaler, named after the whale.
    It left New Bedford in 1818 and arrived with the Equator
    off Honolulu on Oahu Island on 29 September 1819.   Cap-
    tain Elisha Folger of the Equator, with others, heard of
    a report that whales had been seen off the Japanese Is-
    lands, which caused all the whalers in port to race west-
    wards.

BALTIMORE   (Cruiser)
    The first navy vessel, commissioned as a cruiser, to be
    fitted with a heavy steel lower deck, on 7 January 1890.

It served in the Spanish-American War. It was decommissioned to become a minclayer 8 March 1915, seeing service in World War I.

BANGOR (Schooner)
This steam packet was the first substantial twin screw, iron sea-going vessel built in the United States for coast-wide trade. It ran between Boston and Dangor, Maine. It was constructed by Harlan and Hollingsworth Company, a pioneer of large and medium-sized shipbuilding plants in America. Schooner rigged, it registered 450 tons and was launched in May 1844.

BARALT (Dutch Steamship)
The first ship on which a child was born as it passed through the Gatun Locks, Panama Canal. The birth occurred 2 June 1930. The parents, Mr. and Mrs. Niezes, were from Panama.

BEAVER (English Steamboat)
This Hudson Bay Company vessel was the first steamboat to appear on the Columbia River. This side wheeler was built on the Thames River in 1834 or 5, for a man-of-war and trading boat. She left Gravesend, England, on 27 August 1835, without her engines installed, her two 13-foot paddle wheels carefully stowed on deck, 20 tons of coal aboard. Originally schooner-rigged with three masts, she was changed into a brigatine to make the long voyage to Oregon. Staunchly built, double planked, with copper sheathing on her hull and copper fastenings throughout, the Beaver was to see over 50 years of service.
The engines were installed on the coast, the paddle wheels put on and David Hume, her first captain, tested her on short trips to a sawmill downstream, where Indians had told him there were black stones that would burn. The coal however was not found suitable, so wood was burned instead. An excursion was planned with dignitaries and ladies aboard, moving down stream to the mouth of the Willamette River.
The vessel worked on Puget Sound because it drew too much water for convenient use on the Columbia River. She became a tug boat finally, operating until 1888 when she slammed onto Beaver Rock at the entrance of the harbor at Vancouver on the Sound. She couldn't get off and lay there five years. When the tide washed her off, she sank. The Indians called her "Skookum Ship," mean-

ing, "powerful, or strong demon."

BEAVER (Whaler)
  The first whaler out of an American port to round the
  Horn and sail into the Pacific, in 1791.

BEDFORD (Whaler)
  The first American vessel to cross the Atlantic and re-
  sume trade with Great Britain after the Revolutionary
  War, late in 1782. She was the first vessel to display
  the 13 rebellious stripes of America in any British port.
  She arrived 6 February 1783.
  Commanded by Captain Mooers, or Morris, the vessel,
  loaded with 487 butts of whale oil for Europe, stopped at
  a port in France, learned of the peace news, so changed
  her destination for a more promising market, and set
  out for London, on the Thames River. She was the
  first Nantucket, or American whaler in the Thames.
  The vessel was owned by William Rotch who backed Nantucket whalers, resulting in a wide interest in whaling.

BELLE (Steamer)
  The first steamer built to run to the Cascades. The
  second was the Fashion, and the Mountain Buck was
  then built. This vessel was owned by J. C. Ainsworth
  and Co.

BELLINGHAM (Steamboat)
  The first steamboat to ply the upper Yukon River. It
  was packed unassembled, then taken over the mountains,
  assembled on the Yukon.

BENTON (Ironclad)
  The first ironclad vessels were the Benton and the Essex,
  and seven others built for the U.S. government and
  launched 15 January 1862. They were called the Gunboat Flotilla, the Western Flotilla, sometimes the Mississippi Squadron.

BETSY (Ship)
  The first American vessel to put in at San Diego Bay,
  25 August 1800. The captain, Charles Winship, secured
  wood and water, went on to San Blas.

BIG DIPPER (Work Boat)
  The first garbage scow, the Big Dipper, went into operation in 1972 in the Long Beach, California harbor. The

vessel is a trash boat specially designed by John Mar-
riner, naval architect, to keep the waters of Long Beach
Harbor clear of floating trash and debris. Other world
ports have no such craft for harbor cleanups.

It was built by the California Shipbuilding Corporation
in less than four months. A hydraulic basket near the
bow scoops up the debris, which is dumped into two bins.
The bins on the deck, when full, are hoisted off, onto
trucks that take the trash to a land dump. There is a
hydraulic crane with tongs to grip heavy objects, pull
them up out of the water.

BIG HATCHEE   (Steamboat)
This vessel was one of the first steamboats taken from
the Mississippi River to steam up the Rio Grande through
the dunes and marshes, transporting soldiers and animals
to invade Mexico.

BLACK BALL LINE
This was the first transatlantic packet line to keep to
regular schedules between New York and Liverpool. Four
vessels, Amity, Courier, Pacific, James Monroe, would
sail from each place on a certain day in the month
throughout the year, carrying passengers, mail and
freight. Service began in January 1818. The James
Monroe left New York on the 5th of the month, and the
Courier left Liverpool on the 1st of January 1818. Gradually sailings were increased to Havre and London.

BLACK CROOK   (Barge)
The first barge to navigate the Colorado River was de-
signed in San Francisco and built in 19 days, in 1864.
It was used 12 to 15 years.

BLAZING STAR   (Teamboat)
A new ferryboat, that was propelled by six horses on a
treadmill, was invented by Mose Rogers in April, 1814.
It was used in slack water and could carry 800 passengers.

BLESSING OF THE BAY   (Sloop)
The first vessel to be launched by the Puritans, one
year after their arrival, was built to give the colonists
a means of water communication with their neighbors.
It is said to be the third ship built in America. This
ship was built not far from Governor Winthrop's house,
"Ten Hills," within Medford, Conn. by Master Walter

Merry and others, in 1631. It was launched 4 July
1631 at Mystic, Conn.
The makers of this 60-ton, part trader, part fighter,
were blacksmiths, riggers, calkers, etc., who took
their pay in shares. She was built mostly of native
locust. The vessel was used as an armed ship against
pirates and as a trading vessel. Furs, wampum, off-
shore fishing were traded with the Dutch at New Amsterdam. Salted and dried fish were taken to Bermuda,
Barbados, and Europe. In 1633, on its last voyage,
while loaded with fish and furs, it was lost.

BOOKER T. WASHINGTON, S.S. (Ship)
First merchant ship of the United States to be captained
by a Negro, Captain Hugh Mulzac, the first Black man
to hold an unlimited mariner's license. This liberty
ship was launched 29 September 1942.

BOSTON NEWS LETTER
The first shipping news in the period beginning with
1704 was carried in this News Letter, America's first
regularly published newspaper. It started with frag-
mentary shipping reports in the Massachusetts Bay Colony. The other colony ports were considered to be foreign.

BOWHEAD (Whaler)
The first steam whaler on the Pacific Coast. It was
called the "floating tea-kettle of the polar sea," because
it went to the Arctic for whales.

BUENA VENTURA (Ship)
The first ship captured in the Spanish-American War,
taken by the gunboat Nashville on 22 April, 1898.

BUFORD (Army Transport)
First army transport to pass through the Panama Canal
en route from San Francisco to Galveston, Texas, 9
September 1914.

BUSKO (Ship)
The first German ship captured in World War II by the
Coast Guard Cutter Northland.

CADET (Brig)

William Vans claimed in his autobiography that he brought the first pepper to the United States in this vessel in 1788. The brig was fitted out in Boston and was the first vessel to visit the ports on the west coast of Sumatra, opening trade with the island. He brought cassia, cinnamon, gum, benzoin, pepper and other goods to Salem. Jonathan Carnes was also on this vessel. He was at Benkulen in 1793, he said, when he heard of a pepper colony in Sumatra. On this initial voyage he might have been on the Cadet, but it is alleged that the ship to bring the pepper was the Rajah. The Rajah left Salem in November 1795, returned with an $18,000 cargo of pepper which was sold at 700 percent profit at Salem.

The story goes that by the time the Rajah had made three voyages bringing pepper, the mystery of the source of the pepper market was out. This was about 1800. It is said that ten men, lured into a Salem tavern were plied with drinks, so loosening their tongues, making them tell that Sumatra was the source of the pepper they brought back to Salem. Between 1795-1845 around 200 pepper vessels made Salem the emporium of pepper. See also RAJAH.

CALIFORNIA (Steamship)

The first Pacific Mail Steamer to come all the way around Cape Horn, establish a semi-monthly service was the California. The vessel took 144 3/4 days, 76 on steam. She left the East Coast 6 October 1848, and shortly after the Gold Rush started.

On the voyage many adversities plagued the captain. The engine stopped at Virginia Capes. The captain, Cleveland Forbes, became ill. It took the vessel 40 hours to pass through the Straits. The maximum number of passengers allowed were 60, but 150 emigrants were in steerage, and there was a crew of 36. To this number were added 350 passengers taken on at Panama. It was also discovered there were stowaways aboard. More troubles heaped on Captain Forbes at San Francisco for his crew deserted him for the Gold Fields; and he had a difficult time finding a new crew.

This wooden paddle wheel steamer, bark-rigged, registered 1057 tonnage, was built by W. H. Webb in New York. She plied regularly between Panama and San Francisco from 1849-1854. Then until 1875 this vessel was operated coastwise, sometimes as a spare steamer to make occasional voyages. As a bark she hauled lumber and coal. Then she came to an end when she pounded to pieces on the coast off Peru near Picasmayo in December 1894.

CAMACHE (Steamboat)
This vessel, owned by Major Pierson Barton of Reading, Pa., made the longest steamboat trip ever made, 485 miles, from San Francisco to Tehama. This was in 1851.

CAMBRIDGE (Packet)
The first serious packet mutiny occurred on this Black Ball vessel in 1840 with Captain Ira Bursley in command. They were three weeks out. Eight of the crew mutinied, refused to do duty. They threatened to hang Captain Bursley at a yardarm and threatened to stab anyone who came near them to arrest them. Passengers from cabins and steerage helped work the ship, kept watch at night. Captain Bursley cut off the mutineers' food, and in four days six were starved into submission. Two held out against him. They went into the forecastle. Although armed, the mate and the captain finally seized them, confined them below deck. Arriving at Sandy Hook, a revenue cutter carried the mutineers to prison.
This vessel was the first to bring back to New York the news of the Liverpool Hurricane in which she had been caught. The anchors dragged, the vessel drifted closer and closer to a stone pier. The Captain put out a sign offering 1000 pounds to any steamer that would tow him to safety. No one came. At the last minute the anchors held, prevented the vessel from being dashed to pieces.

CAMERONIA, S.S. (British Steamship)
The first ship to enter the port of New York without stopping for quarantine procedure, on 1 February 1937. Passenger vessels which complied with the health requirements were allowed to enter under a system of licenses. This arrangement was later extended to Boston.

CANADA (Packet) see ADDENDUM (p. 146)

CATAMARAN
This jointed vessel, used by life guards at public beaches, was patterned on two parallel hulls by Nathanael Greene Herreshoff of Providence, R.I., on 10 April 1877.

CHARITY (Ship)
The first cattle, a bull and three cows, arrived in New England on this Weston ship, June 1622.

CHARLES (Oil Tanker)
The first oil tanker to voyage between Antwerp, Belgium and the United States from 1869 to 1872. The tanker contained 59 iron tanks arranged in the bottom of the hold, and held 7000 barrels, or 794 tons.

CHARLES DOGGETT (Hermaphrodite Brig)
The American Flag was nicknamed "Old Glory" for the first time when the people of Salem, Mass., presented Captain William Driver, commander of this vessel, with an American flay saying, "Do your best to keep 'Old Glory' flying." The captain was a whaler who was getting ready to sail for the South Pacific in December 1831. The vessel had been launched at Cohasset, Mass., in 1826. Captain Driver carried the descendants of the Bounty mutineers to safety, when they drifted away from Pitcairn Island. See also Part IV under BOUNTY.

CHARLES W. WETMORE (Steamer)
The first whaleback steamer to cross the Atlantic Ocean when it left Duluth, Minnesota, on 11 June 1891 with a cargo of grain for Liverpool, England. Her net tonnage was 1,075 with a dead capacity of 3000 tons.

CHARLOTTE DUNDAS (Steamboat)
This vessel has been claimed as the first practical steamboat. It was built by a Scott for Lord Dundas, a wealthy landowner, who named the vessel for his wife. It was used to tow barges on the Forth and Clyde Canal in 1802, irregularly, as it was feared the sides of the canal would be damaged by the wash from the paddle wheel.
John Fitch made his model steamboat in 1785, and in 1787 tried it out successfully. In 1790 a third Fitch steamboat operated, but failed to meet expenses. In 1807 when the Clermont was launched, 16 steamboats had been built. See CLERMONT.

CHESAPEAKE, U.S.S. (Ship)
The first ship constructed by the U.S. Government. It was built to help protect our commerce from the Algerians. It carried 36 guns. Work began in 1794, but was discontinued because peace came in 1796. Then

the next year work began again on the vessel and it was launched in December 1799.

Captain James Lawrence was ordered to sea before she was properly equipped. At Boston Harbor the 38 gun British Shannon blocked her as she tried to outrun the Shannon. The Shannon closed in and captured her in 15 minutes. The captain, mortally wounded, said, "Don't Give Up the Ship."

CHIEF JUSTICE MARSHALL (Steamboat)
The first steamboat to be used in service between Troy and New York. It was built in 1825. It towed the Niagara through the Erie Canal.

CHIPPEWA (Steamboat)
The first steamboat, a fur company vessel, to ascend the Missouri River to Brulé Bottom, 15 miles below Fort Benton, a distance of 3600 miles, 17 July 1859. It plied upstream with difficulty, with freight on board. The cargo was left on the bank.

In 1860 the Chippewa made it to Fort Benton. The next year it again went up the Missouri River. Near the mouth of Poplar River, at Diaster Bend, the crew upset candles burning on kegs of whiskey. The boat caught fire. The crew got off before the fire reached the powder kegs. After the explosion there was nothing left of the Chippewa. All over the shore were strewn beads, blankets, tobacco and pipes.

CHRYSOPOLIS (Steamboat)
This luxury boat, a side-wheeler, was the fastest steamboat on the Sacramento River the year it was launched, in 1860. The vessel, tonnage 1050, was built at a cost of $250,000 by John North for the California Steam Navigation Company and launched at Steamboat Point on a moonlit night. People crowded along the shores to view this beautiful steamer as it was towed to Benicia for its final touches. She was gold and white, and called "Bride of the Golden River." In the ten years of her heyday, she transported bridal parties for 15 years, between San Francisco and Sacramento.

As you stepped into the spacious salons you were transported into a gold and white Victorian elegance-- plate-glass mirrors, gilt, red plush sofas, chairs, brass lamps and gourmet cuisine. She was a running mate of the Yellowstone in October 1865. And when the Yellowstone boilers exploded, the Chrysopolis picked up the wounded.

She had a long and useful career because North had built her carefully, of the best wood. She was well cared for, the engines were always kept clean, in order. She never raced, so no explosions occurred, that is none that had to do with her. And at least not until St. Patrick's Day, 1869. These were still tense post-war days. Two companies of Emmett Guards decided to march and hold clambakes on this day of this year. They smuggled cannon and a powder keg aboard the Chrysopolis. As they approached the wharf at San Francisco, two guards loaded the cannon. When it went off, the planks of the boat loosened, the red plush seats caught fire and began to burn. Sixteen guards were hurt.

In 1875 she was rebuilt from hull up as a ferry steamer, renamed the Oakland, and plied between San Francisco and Oakland, lasting 30 more years. In 1940 she was lost by fire.

CITY OF PEKING   (Iron Screw Steamboat)
One of the first two merchant vessels to be designed and built for reserve warships, the other being the City of Tokyo. Both were built at Chester, Pa., in 1874. Both were the first vessels to be built for the run from San Francisco to China.

As a trans-pacific liner, it carried large cargoes, burned little coal. This vessel made 12 1/4 knots as against the wooden steamboats that made 9 1/2 knots. The vessel always made schedules and was ahead of schedule sometimes. The run to Yokohama took 16 days. It is said she helped to bring an end to the clippers. The City of Peking was rated as a Navy Cruiser, taken over by the Navy in 1898, then used only as a troop transport.

CLERMONT   (Steamboat)
Robert Fulton did not invent the first steamboat. Eight other men had built workable steam vessels. He built the first practical steamboat, the first financially successful vessel, that started their general use. The snubnosed Clermont made five miles an hour against the current on the Hudson River when it was launched in 1807 by Livingston and Fulton. It ran from New York to Albany and back in 62 hours.

The vessel was 133 feet long, 18 feet of beam, 7 feet deep at first, then it was enlarged to 150 feet. It had two masts, a smokestack. The sails were never used.

Its paddle wheels were first in the open, later covered.
Its low pressure engine was designed by James Watts,
English inventor. Cabins were built on the decks.
Meals were served. Hudson obtained exclusive rights
to sail such vessels up and down the Hudson River. He
has been hailed as the inventor of the "first steam
packet" that was financially successful. The steamboat
was first called North River, as well as Fulton's Folly.
See also CHARLOTTE DUNDAS.

CLIPPER SHIP   (Clipper)
   The first clipper ship was an American creation.   See
   ANN McKIM.

CODORUS   (Iron Steamboat)
   This vessel was the first iron steamboat built in America,
   by Jesse Starr, at York, Pa., in 1825. She was built
   as a sectional, small and light shallow-draft steamboat,
   80 feet long, 9 feet of beam, drawing 6 1/2 inches, with
   its engine on board. The sections were hauled by horses
   to the Susquehanna River; there assembled on the bank
   for service on the upper reaches of that river.

COLONEL WRIGHT   (Steamboat)
   The first steamboat built above the Dalles was the Colonel Wright, to run to Fort Walla Walla, Priest's Rapids
   up to the Snake River. It was constructed in the autumn-
   winter of 1858-9.

COLORADO, U.S.S.   (Ship)
   First naval engagement of the Civil War occurred at
   Pensacola, Florida, on the 14 September 1861 between
   this vessel and the steamer, Judah, lying at anchor.
   Lieut. John Henry Russell took a detachment of men
   from the Colorado, appeared at the Navy Yard at two in
   the morning, burned the Judah, spiked the only gun in
   the yard. Three Union men were killed, four wounded;
   but no Confederates suffered casualties.

COLUMBIA   (Sloop)
   This ship carried the American Flag around the globe for
   the first time with Captain James Kendrick commanding
   part of the way, Captain Robert Gray commanding the
   remainder of the voyage, 1787-1790. Both the Columbia
   and the Lady Washington, as tender, the latter commanded by Captain Robert Gray, were the first North
   American vessels to pass Cape Horn.

While Captain Kendrick remained at Nootka Sound
with the Lady Washington, establishing the first fur post
on the west coast, Captain Gray took the Columbia with
sea otter pelts to Canton and to bring back tea for Boston. Captain Gray returned to Boston by way of Cape
Good Hope. In Boston Harbor, on 9 August 1790, after
completing 41,890 miles, after a three year absence, he
fired 13 gun salutes to the hurrahs of welcome that
greeted him.

With him was an Hawaiian (then called a Sandwich
Islander) who came off the boat with him, which may
have been the first time the Bostonians had seen a native
of Hawaii dressed in a feather cloak of golden suns set
in scarlet and a feather helmet. This first voyage began the northwest fur trade, paved the way for fortunes
to be built with the China trade.

Captain Robert Gray, on his second voyage in 1792,
was the first to discover the Columbia River, give the
United States title to the territory (Oregon) which Lewis
and Clark were to find 13 years later. Gray found the
entrance to the Columbia River in the spring of 1792
when finally a favorable wind took him through the breakers. He anchored 11 miles upstream; then went up the
river and finally landed at the mouth. There he raised
the American flag, named the river Columbia after his
ship. He charted the river entrance and coast. This
vessel was built at Hobart's Landing on the North River
by James Briggs in 1773.

COLUMBIA   (Steamboat)
The first ship in the world to successfully use electricity
for light. On 2 May 1880 a four-dynamo "A" type was
placed in the salons and passenger cabins. This lasted
for 15 years when a larger dynamo was installed.

The vessel was built at Chester, Pa., and plied between Portland, Oregon, and San Francisco, California.
Her net tonnage was 1,746.

COLUMBIA   (Steamboat)
The first Columbia River-built vessel, constructed at
Astoria by James Frost and John Adair, men of John
Jacob Astor's Pacific Fur Company, was launched 3
July 1850. This ferry-like boat, a side wheeler with
machinery bought in California, of odd shape, without
ornaments or trim, clumsy and slow, took 26 hours to
journey from Astoria to Oregon City on its maiden
voyage. The boat worked between Oregon City and the

Cascades. It towed barges, brought emigrants and did
a big business because it was the only steamboat on the
Willamette and Columbia rivers.

COLUMBUS (Packet)
    The first pre-arranged race between packets occurred
    between the Columbus and the Sheridan in 1837. It is
    the first ocean match recorded, although there must
    have been many informal races before. The 597-ton
    Columbus of the Black Ball Line, commanded by Captain
    Depeyster, put up a stake of $10,000 to see which pack-
    et came in first at New York from Liverpool. The new
    895-ton Sheridan of the Dramatic Line, commanded by
    Captain Russel, promised all his 40 crew a bonus of $50
    each if the Sheridan won the race.
    The packets left New York 2 February 1837. The pas-
    sage was 16 days for the Columbus; the Sheridan coming
    in two days later. Later the Sheridan was found to be
    too large for a Liverpool packet and was put in the
    China trade.

CONCORD (Bark)
    The first vessel to sail direct from Europe with the in-
    tent to reach the New England coast. Bartholomew
    Gosnold, a navigator, trader, colonist, with 32 men, in
    1602, crossed the Atlantic from Falmouth to a point near
    Portland, Maine (Casco Bay). He sailed down the coast,
    explored, charted the Northeast American coast. This
    expedition was not a permanent success. He named
    Cape Cod, found Narragansett Bay. He went back to re-
    port the rich resources he had found.

CONESTOGA (Gunboat)
    The Conestoga, Lexington and Tyler were the Union
    Navy's first gunboats used on the Mississippi River.
    This vessel was a packet converted to a gunboat to
    serve during the Civil War. It was squat and black.
    At night it would be anchored in midstream. Once the
    Captain heard hounds baying. A Negro ran ahead of
    them toward the river shore. The captain sent a yawl
    to pick him up.

CONSTANCE (Ship)
    The first American woman pirate during the American
    Revolution took a British armed sloop, the George of
    Bristol, a bark. Her name was Fanny Campbell which
    she changed to Channing. She dyed her skin brown,

cropped her hair, and dressed as a pirate, with the in-
tent of releasing her imprisoned lover in Havana.
When the crew of the Constance mutinied, she took
over as captain, and the Constance became a renegade
ship, sailing under the black flag. She put a friend in
charge of the George, and with it sailed to Havana to re-
lease William Lovell and his companions. Lovell had
left Boston on the Royal Kent for South America, ex-
pecting upon his return to marry Fanny. A friend had
escaped the prison where Lovell was incarcerated, returning to Boston, found Fanny and told her of William's
plight. This was Fanny's first and only experience as a
pirate. Shortly after they returned to America, the two
lovers were married.

CONSTELLATION U.S.S. (Frigate)
The first carronades to be used on an American Naval
vessel were put on this vessel. They were 28 24-pound-
ers on the main deck and 20 long 12-pounders on the
quarter deck and forecastle. This was the first U.S.
Naval vessel to sail around the Cape of Good Hope to the
West Coast, then to China, in December 1840.
It was the first American vessel to capture an enemy
ship, which fired on the Constellation first during the
undeclared war with France, after the American Revolution 9 February 1799, off Nevis Island, West Indies.
Commodore Truxton was in command, met L'Insurgente,
French warship, with Captain Barreault in command.
After an hour and a quarter of fighting, the French ship
surrendered.
The naval battle of the Constellation and the Vengeance, French frigate and privateer, was one of the
bloodiest single vessel engagements in all history. It
ended in victory for the Constellation, but the Vengeance
was able to steal away under the protection of night,
limping along. No trace of her could be found. Captain
Truxton was honored for this victory with a gold medal
from Congress; then given command of the new larger
President.
This frigate had a long distinguished career. She was
called "Yankee Race Horse." She was launched at Baltimore on 7 September 1797, tonnage 1,265.

CONSTITUTION, U.S.S. (Frigate)
The first important naval victory of the war of 1812 was
effected between this vessel and the British 38-gun
H.M.S. Guerrière, in August 1812. This battle proved

that the ships of the American Navy were the best in the
world at that time, for they were better designed, faster
than the English warships. "Old Ironsides," as she was
called, achieved this sobriquet when the British fire fell
off her hull, ineffective, and a seaman of the Guerrière
called her that.

She was one of the three new frigates, with the Constellation and the United States, built by the U.S. at the
end of the Revolution. All three were designed by Joshua
Humphrey and built at Boston, launched in 1798. The
ship had a total of 50 guns, 32 pounders and 8-inch guns;
and weighed 1607 tons. She was built of live oak timbers that came from the islands off Georgia and the
Carolinas, so it resisted rot and insects. Paul Revere
sheathed her with copper after he learned the secret of
rolling copper. Her figurehead was Hercules, carved
by the skilled Bostonian, Simeon Skillin. It splintered
in 1803 and was replaced with Neptune, then still later,
it acquired another Hercules.

These frigates were called by the British, "monstrous
armament, ridiculous in lines, unpractical and incompe-
tent," when they first saw them. A British frigate, re-
puted to be one of the best in West Indian waters, challenged the Constellation to an all-day race. They raced
from sunrise to sunset. The superior sailing qualities
of the Constellation astonished the British captain. She
decisively beat the British frigate. Later 18 British
frigates tried to overtake the Constellation without success.

By March 1813, seven months after the War began,
not one American frigate had struck her flag. England
was amazed for she had expected the U.S. navy to be
annihilated long ago. The Guerrière was the first major
defeat for the British in 14 years. This victory did
much to win enthusiasm from New Englanders when they
heard that the Guerrière came out of the fray looking
like a sieve, sinking rapidly into the sea, its prisoners
brought to Boston.

CONSTITUTION (Packet)
This vessel was the fastest of the river packets of its
period. On opening day of the Erie Canal, it entered
the parade through it.

CONTE DI SAVOIA (Ship)
The first gyro-stabilized vessel to cross the Atlantic
Ocean was commanded by Captain Antonio Lena arriving

in New York Harbor on 7 December 1932.   The vessel
was of the Italian Line.

COURIER   (Ship)
The first vessel designed by Donald McKay, of future
clipper fame.   It was owned by W. Wolfe and A. Foster,
Jr. of New York.   She outsailed every vessel she fell
in with at sea.   She made a great deal of money for her
owners in the Rio coffee trade.   She brought Donald
McKay into the shipbuilding limelight.

COURIER   (Ship)
The first liner to carry mail, passengers and freight
monthly from New York to Liverpool on a regular schedule.   Also the first recorded towing of a vessel occurred
in 1819 when this vessel was towed out of Liverpool, in
January 1819.
The initial sailings of the packets Courier, Pacific,
Jame Monroe, and Amity of the Black Ball Line began
in January, 1818.   The other vessels may also be called
"firsts."   This marks the beginning of the packet service.
New York arrival was 23 February 1818.   This vessel
left Liverpool with apples for New York, trunks and
cases of English woolens and coal.   Westbound winds
made the trip long, 47 days, but a British transient
took 90 days during the same week.   Sailing dates were
known far in advance.   The regularity, rapid delivery,
pleased the dry goods merchants, as the financial re-
turns were quicker.

CROWN GALLEY   (Ship)
The Crown Galley with Vice-Admiral Rhett commanding,
engaged in the first southern fleet engagement, repulsing
a Spanish Fleet of six ships, commanded by a French
Admiral.   One vessel manned by 90 men was captured
off Charleston, S.C. in 1706.

CURTISS, U.S.S.   (Tender)
The first seaplane tender designed and built for the U.S.
Navy was authorized by Congress on 30 July 1937.   She
was launched at the New York Shipbuilding Corporation
Yard, Camden, N.J., on 20 April 1940.   She had a dis-
placement of 8,625 tons and cost $9,943,000.

ADDENDUM
CANADA   (Packet)
This pioneer, outstanding, packet of the Black Ball Line
made the fastest average, and the fastest westbound

time, up to 1827. She was called "the greyhound of the
fleet." She also headed the fleet for the best average
time of crossing. She was a luxury liner, comfortable,
beamy and fast. The passenger quarters were luxurious.
She was the best appointed packet of her day.
She was diverted to California trade from 1840 to
1851; then she became a New Bedford whaler. She was
lost off Brazil in 1856, when she was 33 years old. In
its day the packet was the only communication between
the United States and Europe. European mail came by
packet. The packets drove through ice and snow and fog
and gales to make their schedules. Many of their captains had commanded privateers during the War of 1812
and were veterans on handling a vessel well.

DAISY GRAY (Schooner)
This vessel was the first ocean going lumber schooner
to enter the newly made port, which was still uncom-
pleted, of Stockton, California, on February 1933.

DANUBE (Brig)
The first white person and the first American to be
buried on Santa Catalina Island was Sam Prentiss who
owned and sailed on the Danube. After graduating from
college, Prentiss set out for a life at sea. He arrived
in California in 1824. As his vessel neared Dead Man's
Island, the ship was cast on the rocks during a sudden
storm. He was rescued from the waters where the ship
had been cast. He died in 1854 at the age of 72.

DAVID BROWN (Steamboat)
This vessel was the first steamship to try to provide a
regular fortnightly schedule between the ports of New
York, Philadelphia, Baltimore and the Charleston-Savan-
nah area, which began in April 1833. She was commanded by James Pennoyer. The boat was insufficiently
powered, too small, so when hit by the tail end of a
hurricane, she lost her rudder and was severely damaged on 23 August 1833.

DAVID DOWS (Schooner)
This first five-masted schooner with top masts was
built at the Bailey Brothers shipyard in Toledo, Ohio.
She was launched 21 April 1881. Her first captain was
Joseph Skelton; her owner M. D. Carrington. Her reg-

istered tonnage was 1418. She was lost off Whiting,
Indiana on Thanksgiving Day, 1889.

DE ROSSET   (Iron Ship)
The first iron vessel built of American iron. Of 186
tonnage, she was built by Langley B. Culley at Baltimore and registered there 4 April 1839.

DEAN   (Brig)
The Dean was the first vessel to be built on western
waters, in the Mississippi-Ohio-Great Lakes area by a
Mr. Dean who launched it at an unidentified yard on the
Alleghany River (some sources claim at Alleghany City
in 1806), in January 1803. She sailed from Pittsburgh
to the Cumberland, took on a cargo of cotton to Liverpool. A Liverpool newspaper recorded on 9 July 1803,
that the Dean was the first vessel to come to Europe
from the western waters of the United States.
    She made a voyage to Leghorn in the Mediterranean
in 1807, showed her American papers. When the cus-
tomshouse officer saw them, he said, "There is no such
port as Pittsburgh," the captain had to show him a map
of the United States indicating the new city.

DEFIANCE   (Steamboat)
The first calliope is said to have been installed on this
vessel that plied the Sacramento River. Port officials
told the Captain that he could not carry passengers on
San Francisco Bay. So the passengers were loaded on
barges, the barges swung astern. As the calliope
played, the people sang.

DELAWARE, U.S.S.   (Ship)
The first gyro-compass was installed and tested on this
vessel, at sea 28 August 1911.

DEMALOGOS (or FULTON I)   (Frigate)
The first steam propelled frigate in the world, built by
Robert Fulton for the U.S. Navy was launched 29 October 1814 at Brown's Shipyard, New York. Fulton designed and supervised its building. It was designed for
a floating fort, intended for harbor defense, not sea.
    The vessel was made of five-foot thick wood; it had
center-wheel propulsion; drew eight feet. It carried 30
32-pound carronades, two Columbiads (each carrying a
100-pound red-hot ball). Guns in a battery were protected by the massive wood sides. An explosion of her

powder magazine in 1829 when she was 15 years old,
destroyed her by fire.

DESIRE   (Ship)
    The first Yankee sailing record is on this vessel; which
    records the vessel as trading in slaves.   It may have
    been the first, or one of the first to engage in slave
    trade.
    This 100-ton vessel (or 120) was built at Marblehead
    in 1636-7 for fishing on the Banks.   It fished for two
    years.   In 1638 commanded by Captain William Pierce,
    she brought cotton, tobacco and Negroes to Salem from
    the West Indies.   In 1639 she left Boston for Gravesend,
    England, taking 23 days, as recorded by Governor Win-
    throp.   She had no navigating instruments.   Her records
    were kept with chalk used on a shingle.   The shingle
    was stowed in the binnacle.

DIRIGO   (Steel Vessel)
    First steel sailing vessel was built on the American con-
    tinent at Bath, Maine, by Arthur Sewall & Co., launched
    3 February 1894.   Captain George W. Goodwin was the
    first commander.   Its gross tonnage was 3,004.   It car-
    ried 13,000 square yards of canvas.   The name means
    "I Lead," for the Maine Motto.

DISCOVERY   (Sloop-of-War)
    The first foreign vessel, other than those of the Span-
    iards, to call and enter at Yerba Buena (San Francisco),
    was on 14 November 1792, after leaving Nootka Sound.
    Captain George Vancouver, English navigator, commanded
    the vessel.   He remained 10 days, then sailed south.   At
    San Juan Capistrano Mission, he gave the mission a bar-
    rel organ.
    This vessel was the first vessel to enter San Diego
    Harbor, where Spanish officials were a little perturbed,
    although he was treated with courtesy.   He had on board
    geologists, botonists, astronomers and geographers for
    this was his famous around-the-world voyage of 1790-
    1794.

DISCOVERY   (Pinnace)
    This vessel, with the Godspeed and the Susan Constant,
    brought the first permanent settlers to Jamestown in
    1607.   This 20-ton pinnace was a companion to the flag-
    ship, Susan Constant.   She was commanded by John Rat-
    cliffe, an English mariner.   The plan was to leave her

in America as an exploring boat. She was buffeted by
storms so bad that Ratcliffe wanted to turn back. But
the Admiral of the Fleet, Captain Christopher Newport
in the flagship, would not hear of it. Finally the fleet
sighted land, Cape Henry, 26 April 1607. She had left
England in January of that year. See GODSPEED,
SARAH CONSTANT.

DONALD McKAY (Clipper)
    This ship was the first in size of all sailing ships in the
    world--2598 tons--for many years. She spent her last
    days as a Quebec lumber trader.

DRAGON SHIPS (Ships)
    The dragon ships of the Norsemen who sailed the New
    England coasts in the 10th and 11th centuries may have
    been the first vessels to land, explore and colonize in
    New England. It is said that in 1005 Thorwald, brother
    of Lief Ericson, built the first ship on the coast of New
    England. An old keel was raised on the head of Cape
    Cod, as a landmark, and the place marked on Norse
    maps as "Keel Cape, " or "Keelness. "
    The Viking Danes sailed to Greenland where they
    founded a colony. It is believed they copied their dragon
    ships design from the large dragon boat of King Alfred
    of England; and sailed to North America in them hun-
    dreds of years before Columbus.

DREADNAUGHT (Clipper)
    The first clipper to carry a brass band to attract first-
    class trade.

DUNDERBERG (Screw Ironclad Ram)
    This is the first warship to be fitted with a double bot-
    tom. She was the most powerful war vessel of her day,
    the largest, the speediest. She was the first to have a
    complete system of water-tight bulkheads, transverse
    and longitudinal. The armor on the hull was 4 1/2
    inches thick.
    Secretary Wells asked William Webb's shipyard to
    build a "monster ironclad" for the U.S. government.
    This long, powerful ram was laid down in July 1862,
    completed in the middle of 1865, too large to be built
    quickly and too late for the war was over. It could
    make 15 3/4 knots due to having two ship's engines of
    5000 horsepower; its tonnage was 5250. Webb sold her
    to Napoleon III. She was renamed Rochambeau in 1866.

Her features were copied in the future French ships.

EAGLE   (Brig)
   The first Chinese to come to America's shores are said
   to have come on this vessel in 1848.   Later thousands
   of Chinese, and other nationalities were drawn to California when gold was discovered at Sutter's Mill.

EDWARD   (British Ship)
   This vessel was the first warship captured by a commissioned U.S. Navy officer, Captain John Barry, of
   the brig, Lexington, who took this 16-ton vessel off the
   coast of Virginia 17 April 1776.   Then he brought her
   to Philadelphia.

EDWARD EVERETT   (Ship)
   One of the first ships to sail from Boston.   The vessel,
   named for the Harvard College president, was commanded by Captain Henry Smith.   The vessel sailed 13
   January 1849 with a regularly organized company of
   150, and arrived in San Francisco Bay 6 July 1849.

EIGHT COLONY   (Boats)
   Paving stones for guns were used by 64 men commanded by Captain A. Whipple, probably for the
   first time, in 1772, in the first overt act of resistance,
   and commencement of our struggle with Great Britain.
   On 18 June 1772, they captured the schooner Gaspé,
   tender to the British squadron.   She was in chase of the
   packet Hannah, with Captain Linzee, master.   There
   were 27 armed men on the Gaspé.   The vessel ran a-
   ground and was captured by boarding, set on fire.   She
   later blew up.

ELIZA   (Whaler)
   The first American ship to be chartered by the Dutch
   East India firm to go on the annual cruise of one ship
   a year from Batavia to trade at Nagasaki, Japan.   So
   under the Dutch flag the Japanese saw an American vessel for the first time, in 1798.   Historians differ on
   this.   There is a Japanese painting showing this vessel
   off the rocks, being unloaded or loaded by several dozen
   small craft in Nagasaki Harbor.   See LADY WASHING-
   TON; MARGARET.

ELIZA ANDERSON   (Side-Wheeler)
This vessel may have been the oldest vessel on the
Pacific Coast because it had been built 40 years before
she became a gambling hall tied up to the Seattle river
bank, after which she was readied for the Klondike Gold
Rush in 1896. The Eliza Anderson was refurbished in
a hurry. The boilers were old. There were no pro-
pellors, no ship's compass--and she was going on a
3000-mile voyage to the Bering Sea, as the flagship of
a flotilla of five decrepit vessels.

This small craft was stuffed with pots and pans, tents,
cups and dishes, patent gold rockers, stoves, sleds,
provisions and clothing, as well as twice as many people as she should have carried when she set off ahead
of a tug pulling three other craft. One of these carried
a cargo of tin goods lashed to the deck. One was a
coal barge and the last a yacht, privately owned.

The first mishap came after stopping for fuel on Vancouver Island. The inexperienced crew loaded the coal
unequally so that the vessel listed, and the rudder would
not work. Then the Eliza Anderson drifted into a clipper, Glory of the Seas, shattered her paddlebox. The
passengers grew alarmed, demanded that the captain
turn back, but he would not.

Then the ship ran out of coal, for the lazy crew had
stowed only half of the assigned amount. So wooden
bunks, furniture, stateroom partitions were torn away
to feed the furnace. Rain began to pelt down on the
flotilla, strong winds tossed the vessels about. The
storm raged. When the crew went to get out the life-
boats and rafts, they were gone, swept away by the sea
and storm. The passengers were even more frightened
now. They wrote farewell notes and stuffed them in
empty whisky bottles, of which there were aplenty. By
this time the Eliza Anderson was out of control, and
Captain Tom Powers gave the order, "Abandon Ship."

Then suddenly out of the storm appeared a mystery
man in oilskins, rubberboots, with white beard and
hair. He took the wheel, steered the vessel into a
cove on Kodiak Island. Then he vanished. No one
knew where he went, or who he was. Later it was
discovered that he was a stowaway who lived on Kodiak
Island who wanted to get to Unalaska. On Kodiak Island coal was found and loaded on the vessel. The
Eliza Anderson continued her voyage hugging the coast.
At Dutch Harbor she swung into the docks. Wood
splintered, a boiler pipe burst and scalding steam

gushed everywhere.
    Some of the passengers, disgusted, left the vessel,
and took a whaler, the Baranof, to finish their journey
across the Bering Sea. Some sailed for home. The
rest sailed on to find that at their last stopping place,
there would be 1700 more miles to go--on foot.

EMELIA
    First whaleship to round Cape Horn with James Shields
    as commander, in 1788.

EMERALD (Packet)
    This vessel voyaged from Liverpool to Boston in 16
    days, the only record passage like it being in 1860
    when the powerful clipper Andrew Jackson ran it in 15
    days. This was a packet of the Jewell Line, com-
    manded by Captain Fox.

EMILY (Whaler)
    The first woman to go on a whaling voyage was the wife
    of Captain Joseph Russell of Nantucket, commander of
    the Emily. She left home in 1822 to join her husband
    in London for a trip to the Japanese whaling grounds.
    After that many wives went to sea with their husbands.
    At this time whalers considered a woman on board any
    whaler bad luck.

EMPRESS OF CHINA (Privateer)
    This vessel is America's first trading ship, which was
    first in the Canton china trade. It was the first suc-
    cessful trader to fly the American flag at Canton.
        It sailed from New York on Washington's Birthday,
    1784, under Captain John Green to open trade for tea
    and silks. She arrived in the Pearl River, 28 August
    1784. She left the River 28 December and arrived in
    New York 11 May 1785. She returned around the Cape
    of Good Hope, taking three years with stop-overs.
        The venture was the result of a need to find new
    markets after the American Revolution when the Ameri-
    can colonies had broke with Great Britain, closing their
    trade with the British West Indies. So the Yankees,
    without maps and charts, sailed away to faroff ports to
    trade wherever they could. The merchants of New York
    made this supreme effort by fitting out a privateer, re-
    naming it Empress of China, and sent her to Canton.
    Trade grew. By 1789 American ships from the Atlantic
    seaboard crowded Canton harbor. Fifteen American ves-

sels were there in the roads at one time.

Tea, silk, chinaware, art objects, copper, bronze, ivory and porcelain were obtained for seal and otter furs, sandlewood, mirrors, metal tools, knicknacks. American-made goods were exchanged for the furs, sandlewood, which in turn were exchanged for China goods. This made a three-way trade deal.

On 22 February 1789 the Empress of China was stranded on the Irish coast, seven years to the day from the time she sailed for China. She came off the coast as the ship Clara. As the Clara, she registered 368 1/4 tons, indicating that this was the tonnage of the Empress of China also. Her records had been lost, and no one knew the exact tonnage. It is said that the China trade eventually paid the greatest share of Federal income which enabled the United States to buy the Louisiana province from France.

ENDEAVOR   (Ship)
The first passage through the Straits of Magellan by a U.S. vessel was made in 1824 when she voyaged from the Atlantic to the Pacific with Captain David Elwell as commander.

ENDEAVOUR BARK   (Collier)
Captain James Cook, English navigator, was the first to discover that North and South islands of New Zealand were insular, on Cook's first voyage when he left Plymouth, England, 25 August 1768 to return in the Downs 12 July 1771. He also discovered Cook Strait in 1769. On his third voyage on this vessel, Cook discovered the Sandwich Islands (Hawaiian Islands) 18 January 1778, and died there 14 February 1779. He also discovered Cook Inlet, a bay in Alaska, in 1778 on this third voyage.

On the first voyage Sir Joseph Banks, English naturalist, headed an eminent scientific staff. It is recorded that he fitted the Endeavour at his own expense. He made the marsupial fauna of Australia known to western science for the first time. The breadfruit tree was introduced into the West Indies through his influence. The purpose of this third voyage was to see what communication existed between the Atlantic and Pacific Oceans in the Arctic regions. A result of this search for a Northwest passage was the opening up of the Northwest American shore to trade and colonization.

This 368-ton Whitby collier, named Earl of Pembroke, was purchased and renamed Endeavour in 1764, was of

strong construction with great stowage capacity, and
shallow draft. The ends were short, snubbed, and it
was a ship rigged with three masts, and mounted a few
light guns. She was not a bark. Because the English
Navy had a fighting vessel Endeavour, the name of
Endeavour Bark was given the collier. In the 16th century onwards "bark" meant a minor subsidiary. This
vessel was layered with tarred felt to protect her from
the teredo worm. The ship is one of the world's most
famous vessels. See also: RESOLUTION, for the
"firsts" of Cook's second voyage.

ENTERPRISE   (Steamboat)
    This vessel was the first steamboat to demonstrate the
    practicality of steamboats for towboats. She towed the
    brig Arethusa, bound for New York from Charleston,
    down to the outer buoy in an hour and a half. On 11
    May she towed the Georgia from Savannah to Five Fath-
    om at five miles an hour.

ENTERPRISE #4   (Steamboat)
    The first steamboat to complete return trip between two
    points, Pittsburgh and New Orleans, 1815, taking 25
    days covering 1500 miles. She loaded military stores
    at Pittsburgh and delivered the cargo to General Andrew
    Jackson who was defending New Orleans from the Brit-
    ish. Then Jackson used her as a patrol boat transport-
    ing troops, arms, ammunition on the lower Mississippi.
    Later she was wrecked on the rocks at Louisville.
        She was built by D. French at Brownsville, Pa.,
    under his patent, in 1814, tonnage 75. Captain J. Gregg
    commanded her. The vessel was built to run on ex-
    tremely shallow water. Its hull was like a keelboat.
    See also GEORGE WASHINGTON.

ERICSSON   (Torpedo Boat)
    The first warship, a torpedo boat, to be built on inland
    waters, was launched 12 May 1894 on the Mississippi
    River at Dubuque, Iowa. It was a triple screw steam
    vessel, of 120 tonnage, three guns, with a crew of 23.
    Cost was $113,500.

ERIE   (Whaler)
    The first American ship to take up bay whaling on the
    "greasy" hunting grounds in the South Island region of
    New Zealand. This Newport, R.I., whaler left port in
    April 1832, found the new area, returned in June 1835

with 200 barrels of sperm, 1800 barrels of black oil,
and the news of discovery. She was lost in 1841.

ESEK HOPKINS
This man was the first commander-in-chief of the Continental Navy, appointed 5 November 1775 and holding office until 1777. He came from Rhode Island.

ESSEX, U.S.S. (Frigate)
The first American naval vessel to show the American
flag around Cape Horn was commanded by Captain David
Porter. She was the first vessel of war that doubled
the Cape of Good Hope (1800) and Cape Horn (1813).
Captain Edward Preble commanded. She was built in
1799 at Salem, Mass., by Salem citizens, at their own
expense. She had 32 guns; tonnage 300; speed 12 knots.
This vessel was the most successful commerce raider
in winning the War of 1812.

EXCELSIOR (Steamship)
This vessel was the first to bring the news of gold in
the Klondike to San Francisco. She beat the Portland
for Seattle, from St. Michael on the Bering Sea, arriving two days earlier. The most frenzied of gold
rushes began immediately, with the arrival of these two
vessels, and lasted until the next spring, when the
Spanish-American war broke out. Then the fever died
suddenly.
The stubby Excelsior, a two-masted vessel, stained
with rust marks, poured out passengers in working
clothes, caked with mud, sun-burned black faces, griz-
zled and unshaven. They came off staggering under
heavy bags and suitcases of gold. When the Portland
arrived the crowds really went into a frenzy when they
heard she carried a ton of gold on board.

EXPLORER (Iron Steamer)
The first little iron steamer to explore the canyons on
the Colorado and Gila Rivers was built in Philadelphia
in September 1857 for exploring, by the War Department. Its hull was iron. She made a trial run on the
Delaware River, then was dismantled, shipped to San
Francisco, reshipped to the mouth of the Colorado
River; reassembled. She was launched at high tide by
moonlight.
Captain Ives, commander, took three days to voyage
nine miles. When he ran aground, he tied the vessel to

a tree and left it, stranded.   In 1930 a survey party
discovered the rusted iron plate, shaped like the hull
of a boat, in the middle of the desert--the remains of
the Explorer embedded in sand, which once had been
the bed of the Colorado River.

F-4 (Submarine)
       The first submarine disaster occurred on 25 March 1915
       when the vessel, commanded by Captain Lieut. Alfred L.
       Ede, sank with a loss of 21 men.   She was one and a
       half miles out of the harbor at Honolulu, Hawaii.

FAITH
       The first concrete ship to cross the Atlantic Ocean.
       She was built in Redwood City, California, on 14 March
       1918, launched six weeks after the concrete was poured,
       at a cost of $750,000.   The builder-owner is W. Leslie
       Comyn of San Francisco Shipbuilding Co.

FAME   (Privateer)
       The first privateer of the 1812 period to fit out from
       Salem, Mass.   She was a new Gloucester-built Chebacco
       boat of 30 tons, owned by William Webb, and had a
       crew of 24, ex-shipmasters.   She was launched 1 July
       1812 and returned in eight days with a 300-ton ship, a
       200-ton brig, prizes taken off Grand Manan without firing
       a shot.

FANNING, U.S.S.   (Ship)
       First navy vessel, with the U.S.S. Nicholson, to sink
       an enemy submarine.   While in convoy, 17 November
       1917, the Fanning sighted a submarine.   Arriving at the
       spot, depth charges were dropped.   The U58, German
       submarine surfaced.   The Fanning fired her bow gun;
       the Nicholson shot her three times from the stern.   The
       U58 crew came on deck, surrendered.   A short time
       later the U58 sank.   Commanders were: Nicholson--
       Lieut. Commander Frank Dunn Barrien and Fanning--
       Lieut. Commander Arthur Schuyler Carpenter.

FANNY (Ship)
       The fastest sailing merchantman of the 1750's.   It made
       its maiden voyage from Philadelphia to Cowes in 17
       days.   A Mr. Grice built it for Captain Charles Ma-
       calester.

FANNY   (Pilot Boat)
    The first wreck at San Diego Harbor occurred when this
    vessel had been cruising for the Northerner on 24 De-
    cember 1851.   It anchored outside Ballast Point.   A
    gale rose, drove her ashore, and she was lost.

FANNY, U.S.S.   (Ship)
    The first transport to carry a balloon attached to a
    windlass at the stern on 3 August 1861.   The balloon
    observed military positions at Fort Monroe, Virginia,
    at 2000 feet.

FAR WEST . (Steamboat)
    The first news of Custer's massacre was brought to
    Bismarck, North Dakota, on this fast stern wheeler.
    It was the first vessel to carry two capstans on her
    bow.   She was built in 1870 for trade on the upper Mis-
    souri.   She was a trim, speedy, easy to handle boat.
    She served on the river during the Indian wars, carrying
    army officers and supplies to the upper posts.   The
    army chartered her for $360 a day in 1876 when, up
    the Yellowstone, she ferried wagons, troops, set up
    new bases of supply; ran patrol.
        General Custer and General Gibbon were encamped
    at the mouth of Rosebud Creek, and used her when
    working on campaigns.   To this vessel came a Crow
    Indian scout with the news of Custer's ambush and dis-
    aster, which he made in picture form.   She carried the
    wounded of Reno's 7th Cavalry, even Captain Keogh's
    horse, Comanche, that came down to Fort Lincoln on
    her stern deck, the only survivor from Custer's Last
    Stand.

FELLOWSHIP   (Ship)
    The first important vessel built at New Haven, Conn.
    It was 100 or more tonnage.   It suggests community
    interests.   It is the vessel that H. W. Longfellow wrote
    about in The Phantom Ship.

FIGUREHEADS
    The first figureheads for ships were carved by the early
    colonists, were of women and often with breasts as
    large as pumpkins.   Usually there was some connection
    between the carved image, head or bust and the name
    of the vessel.   It was placed above the cutwater, which
    is the forepart of a ship's stem or prow which cuts the
    water.

The clippers were speedy; therefore their names represented speed and the figurehead coincided with the idea of the name. The Nightingale had a carved image of Jenny Lind, the famous singer, on her prow. The Flying Cloud carried a finely carved angel blowing a trumpet. Flying Fish had a replica of an aerial fish whose flight is rapid, and which was done in green and gold. The Sea Witch figurehead was a bright beautifully carved and aggressive dragon, gilded black, symbol of the Chinese Empire. The hull was black with yellow stripe around her strakes. The Witchcraft had a crouching tiger and the vessel was richly decorated around the bow.

The first to introduce upright figureheads on ships is said to be William Ruch, born 4 July 1756, the son of a carpenter in Philadelphia. He was considered the best carver of his day. Another source claims Edward Catush of London to be the first person to introduce the upright figureheads.

FISHAWK (Ship)
The first federal fish hatching vessel was authorized by Congress on 3 March 1879, at a cost of $45,000. It had a complete hatchery; a laboratory; dredges; trawls; hoisting engine; deep-sea thermometers; designed by Charles W. Copeland. It was launched 13 December 1879 and given to the U.S. Fish Commission on 23 February 1880. She had an iron hull sheathed with yellow pine below the main deck.

FLEET, A (Vessels)
The first Northern fleet engagement against the French at Port Royal, N.S., occurred in May 1645. It was the first affair only and was successful. There were 45 large and small Colony vessels with 2800 men and Sir William-Phipps as commander.

FLOATING CIRCUS PALACE (Showboat)
The first big circus boat of the Spaulding and Rogers firm was built in 1851 in Cincinnati, Ohio. It was twice as large as the St. Charles theater in New Orleans. The boat played the major cities along the Mississippi River. It was brilliantly lighted. It had a pipe organ, set of chimes, a 12-piece band and a calliope. In 1862 the Confederates confiscated it, converted it into a floating hospital near New Orleans.

FLYING FISH   (Extreme Clipper)
    This clipper made the fastest westward Cape Horn cross-
    ing of all time. It is considered Donald McKay's "finest
    and fastest creation."

FLYING FISH   (Pilot Boat)
    The American Flag was planted for the first time at
    Antarctica by Charles Wilkes, explorer, who used this
    vessel in 1840.

FONTANELLE   (Steamboat)
    This steamer was the first on the upper Missouri River
    and was used as a mountain boat before the railroads
    came in.

FORTY NINE   (Steamboat)
    The first steamer to cross the 40th parallel. Captain
    White carried gold seekers headed for the Big Bend dig-
    gings. It was the only steamer on the far upper river
    for a long time. It is reported that this Fort Colville,
    Washington built boat (1865) hit a rock and sank in shal-
    low water.

FRANKLIN   (Brig)
    The Franklin opened Cochin-China to American com-
    merce when it sailed up to Saigon in 1819, as recounted
    in the diary of Lieut. John White, U.S.N., called "The
    History of a Voyage to the China Sea."

FRANKLIN   (Frigate)
    The first keel laid down at the U.S. Navy Yard was for
    this vessel which was launched at Philadelphia 25 August
    1815. It had 74 guns. This occurred 16 1/2 years
    after Congress appropriated funds for building 12 ships
    of war and two docks for repairing ships.

FREDDIE   (Excursion Packet)
    The first excursion packet of the Streckfus Line.

FREMONT   (Steamboat)
    One of the first steamers on the steamship line plying
    from San Diego to San Francisco in 1850.

FRONTENAC   (Steamship)
    The first steamer on the Great Lakes in 1816. She
    was built near Kingston, Canada, employed on Lake
    Ontario as a freight and passenger vessel from Niagara

to Ogdensburg. The second boat was the <u>Ontario</u> built at Sackets Harbor in 1817.

FRONTIER   (Steamboat)
The first steamer to enter Rock River in 1836. It was brought up the Mississippi River by Captain Harris, who sold the boat at St. Louis. The Captain was given a townsite on Rock River for being first to enter the River.

GALENA   (Warship)
The first sea-going warship of the U.S. Navy. She was built at West Mystic, Conn., about 1860 by Cornelius Scranton Bushnell, New Haven, Conn. She had ten guns, was designed by Samuel Hart Pook, architect of Boston. She was covered with railroad iron one inch thick, with an armored boiler plate.

GANGES   (Whaler)
The <u>Ganges</u> was the first vessel to open up the Gulf of Alaska coast fishery. In 1835 Captain Barzillai T. Folger captured the first whale on the Kodiak (Alaska) ground. The vessel was built in Nantucket, Mass., 1815, rebuilt and enlarged in 1840. It was condemned in 1858 at Talcahuano.

GARRICK   (Packet)
The fastest packet of the Dramatic Line which began operation with the <u>Garrick</u>, Nathaniel B. Palmer, commanding with a crew of 36 in 1836. The fastest trip was in the autumn of 1841 when she took 15 days and four hours to voyage from Liverpool. The only serious accident, except that of her demise, was at the time she came into a heavy fog and grounded on Deal Beach in January 1841.
The captain was able to get all his passengers (67) ashore safely through the turbulent surf. It was a bleak and dreary part of the New Jersey coast where only barns could be found as shelter. The cows were turned out and everyone sang, "Hail Columbia," for they were all safe. The vessel had been bilged, but after several months of repair work she was ready to sail again. She cleared the sands, sailed for Liverpool. The <u>Garrick</u> was wrecked near Cardiff in January 1857. It was valued at $70,000; her cost had been $80,000.

GASPÉ (British Schooner)
   The first blood of the American Revolution was shed
three years before Lexington. The town crier marched
through the streets of Province Town. Before him went
his drummer. "Gaspé aground! All men willing, join
to rid ourselves of the 'fire-eating seadog,' meet at
James Sabin's."
   That night Sabin's house was filled with patriots, who
had brought bullets and guns and powder horns, and
were now casting bullets in the kitchen. At 10 o'clock
they went to Fenno's Wharf, got on the Gaspé, no more
than 60 yards beyond, taking three boats headed by Hopkins, Whipple and Dunn, clubs, paving stones and whatever
they could lay their hands on.
   The man on watch challenged, "Who goes there?" No
answer. Then Whipple said, "I'm Sheriff of Kent County.
I order you to surrender." The watchman crumpled from
a shot, wounded. The patriots boarded the Gaspé.
Quickly and quietly they ordered the crew into their
boats. The chief was taken to the home of Joseph
Rhodes. Now only the leaders were left. They set fire
to the Gaspé which burned to the water's edge.
   This armed, British sloop-of-war entered Narragansett
waters in 1772 to enforce the payment of duties, ruth-
lessly stopping all vessels. When the packet sloop, Hannah, a ferry operating between Newport and Providence,
was chased by the Gaspé, the American vessel led the
British schooner over a shoal off Namquit Point where
the vessel went aground. So the citizens were roused;
resentment increased, and their fighting spirit at breaking point they set out to rid themselves of the Gaspé.
The Gaspé affair encouraged the colonists to bring about
the Boston Tea Party.

GENERAL JESSUP (Side-Wheeler)
   The General Jessup was the first vessel to navigate the
Colorado River successfully. It was built in January
1854. Later it was lost by explosion in 1859.

GENERAL MOULTRIE (Dredge)
   The first steamer dredge, converted from a commercial
steamer by installing centrifugal dredging pumps, piping,
and constructing bins in her holds. It was used in
Charleston, S.C., harbor. This vessel was built in
1855 by William Colyer in New York City. Tonnage 365.

GENERAL PIKE (Steamboat)
This vessel was the first middle western steamboat
built for passenger traffic exclusively. She was the first
ship of the U.S. Mail Line. She was launched at Cincinnati, Ohio, in 1818. The vessel was ornate and fast.

GENERAL PIKE, U.S.S. (Ship)
One of the first two ships to be constructed on Lake
Ontario in the winter of 1812-13. The other was the
U.S.S. Madison. She was laid down at Sackett's Harbor,
had a single deck with 24 short 32-pounders. Both ves-
sels were used in the War of 1812.

GENERAL SLOCUM (Ship)
William H. Van Schaick, captain, was the first American
merchant captain to be sentenced to federal prison for
failing to train his crew at fire drills, and keeping the
vessel's fire apparatus in shape, 27 January 1906.
There was a disaster at sea because of negligence. The
sentence was ten years in jail. He was called a "scape-
goat" by some.

GEORGE HENRY (Bark)
This vessel brought the first machinery for erecting a
steam flour mill, saw mill, shingle mill, and distillery,
as well as the first engineer and machinist to put them
together.
The vessel put into Monterey on 10 May 1843, having
left Baltimore in April 1842. Captain Stephen Smith,
native of Baltimore, owned the vessel and most of the
cargo. He had visited California, obtained a promise
of lands on which to erect his mills from Alvarado.
This was the first steam engine for saw mills and grist
mills, ever seen in California. The captain also
brought the first pianos (three) to California on this vessel.

GEORGE W. WELLS (Schooner)
This vessel was the first six-masted schooner and was
built by Holly Marshal Bean at Camden, Maine, for
George W. Wells of Southbridge, Mass. She was
launched 1 July 1900. Net tonnage 2,745. Cost:
$125,000. Commander: Captain John G. Crowley.
She was built along with the Eleanor A. Percy, and
had the first gigantic hull. One night in 1901 off Cape
Cod these two schooners crashed into each other. The
George W. Wells fared the worst damage. In 1918 the
Eleanor A. Percy foundered in the Atlantic.

GEORGE WASHINGTON (Steamboat)
This vessel is considered by some the first real steamboat as it corrected the flaws of the Enterprise. It became the prototype of 5000 or more steamboats. This vessel was the first double decker steamboat.
For the first time high pressure engines were placed on the deck instead in the hull of the vessel. This ship was launched in June 1817 by Henry Shreve and had a hull like a keelboat. See also ENTERPRISE.

GIFT OF GOD (Pinnace)
This vessel came with the Mary and John, the first ships to arrive at Sagadahoc (Kennebec) River in the spring of 1608, to establish the first colony in New England.
It was a fly boat intended for shore exploration. It was smaller, lighter than the John and Mary, and flat bottomed. Both vessels were sent by the Plymouth Company to found a fishing colony on the Maine Coast, on the west side of the Kennebec River. There they erected a church, storehouses within a stockade. They also built the pinnace Virginia for coastal trade. Captain George Popham commanded Gift of God. See also VIRGINIA; MARY; and JOHN.

GODSPEED (Ship)
One of the first three ships to bring the first permanent settlers to Jamestown in 1607. The others were the Susan Constant and the Discovery. This 40-ton vessel carried wheat seed, oats, barley, tools, wine and beer. Captain Bartholomew Gosnold was commander. He was a promoter of the Virginia enterprise. 52 persons came on the vessel. Their food was thin porridge made from meal or flour and water. See Pt. III--SUSAN CONSTANT.

GOLDEN HIND (Ship)
The first English vessel to circumnavigate the globe. Originally this vessel was called the Pelican then rechristened the Golden Hind by her commander Sir Francis Drake while in the Magellen Straits. The figurehead was that of the pelican, its beak extended forward from the stem taking a small animal, such as a golden hind.
Drake left Plymouth, England, 13 December 1577 with the Elizabeth and several smaller vessels, sailed up the South American Coast, plundering Spanish treasure

ships. He arrived near San Francisco 15 June 1579.
He returned by way of the Cape of Good Hope, arriving
at Plymouth, 26 September 1580. The expedition was
intended to open the Pacific and Oriental trade, break
the colonial and commercial monopoly of Spain.

GOLIATH   (Steamboat)
One of the first steamers on the first steamship line
between San Diego and San Francisco, operating in 1850.
It was a side wheeler of 235 tonnage and built on the
east coast in 1849.

GRAND TURK   (Ship)
The first Massachusetts vessel to visit the Far East.
This Salem vessel owned by Elias Hasket Derby came
into Canton by way of Good Hope, after the first American ship, Empress of China.

GREAT EASTERN   (Ship)
The first newspaper to be published at sea was on this
vessel, the cable-laying ship commanded by Captain
James Anderson. The series sold for five shillings
and was published on 29 July 1865, 5 August 1865,
12 August 1865.

GREAT REPUBLIC   (Extreme Clipper)
This extreme clipper, considered Donald McKay's masterpiece, was the world's largest wooden ship. (4555 tons
register) This leviathan was built by McKay at East
Boston in 1853. When she was loaded and ready to go
to sea, a warehouse a block away caught fire, sent
sparks into her canvas and tarred rigging. Her four
masts were a mass of smoke and flames. She burned
two days, to the water's edge. Her hull was saved by
sinking her to the bottom of the East River. The grain
cargo had swelled and gutted her hull. Captain Nathaniel
B. Palmer bought her; rebuilt her at Green Point, L.I.;
sold her to A. A. Lowe and Brothers, New York.
Now she was rigged conservatively; became 3356 tons;
but she remained the largest clipper afloat. She still
drew too much water, which handicapped her. A steam
engine on the deck and double topsails helped economize
in crew. For a figurehead the American Eagle emerged
below the bowsprit. Another eagle 36 feet between the
tip of the wings spanned the stern semicircularly.

She made many fast passages. One in 92 days, San
Francisco to New York. Her best run was 413 miles
in one day. She is among the other six immortals, as
to runs. The Great Republic was chartered as a transport ship to the French Government during the Crimean
War. She foundered off Bermuda in 1872.

GREAT STONE FLEET (Barges)
The first great stone fleet so called because it consisted
of wooden vessels, dismantled whalers, and barges, all
filled with stones by the Union Army and sunk in the
mouths of southern harbors to block the southern fleet,
in 1861-65. This was the first fleet of its kind. The
men filled the holds with Yankee stone walls, which
farmers sold for $.50 a ton.

GREAT WESTERN (Steamboat; English)
The first regular English steamboat service across the
Atlantic began with this vessel sailing from Bristol for
New York, arriving on the 23 April 1838. She com-
pleted the trip in 15 days. The Sirius left London and
completed the trip in 19 days. Both vessels arrived in
New York on the same day, and both were built by
Isambard Kingdom Brunel, English engineer.

GREY EAGLE (Steamboat)
This vessel was the first to bring a royal message con-
cerning the completion of the Atlantic telegraph cable in
the fall of 1858, sent by Queen Victoria to St. Paul,
Minnesota. The newspaper containing the news was delivered wrapped around a piece of wood, tossed to an
agent on the docks.

GRIFFIN (Bark)
The first sailing vessel on the Great Lakes. This small
vessel of 45 tons was laid down in a clearing on the
east bank of the Niagara River by De Tonty for the
French explorer, Sieur de René Robert Cavalier, or
LaSalle, in 1679. The town of LaSalle claims the site
of this historic shipyard.
LaSalle set sail for Green Bay, Wisconsin, 7 August
1679 with a crew of 34, crudely outfitted. There the
vessel was loaded with rich furs, worth $12,000 in
gold, to meet claims of his creditors at Montreal, and
sent back to Niagara 18 September 1679. On the return
journey a strong gale came up during the night and the
vessel was lost.

GUADALUPE (Ship)

The first ship constructed in San Pedro Harbor. It was built in honor of the patron saint of Mexico in 1831. It is also called the Refujio by historians.

HANCOCK (Steamboat)

Nantucket's first steamboat, once called the Eagle. She was built at Norwich, Connecticut. 80 tons.

HANNAH (Schooner)

The Hannah was the first schooner to be commissioned as a privateer of the War of the Revolution. She was fitted out at Beverly, Mass., with provisions, arms, ammunition in September 1775. She had been owned as a fishing schooner by Colonel John Glover. She was commanded by Captain Nicholson Broughton of Marbleheader, Mass., a crew of army officers with maritime experience, took the ship Unity off Cape Ann.

HARMON, U.S.S. (Destroyer)

The first warship to be named for a Negro. Leonard Roy Harmon from Cuero, Texas, a mess attendant, shielded a shipmate from enemy fire at the Battle of Guadalcanal, 12-13 November 1942. The Navy Cross was awarded him posthumously. The Harmon was launched 25 July 1943 at Quincy, Mass.

HARRIET LANE (Steamboat)

First Federal steamboat named for a woman. She was the niece of President James Buchanan. This sidewheeler, of 500 or 670 tonnage, eight guns was built by William H. Webb in 1857 as a revenue cutter for the Treasury Department. This vessel fired the first shot in the War between the States on 12 April 1861 at the steamboat Nashville, to force her to show her colors. She was captured by four confederate cotton-clads in Galveston Bay.

HARVARD, THE (Shell)

The first racing shell was six-oared, rudderless, of white pine, round bottomed and 40 feet long. James Mackay built her in 1857 for the Harvard Boat Club of Harvard College, Cambridge, Mass.

HELIOPOLIS (Snag Boat)
    The first snag boat invented by Henry Shreve to clear
river bottoms of snags between New Orleans and Louisville. Shreve built the first shallow draft steamboats
that floated on water instead of cutting through it. He
cleared many Mississippi River crossings. A solid
mass 100 miles long was removed from the Red River.
    The vessel had an M-shaped, iron-plated bow. The
great jaws wrenched and broke off the snag from the
river bottom. Hooks lifted this timber; a windlass
dragged it aboard where saws cut it; rollers passed it
out the stern. Roots and stumps were shredded, sank
to the river bottom to cause no harm. The cordwood
fed the snag boat's furnaces. Wrecks diminished; steamboats multiplied on the river. In 1832 no boat was lost
due to snagging. By 1834 boats ran through channels at
night that once were dangerous in daylight.

HERCULES (Whaler)
    The first (with the Janus) to take bowhead whales off
Kamchatka, Siberia, in 1843. Also called Herkules.
This 334 ton whaler was built by John Lozier at New
York in 1816, for the New York-Liverpool Star Line.
It was relatively slow as a transatlantic sailing packet
so became a New Bedford whaler after 11 years as a
packet in the North Atlantic trace. Captain Ricketson
on the Hercules; Captain J. K. Turner on the Janus
shared honors in being the first to catch these whales.
The Hercules took home 1900 barrels of whale oil, 200
barrels sperm oil and 12,000 pounds of bone, reaching
the East Coast 3 April 1845. The Janus returned to
New Bedford 9 June 1845 with 1600 barrels of whale oil;
270 gallons of sperm oil and 20,000 pounds of bone.

HERO (Sloop)
    Captain Nathaniel B. Palmer was the first to find the
Antarctic continent in this vessel. Eldredge Parker
built her in 1800. 40 tons. She was a Mystic, Connecticut privateer during the War of 1812, giving good
service. Then Palmer was given command of the Hero
to hunt for seals. As a tender to the Hersilia in 1819
both ships returned with full cargoes of seal skins.
Palmer returned in 1821 with six vessels commanded by
Captain William Fanning of the brig Alabama Pocket.
By this time there were few seals left. They searched
for other sealing grounds. While seal hunting, the Hero,
Huron, Huntress were searching near the Antarctic Con-

tinent and discovered it on 18 November 1820. Maps
today show Palmer Peninsula and Palmer Archipelago.
Voyages Around the World by Edmund Fanning gives an
account of these explorations.

HIGHLANDER (Steamboat)
This vessel started a regular packet service as far up
the Wabash River as Terre Haute and Lafayette, after
1823.

HOOSIER (Steamboat)
The first steamboat to work on the upper Williamette.
She was built at Portland, Oregon, in 1851. The noisy
tiny vessel of five tons, 50 feet long, was built out of
a ship's longboat and powered by an engine from a pile
driver. While trying to go over a shoal below Salem,
the shaft broke. The two pieces were taken to Salem to
a blacksmith, welded together then taken back to the
boat and put in. The vessel was wrecked in 1853.

HOPE (Ship)
This vessel was mastered by James Magee, who established the first American Commercial House in China.
He represented the ship owners of the Empress of China
that brought back a cargo proving America need no longer pay tribute for silks and teas to either Dutch or
English.

HUNTSVILLE (Whaler)
First whale oil said to have been taken by this vessel
in Okhotsk, Siberia Sea, about 1843. The Asia (French)
commanded by an American also claimed the first whale
taken from the same area. The Huntsville was built in
1831, of 522 tons by Ficketts for the New Orleans Line.
From 1831-44 it operated as a trader, then left the
trade, as a coastal packet. It was the pride of the
fleet for its speed. When she was 39 years old in 1870,
she was registered at San Francisco.

ICE YACHT (Yacht)
The first ice yacht was built out of a square box,
mounted on three runners, covered with iron and having
a sail, a rudder post and a wooden tiller. It was built
by Oliver Booth at Poughkeepsie, New York, in 1790.

INDEPENDENCE (Packet)
The first 700 ton packet afloat. She ran in the Liverpool Line in 1834. Her first commander was Ira Barsley from Cape Cod. She was one of the fastest transAtlantic packets of her time.

INDEPENDENCE (Steamboat)
First steamboat to attempt ascending the turbulent Missouri River from St. Louis to Chariton, Mo. At Franklin, Missouri, the head of the Santa Fe Trail, the Independence stopped to unload cargo. There Kit Carson, then a 10-year-old boy, welcomed the vessel. The vessel crept up to Chariton for another celebration. It took 13 days to make the trip; six were sailing days, the other seven were spent aground. The upper Mississippi was not penetrated until 1823. See VIRGINIA.

INDUSTRY (Schooner)
The first vessel to go to the West Indies from the Kennebec River. She was built in Topsham, in 1772.

IRON AGE (Bark)
The first iron sailing vessel built on the Delaware River which was in 1869. She was three-masted.

ISOBEL [ISABEL] (Schooner; Canadian)
The first Canadian vessel to go through the American Locks in 1856. She was launched between 1851 and 1853. She plied Lake Superior until 1863. Capt. Tozen commanded.

J. W. VAN SANT (Steamboat)
This stern wheeler set the pattern for rafting boats on the upper Mississippi River. The sturdy vessel had large, outsize boilers, a big stern wheel. It carried timber on its first run. The boat was deft at guiding her tow between the Rock Island bridge piers. She was built in 1869.

JAMES P. FLINT (Steamboat)
This small iron propellor built in the east was the first steamboat to ply the Colorado River above the Cascades. She was hauled up over the rapids to run the Dalles in 1852. On the down trip she brought emigrants and stock, and on the upward run she took troops and army

supplies. When business slackened, the owners put
skids on the vessel, pulled her around the rapids. Below the Cascades again, she went back into service.
She struck rocks near Cape Horn in September 1852,
sank. The upper part of her boat remained above water
and the following January she was pumped out, taken to
Vancouver and renovated. The Columbus engines went
into the Flint and she became the Fashion, which continued as a trader until 1861, when her fittings were
stolen. Then she was junked.

JEANNETTE   (Bark)
    A tiny vessel under the command of Captain Ward was
    the first American vessel to get away from Hongkong
    with her holds full of tea. She was not the first to port.

JEANNETTE   (Steamer)
    The first wreck in arctic waters occurred when this ves-
    sel under Lieutenant George Washington DeLong was try-
    ing to find a passage through the ice to Greenland. He
    had voyaged by way of Bering Straits, leaving San Fran-
    cisco 8 July 1879. The vessel locked in the ice for two
    years, drifted about from 6 September 1879 to 13 June
    1881, and was finally crushed, sank 13 June 1881. Of
    the 31 men, 13 survived after crossing ice and open
    water to get to land. First steamboat to use electric
    lights.

JEFFERSON   (Yacht)
    The first American yacht was first owned by Captain
    George Crowninshield, Jr. She was built in Salem,
    Massachusetts, by Christopher Turner in 1801. The
    owner cruised in it for many years. Then during the
    War of 1812 she went into service as a privateer.
    Crowninshield had his yacht decked over, armed her
    with several guns and sent her out after prizes with 30
    men aboard. She brought in the second lot of prizes.
    The first had been the Fame.
    At the end of 1812 Salem privateers had captured 87
    prizes with some cargoes worth a half million. The
    enemy took $900,000 of Salem property. As the Fame,
    this vessel also was rigged like a Chebacco boat. See
    also the FAME.

JERSEY   (Catamaran)
    First steam ferry put in service in America by Robert
    Fulton. It ran from New York to Jersey City, early in

1812. 118 tons. Two more were built by Fulton, the
York in 1813 and the Nassau in 1814.

JOHN ATKINSON   (Steamboat)
The first vessel to shoot the rapids at the Falls of the
Ohio at Louisville, April 1807. Three tall masted vessels built at Marietta, Ohio, for ocean commerce tried
to run the rapids before the summer drought and falling
waters. These were the Rufus King, the Tuscarora and
John Atkinson. The latter went down the chute first taking the Indiana side. It struck rocks three times, shud-
dered, but kept to the channel. She then dragged anchor,
lost it after she coasted into a lee of Sandy Island, and
went aground on a shoal. She came out of it without
damage and no lives were lost.

JOHN D. ARCHIBALD   (Ship)
The first gyro-pilot called "Metalmike, " or automatic
steering gear, was installed on this vessel and tested
7 April 1922. The ship was owned by Standard Oil
Company of New Jersey.

JOHN RANDOLPH   (Iron Vessel)
First iron vessel, built in 1834, by John Caut, at Savannah, Georgia. The iron was manufactured in England,
plates being shipped in sections to Savannah where they
were riveted together.

JOSHUA HUMPHREYS
An American shipbuilder who was the first builder of
war vessels for the colonists, and so is called the "father of the American Navy." First naval constructor
of the U.S. Navy. He designed the Chesapeake, United
States, President, Congress, Constellation, Constitution.

JULIA PALMER   (Steamboat)
This vessel was the first steamboat in Thunder Bay, ar-
riving in 1846. She was commanded by Captain John J.
Stanard.

JUPITER, U.S.S.   (Ship)
First electrically propelled ship of the U.S. Navy was
built as a collier at Mare Island, California. It was
launched 24 August 1912. Converted to an aircraft carrier 11 July 1919. The name was changed to Langley
21 April 1920.

KODIAK (Ship)
      This vessel brought the first Russian sea otter hunters
      from Sitka with Ivan Aleksandrovich Kuskov as com-
      mander. Originally two vessels left Sitka in 1808, but
      one was shipwrecked near Columbia. The Kodiak dropped
      anchor in Bodega Bay, California, in 1809. 130 hunters,
      20 native women and 40 Russians came on the ship.
      Shelters were set up on shore, and the hunters went to
      work to kill the sea otter, securing 2350 pelts which they
      took back to Sitka. This unoccupied area afforded pos-
      sibilities of a Russian outpost, which became Fort Ross.
      In San Francisco Bay the Spanish fired on the hunters,
      killing four, wounding two. The Spanish took the 2000
      pelts the Russians had secured in that area.

LACONIA (Ship)
      The first cruise ship to circumnavigate the globe left
      New York 21 November 1922 with 440 passengers, re-
      turning 30 March 1923, a 130-day cruise.

LADY PIERCE
      The first merchant to trade with Japan is Silas E. Bur-
      rows, who sailed on this vessel immediately after Per-
      ry's expedition.

LADY WASHINGTON (Sloop)
      The Japanese may have seen the American flag in 1791
      for the first time if this vessel accompanied by the
      Grace entered the Harbor at Nagasaki. Sources feel
      the Eliza was the first since Captain Kendrick of the
      Lady Washington with his sea otter pelts could not sell
      his furs, as the Japanese did not know what to do with
      the pelts. The Lady Washington being unsuccessful in
      her effort to trade in the 1790's, was ordered to leave
      Japanese waters with despatch.

LAGODA (Ship)
      The first vessel to bring a printing press and types; a
      standing press, cutting press, book binder's press,
      shears and paper to the Pacific coast. The ship left
      Boston 23 April 1833, arrived in Honolulu 4 October
      1833. She carried the material for the American Mis-
      sion Print Shop. The commander was Captain John
      Bradshaw. The press was sold to Zamorano who, in
      1834, started a print shop for government printing. An

arithmetic and a catechism were printed on it. Then the
new revolutionary government took it in 1836 and operated it until 1845.

LAWRENCE (Steamboat)
The earliest, or one of the first, pleasure seeking trips
on record was made by this steamer, which went to the
Falls of St. Anthony, Minnesota, in 1826. After the
Blackhawk War many pioneers sought land and were
eager to view the beauty of the Mississippi River. There
were many who took trips on the upper river craft. It
was George Catlin who proposed a "fashionable tour."

LEE (Schooner)
This is the first cruiser to sail with a commission and
general instructions from George Washington. She had
four guns, 10 swivels and 50 men under Captain John
Manly. This schooner with five others, Harrison, War-
ren, Lynch, Franklin, Washington, made our first navy.
They captured 14 British transports, storeships when
the British evacuated Boston in 1776.

LELIA BYRD (Brig)
First American ship to anchor off Santa Catalina (1805).
The commander, Captain William Shaler, called the island Rouissillon, after his Polish friend, a Count, but
the name didn't catch on. The captain was a New England fur trader in the California otter trade. The Lelia
Byrd dealers aboard were shrewd. They drove a fast
bargain and became so well known for it that the ship
was nicknamed El Pájaro, meaning "The Bird."

LIFEBOAT (Lifeboat)
The first lifeboat in America was built by William Raymond at Nantucket, Massachusetts, in 1807. She cost
$1433.11, taking an additional amount of $160 for a
shed to house her at Cohasset, Massachusetts. There
she remained until 1813. It is recorded that in 1785
Lionel Lukin, an English coach builder built the first
distinctive lifeboat, which he called an "immergible,"
using cork to give it the non-capsizable qualities.

LIGHT HORSE (Bark)
This vessel was the first to fly the Stars and Stripes in
the Baltic Sea. She was sent to St. Petersburg, Russia,
from Salem on a pioneer trading voyage by Elias Hasket
Derby in June 1784 with a cargo of West India sugar.

The vessel was rebuilt in 1784, 266 tons. She had been
a British ship captured in the Revolutionary War, bought
and refined by Derby.

LIGHTNING (Extreme Clipper)
   This vessel was the first clipper ever built to become
   the fastest. Launched at E. Boston 3 January 1853.
   The need for speed came when gold was discovered in
   California and Australia, so clippers were built. Yankee
   clippers made fine runs around the Horn. No English
   ship was fast enough so James Baines ordered a fleet
   from Donald McKay, master ship-builder. The Lightning
   became the fastest of his fleet; made a record never
   equalled in sail. She made 436 miles in 24 hours--a
   record for sailing ships. Thirty years would pass before the steamships did better. In 1869 flames burst
   from her forehold. She was towed from the wharf;
   scuttled. She sank in 24 feet of water.

LIGHTNING (Torpedo Boat)
   The first torpedo boat was built at Bristol, Rhode Island in 1876 by John Brown Herreshoff and Nathanael
   Greene Herreshoff. She attained a speed of 20 miles
   an hour.

LIGHTSHIP
   The first lightship was placed in Elizabeth River, off
   Cravey Island, Virginia, 14 July 1820, at a cost of
   $6000. Her displacement was 70 tons.

LILY (Steamboat)
   The Lily was one of the first lighthouse tenders. This
   sidewheeler was built in 1875 at Jeffersonville. She
   had to push against the stream on her inspection trips.
   The vessel took supplies to the lighthouse keepers, paid
   the salary of the keepers, etc., at Snag Bar, Four Mile
   Bar, Nine Mile Bar. She stopped at Hanging Rock for
   coal at 5 cents a bushel, then went on to Twelve Pole,
   Straight Ripple, Green Bottom, and Raccoon Island.
      The beacon lights were mounted on six foot to sixty
   foot poles. And when the tender signalled a long and
   three short blasts, a long, then the keepers came out
   with lamps and oil cans. Wicks were replaced, cans
   filled with a supply of oil to last three months. The
   lightkeepers were sometimes farm wives and widows
   living at such picturesque places as Hardscrabble, Poor-
   house, Big Bone, Old Mail and Hole-in-the-Wall. In

1789 there were 15 lighthouses in all the U.S. They
were taken over by the government, as dim whale oil
lights were not satisfactory.

LIVELY   (Whaler)
The first vessel to discover Thompson Island, northeast
of Bouvet, near three rocky islets, which the captain
called the "Chimneys."

LIVERPOOL   (Steamboat)
This steamer was the first three-decker steamboat to be
built. It was built by Brown and Bell in N.Y., launched
early in 1843. Tonnage over 1077, probably 1364.

LLAMA   (Junk)
The first record of a wrecked junk on Cape Flattery was
found in an old document. It occurred 9 June 1834 with
three individuals surviving. It is assumed that a typhoon
blew it off course and that the Japanese current carried
the junk across the Pacific Ocean. The three survivors
were taken to Fort Vancouver, unable to speak or under-
stand new world language. From there they were sent
to China, from there they got back to Japan. No foreign
vessels were allowed to enter Japanese ports at this
time.

LÔMA   (Schooner)
The first vessel built in San Diego Bay. She was built
by Captain James Keating's shipyard, launched 13 August 1857.

LORIOT   (Brig)
The first American vessel to enter the Columbia River
after the arrival of the missionaries without the purpose
of trading. She was commanded by Captain Bancroft.

LYDIA   (Bark)
The first vessel to display the American flag to the
natives of Guam in 1801-2, when on a trading voyage.
The Lydia, Salem built, left in January 1802, with Captain Moses Barnard commanding, on a trading voyage
from Manila. She had been chartered by the Spanish
government to take the new governor of the Marianas,
his family and servants, to Guam. The Captain took
them to Agana, capital of Guam. There he received
his charter fee of $8000. The old governor was asked
$4000 for his return passage, but he refused to pay it.

He offered the captain $2000. The Lydia steamed away
leaving him standing on the shore.

MACHIAS
    The first clash of arms at sea in 1775 came between
the patriots of the little settlement of Machias and the
British in the Unity and the Margaretta. Machias was
a faraway outpost of the colonists. It was the farther-
most point in Maine where white men lived.
    The British needed lumber for barracks in Boston,
and asked the Machias citizens for it, in exchange for
supplies which were needed by the settlement due to the
British blockade of the Maine coast. The British had
two 80-ton sloops, with supplies. On these they intended to take the lumber. One of the sloops was the
Unity, the other belonged to a Tory from Boston. Both
sloops were protected by the British armed cutter, the
Margaretta.
    The British didn't think that the news of the Lexing-
ton incident had reached Machias yet, though it had occurred 44 days before. But the people of the village
had heard rumors, so they refused the British. The
Margaretta then anchored off the village, pointed her
guns at the houses. A second meeting was arranged between the settlers and the British. Meanwhile the citizens held a secret meeting in a woods, 11 June 1775, to
discuss how they could capture the British vessels.
They also despatched messengers to other nearby vil-
lages and settlements for reinforcements. They came,
bringing guns. They placed themselves on the heights
above the Narrows, shot at the Margaretta. Captain
Moore of the Margaretta promptly moved his vessel below the Narrows, and threatened to destroy the people
and the town.
    The patriots seized the Unity, which had no cannon.
They swarmed aboard, and out of the 40 there were 38
who had never seen military service. They carried 20
fowling pieces with three pounds of ammunition each,
13 pitchforks, a few scythes, 10 or 12 axes. And with
only pine board breast works for a screen from the enemy, the Americans in the lumber sloop went after the
Margaretta. This vessel had four three-pounders, 14
swivels, small arms and plenty of ammunition and it
was well-manned. At the harbor entrance the vessels
met. The sloop kept away from gunfire, maneuvered

for boarding the Margaretta. The Americans had au-
dacity, superior marksmanship and wasted no shot. In
one hour they captured the Margaretta, brought her to
port, transferred her guns to the Unity. Machias was
prominent in American Revolution history for its partici-
pation in harassing the British. Reprisal came when
the Ranger partly burned the town.

MACHIAS, U.S.S. (Steamboat)
The first iron or steel vessel built by the Bath Iron
Works in the state of Main, 1890-92. It was the first
gunboat built for the "new" U.S. Navy.

MAINE, U.S.S. (Ship)
America's first armored cruiser, authorized in the late
1880's. First so called second-class battleship. She
had been ordered to Havana to protect American lives
and property in January 1898. The Cubans had revolted
against Spanish mis-rule in 1895, and Cuba was brought
to ruin. Now Spanish loyalists began rioting in Havana
in protest against the Spanish government's new moderate
Cuban policy.
    The vessel was mysteriously destroyed by explosion
in Havana Harbor, Cuba, on the night of 15 February
1898. Two explosions wrecked the entire forward part
of the ship, killing 260 officers and men, sinking the
ship. A U.S. Naval Court reported the loss was due to
a submarine mine. No evidence was obtainable for fix-
ing the responsibility. Her sinking triggered the Spanish-
American War.

MALTA (Steamboat)
For the first time spring mattresses were used on
steamboats.

MANASSAS (Ironclad)
The first Confederate Ironclad. This vessel had been
an ex-steam tug, the Enoch Train. Private subscription
enabled it to be rebuilt like an armadillo, boiler-plated,
with a bow-mounted, plough-like underwater ram. It
had one gun, a 32-pounder. It had an iron eyelid to
shield its gun hatch. It was finished five months before
the Merrimac (rebuilt from the Union Merrimack's
hull). 387 tons. She was commanded by Captain John
Stevenson and went into action 12 October 1861. She is
said to have contrived a fast naval "Bull Run."

MARGARET (Ship)
   This vessel is credited with being the first vessel sailing
under the American flag to attempt trade with Japan and
being amically received in 1801. The vessel carried six
guns, 20 men, 295 tonnage. She was Salem-built and
owned; built in 1800. On 25 November 1800, she left
Salem with Captain Derby, arrived at Batavia and there
agreed to take annual freights to and from Japan. He
carried sugar, spice, sapan-wood, sandlewood, rattans,
medicines, cloth, glassware to Nagasaki. He brought
back lacquered wares, brooms, tables, boxes, writing
desks, tea caddies. The ship always sailed on a certain
day regardless of storms. In a one-month passage,
Captain Derby returned to Batavia. See also: LADY
WASHINGTON, ELIZA.

MARINER (Tug)
   This was the first vessel to make a continuous voyage,
ocean to ocean, through the Panama Canal on the 19th
of May 1914.

MARTIN WHITE (Steamboat)
   The first side-wheeler to tow the first barge ever
brought up the Sacramento River.

MARY & HELEN (Whaler)
   The first steam whaler built as a whaler in 1879. It
was built at Bath, Maine, in 1879, of oak, yellow pine
and hackmatack. It cost $65,000. 420 tons. She was
rigged with full sails, carried coal bunkers and a small
engine with screw propellor. She made six to eight
miles an hour. She was a pioneer steam auxiliary sailing vessel for arctic whaling.
   Captain Leander C. Owen left New Bedford 9 September 1879 to find whale oil in the North Pacific. She arrived at San Francisco 10 October 1880. After her
maiden voyage she was sold to the U.S. government.
She was used to search for the survivors of the Jeannette expedition. On 30 November 1881 she was burned
accidentally. See also JEANNETTE.

MARY & JANE (Ship)
   The first vessel to sail on the first contingent of the
Great Emigration from Plymouth to Nantasket. 140 pas-
sengers were aboard.

MARY & JOHN   (Pinnace)
   The Mary & John with the Gift of God sailed the stormy
sea across the Atlantic to arrive at Sagadahoc (Kennebec)
River in the spring of 1608 to establish the first colony
in New England.   The first colony in New England was
called the Popham Colony.   The location is now known
as Popham Beach.
   Captain Raleigh Gilbert commanded the Mary & John.
The vessel was blown off course, got separated from the
Gift of God, and the first land they saw was Nova Scotia.
They came down the northeast coast, to an island where
they set up a cross.   The next day they reached Ile De
Monhegan where they met Gift of God, which had headed
for the island during the bad weather.   This island had
been a rendezvous for English traders and fishermen
early in the 1600's, having been discovered by Weymouth.
It was free of Indian threat.   Upon arriving at the mouth
of the Kennebec, Fort St. Georges was built.
   A Jesuit explorer, Pierre Biard in 1611, sent by
France to follow up Champlain's discovery in 1605,
visited the abandoned fort on 28 October 1611.   He reported the colony had built the fort trenched and stock-
aded, with houses, church, assembly hall, storehouses
inside it.   He reported that the colony had built for
defense, not farming; that it was not a settlement of
home builders.   The soil was rocky and sandy for six
leagues around.   The colonists spent a savage winter in
America.   And since the colony seems to have been
made up of the inmates of English jails, there were
quarrels and many were sent home.   There were well
trained mechanics and real workers among these workers.   Morale was affected at the loss of their backer
and leader, so the Mary & John sailed home in 1607
with the new pinnace, the first ship to be made in
America, with them.   See also VIRGINIA; GIFT OF GOD.

MARY POWELL   (Steamboat)
   The first, best-loved river boat and family boat that
was the fastest and smoothest on the Hudson River,
therefore was called the Hudson River Queen.   She was
comfortable, neat and clean of line, not gaudy, and always dependable.   A Negro boy is supposed to have kept
the flies from lighting on her rail which would have
slowed her down with their weight.   She was built in
Jersey City around 1861.   Only once was she beaten in
a race.   The yacht, Stiletto from Bristol, R.I., raced
the Queen then 25 years old.   The Mary Powell came

in after the yacht only by five minutes. She ran 60
years between New York and Kingston.

MASSACHUSETTS (Revenue Cutter)
The first revenue cutter keel was laid at Newburyport,
Mass., in 1791. She had one deck, two masts, and
cost $1440, to be paid for out of duties on imported
goods.

MASSACHUSETTS (Ship)
This ship was the largest merchant vessel built in
America up to her time, 1789. She was modeled after
a British East Indiaman, launched at Quincy in 1789. She
was Boston owned. 800 tons. Captain Job Prince sailed
from Boston 28 March 1790 carrying a general cargo to
be exchanged at Batavia. The Dutch wouldn't give her
a permit so when she arrived in Canton she was turned
away. Later she was sold to the Danish East India
Company for $65,000.

MASSACHUSETTS (Steamboat)
The first steamboat to be built for Salem and Portsmouth
owners in 1817. She made 6-7 knots. She ran in the
steam packet service between Boston-Salem.

MATTHEW TONTAINE MAURY
The first person to prepare wind and current charts that
have been a boon to sea captains. These charts enabled
seamen to lessen the length of the trips by 25 days.

MAYFLOWER (Bark)
The Pilgrims, who came on this vessel, were the first
to establish a permanent settlement in New England at
Plymouth, Massachusetts, 21 December 1620. The vessel was three-masted: main mast, middle one, main
topmast. She was a double-decked, bark-rigged merchant ship of 180 tons; normal speed was 2 1/2 miles
an hour. Her overall length bow to stern was 90 feet;
her beam, extreme breadth 25 feet; depth of hold from
top deck to inside of keel, 17 feet. Loaded, she drew
two fathoms (12 feet). Below the main deck was a gun
deck. Below it, the hold. Captain Christopher Jones
commanded the Mayflower. There were 102 passengers
and officers and crew of 40 aboard.
    The Mayflower left Southampton, England, 15 August
1620 with the Speedwell. Eight days out the latter began to leak. She had to turn back. Both ships put into

Dartmouth Harbor. About the 2 September they set sail
again, after repairs had been made. The Speedwell
proved unseaworthy again, so she turned back after
transferring her passengers to the Mayflower. Now the
Mayflower sailed out alone on 6 September with passengers and crew. They sighted Cape Cod 19 November
and dropped anchor at Provincetown Harbor at the point
of the Cape on 21 November. They took on food and
water, mended the shallop which had been stowed in the
main hold and explored the bay and land, and so on 21
December 1620 reached Plymouth. It had taken her 65
days to get to America. Then on 5 April 1621 she left
for England arriving safely. The return voyage took 31
days.

There was a birth at sea. Oceanus Hopkins was born
on the Mayflower. The first white child born in New
England was Peregrine White who had come on the Mayflower. The land that the Pilgrims came to had been
mapped by Captain John Smith six years before. He had
charted and made maps of the coast from Penobscot to
Cape Cod, and called it New England. He gave the
name Plymouth to the mainland opposite Cape Cod, and
that is where the Mayflower colonists landed.

MEMNON   (Clipper)
This clipper was the first to make the record passage
of 120 days from New York to San Francisco, prior to
1850. She cut down the time of 6 to 9 months to 120
days. First American clipper to enter Liverpool or any
British port. She was built by Smith and Dimon in 1848;
1068 tonnage; for rapid delivery of tea, silks, spices in
the China trade. On her first voyage she was commanded by Captain Oliver Eldridge. She was lost in the
Gaspar Straits 14 September 1851, in the British China
tea trade.

MEUSE   (Ship)
The first immigrants coming directly from Havre,
France, arrived in San Francisco, September 1849 on
this ship.

MICHIGAN   (Iron Side Wheel Steamboat)
One of the first iron vessels to be built for the U.S.
Navy was an iron side-wheeler steamer. She is alleged,
with one minor exception, to be the first iron warship
in the world. She was built at Erie, Pa., by Stock-
house and Tomlinson, and begun in 1842. She was con-

structed in sections which were taken to Erie, Pa.,
where on 5 December 1843, she was launched. Her
cost: $165,000. She was renamed the Wolverine in
1905.

MIDWAY (Airplane Carrier)
   The first ship from which a long-range rocket was
   launched 6 September 1947. A V-2 rocket captured
   from the Germans was fired from her flight deck while
   the carrier was several hundred miles off the east coast
   of the U.S. It travelled six miles. Rear Admiral John
   Jennings Ballentine was commander of the task group.
   The flagship, the U.S.S. Midway, was commanded by
   Captain Albert Kellogg Morehouse.

MINE LAYER (Steam Launch)
   This vessel was the first mine layer. It was a 32-foot
   launch that made eight knots, carried 12 men, was used
   by the Engineer School of Application in August 1872.

MISSISSIPPI (Sloop)
   The first vessel to explore the Natchez country by the
   Connecticut Military Adventurers. They laid out 23
   town sites, then returned in August 1773.

MISSISSIPPI, U.S.S. (Battleship)
   The first battleship to visit an inland city when she
   sailed up the Mississippi River, 300 miles, to Natchez,
   Mississippi, 20 May 1909. She left for New Orleans the
   24 May 1909.

MISSISSIPPI, U.S.S. (Steam Frigate)
   The first steamship to go all the way around the world.
   She was the third steam vessel of the U.S. Navy. Fulton
   I was first, Fulton II was second, an experimental vessel.
   Perry battled Congress for a real steam frigate. He
   used the vessel as a flagship in the Mexican War. It
   went to the Orient to negotiate the U.S.'s first treaty
   with Japan. Her career ended in 1863 when she was
   burnt to keep her out of the hands of the Confederates
   at Norfolk.

MONITOR, U.S.S. (Ironclad)
   First of the ironclads (called the "Yankee cheesebox on
   a raft"). John Ericsson, Swedish engineer, built it upon
   order, of President Lincoln, who asked for three ironclads. It was the first to have a rotating turret that

could be fired in any direction. It battled the Merrimac
(by then officially called the Virginia) on 9 March 1862
at Hampton Roads, Virginia, the first conflict ever between ironclad ships.

MONUMENTAL CITY   (Steamboat)
    The first steamboat to cross the Pacific Ocean.

NANCY   (Whaler)
    The first American whaler to go to Resolution Island.
    On the home run she was captured by a French priva-
    teer, the Reliance. Then she was re-captured by the
    American brig, the Eagle. Others claim the Asia and
    the Alliance as first to go to Resolution Island, in 1792.

NANCY   (Schooner)
    One of the first three Richard and Elias H. Derby ves-
    sels to be armed in June 1776. Peaceful trade up to
    this time had been engaged in by the Derbys. Then
    Captain Allen Hallett was sent to Haiti with cotton,
    sugar, molasses, cocoa, powder, linen for shirts, pins,
    silks, writing papers and much needed worsted stockings.
    He returned home safely, with a full cargo, on 20 March
    1776. But two other Derby vessels were seized by the
    British. So in June 1776 the owners armed their first
    vessels. See also STURDY BEGGAR.

NANTUCKET CHIEF   (Tanker)
    The first American ship attacked by a German submarine,
    and torpedoed off the Scilly Isles, 1 May 1915. A 5789-
    ton tanker. This vessel was christened Gulflight in 1913.

NASHVILLE   (Packet)
    One of the first packets to be built with full poop decks.
    By 1831 the fashion in painting changed. Ports were
    painted and the green inside was changed to white and
    light shades. Built in 1831; 513 tons, for the New Or-
    leans Line from New York. It served 10 years. See
    also NATCHEZ.

NATCHEZ   (Packet)
    One of the first packets with full poop decks, a new
    feature. Captain Robert H. Waterman took her around
    the Horn in the China trade. She took 78 days from
    Canton to New York, a day behind the Sea Witch record.

This clipper had made the fastest clipper passage ever
sailed with Captain Waterman in command.   See NASH-
VILLE.

NATHANIEL BOWDITCH
The first to discover 8000 errors in the old standard
English book on navigation.   His The New American
Practical Navigator (1802) expanded J. H. Moore's The
Practical Navigator, and was made the standard authority
of the U.S. Navy Department on the subject of navigation.
Over 60 editions have been printed.

NAUTILUS, U.S.S.   (Nuclear Submarine)
The Nautilus was the first submersible vessel to use an
atomic reactor instead of the conventional engines, running on the power of the atom itself.   It was first to
voyage under the North Pole, 3 August 1958, commanded
by Captain William R. Anderson.   It was launched at
Groton, Connecticut, 21 January 1954.

NEPTUNE'S CAR   (Clipper)
The first and only large clipper built in the state of
Virginia, at Portsmouth, in 1853.   She won sailing
honors on one occasion in the China trade.   The vessel
was sold in Liverpool at auction in February 1863.   She
sailed under the British flag nine years.   She was renamed the Mataura.

NESTOR   (Packet)
First liner of the Black Ball Line on the New York-
Liverpool run to be wrecked.   On Christmas morning
at 3 A.M. in 1824, the vessel was wrecked by grounding
at Fire Island Inlet, Long Island, when approaching New
York.   She quickly bilged, her hull punctured.   No lives
were lost.   She was in service four years.   A 481-ton
liner; launched in New York in 1815.

NEW IRONSIDES   (Ironclad Steamer)
The first ironclad launched at Kensington on 10 May 1862.
This vessel was the most powerful of any northern ship;
the most dreaded.   She fought in more battles; took
severe shelling better; piled up more damage to southern
ships than any other vessel in the fleet.   She was built
by William Cramp who changed his yards to build iron
vessels during the Civil War.   This vessel had a wood
hull with iron plating bolted over it.

NEW MEXICO, U.S.S. (Warship)
    The first warship propelled by electricity. She was
    built in the N.Y. Navy Yard, launched 23 April 1917.
    She carried 12 14-inch guns and 12 five-inch guns.
    Tonnage: 30,000.

NEW ORLEANS (Steamboat)
    The first steamboat west of the mountains to sail down
    the Ohio and Mississippi Rivers and pioneer a fleet of
    large, faster vessels. The clumsy boat belonged to
    Nicholas J. Roosevelt who took his wife, child, New-
    foundland dog, cook, waiter, six sailors, pilot, engineer
    and captain aboard on this first trip. They left Pitts-
    burgh in September 1811 and arrived in New Orleans 12
    January 1812, three months later. Roosevelt outfitted
    the stern wheeler at a cost of $38,000 (some sources
    say $40,000). It had two masts with sails, one deck
    and sat deep in the water. It was a duplicate of Fulton's
    Hudson River steamboat. In the bow it carried the
    freight. The engine was exposed and the smokestack
    was in the middle; the cabin in the rear.
    Roosevelt had come west to the Mississippi River in
    1808 to look for transportation by way of the River. He
    found trade carried on by keelboat down current, but up-
    stream it had to be towed, or poled. So Fulton and
    Livingston set up yards at Pittsburgh to build steamboats
    for the western rivers with Roosevelt in charge. Before
    this trip, the vessel had a trial on the Monongahela, but
    without passengers.
    The boat ran into the Mississippi earthquakes of the
    fall of 1811. At New Madrid the quake was severe, but
    the vessel outran it. It was discovered that it couldn't
    go upstream, as the engine was too weak and the keel
    dragged. So it plied in deep water between New Orleans
    and Natchez till 1814 when the boat was impaled on
    stumps at Baton Rouge, and became a total wreck. It
    was not a true Mississippi River boat.

NIAGARA (Brig)
    For the first time in history a British squadron with a
    force of 10 vessels on Lake Ontario was forced to sur-
    render to an enemy by the Niagara, commanded by
    Oliver Hazard Perry.
    The battle on Lake Erie had been raging. The Law-
    rence was reduced to a wreck by the British. Perry
    then boarded the Niagara and with the schooner caused
    all British ships to strike colors except the Little Belt

and Chippewa. These were captured while trying to escape. So control of Lake Erie was wrested from the
British and the dream of British conquest of interior
America ended. The Northwest territory was saved for
the U.S. Perry returned to the Lawrence from which
he sent his message to General William H. Harrison,
"We have met the enemy and they are ours, two ships,
two brigs, one schooner, one sloop."

NOAH'S ARK (Showboat)
      This little broadhorn may have been the first floating
      theater with professional actors on the western rivers.
      Noah Ludlow, in 1817, bought the boat, floated 260 miles
      to Pittsburgh. The troop of eleven slept in taverns. At
      New Orleans he purchased a keelboat, voyaged to Natchez
      where the cast performed the "Honeymoon." On their
      way there, having heard stories of river pirates, they
      got out their stage properties--cutlasses, poinards,
      swords, rapiers, sabres, dirks to repel them, but there
      were none.
      Newspapers wrote of several stops they made at way
      stations, seeming to indicate the possibility that per-
      formances may have been given on the keelboat. If so
      this boat could be the first showboat. See also FLOAT-
      ING CIRCUS PALACE; SHOWBOAT.

NONSUCH (Ship)
      The first ship to sail directly into the Hudson Bay. The
      result of this ship's successful voyage in 1650 was the
      founding of the Hudson's Bay Company.

NORTH AMERICA (Ship)
      Christian Bergh's first ship for the Atlantic trade. This
      vessel was built in 1804 by one of New York's two most
      important early ship builders. 400 ton.

NORTH WEST AMERICA (Schooner)
      The first American ship built on the Pacific Coast.
      This 40-ton vessel was built, launched, equipped in
      King George's Sound, now Nootka Sound, British Colum-
      bia, in 1788. Her master was Captain Robert Funter.
      She was captured by Spain on 9 June 1789.

OCEAN PEARL (Ship)
      First vessel to bring the news of the treaty between

China and the Allies British and French (25 October
1860). She left Hongkong with a cargo of rice, sugar,
tea and 52 boxes of opium; arrived at San Francisco 19
January 1861 with the news. Launched at Charlestown,
Massachusetts in 1853.

OHIO   (Steamboat)
One of the first steamers on the first steamship line
from San Diego to San Francisco. She voyaged in the
1850's and on. The line was owned by Mr. Wright who
was in the California trade.

OLIVE BRANCH   (Steamboat)
The first independent steamboat to run between New
York and Albany. The vessel was built in New York in
1815. It plied the river during the last part of June
1824, carrying 600 passengers.

OLYMPIAN   (Steamboat)
The first vessel to open a way through the ice to the
Cascades. With its iron hull it went full speed through
the ice. When her bow rode up on the ice, the weight
of the boat smashed sheets of ice. She brought mail
and passengers from the Cascades. Then wooden steamers were used after the ice opened and melted. It was
too expensive to operate except in emergencies.

ONRUST   (Ship)
The first decked vessel in America. Adrianen Blok, a
Hollander and Dutch lawyer, built the vessel in 1614 to
replace his sloop, the Tiger of which he had been captain. This vessel had been a Dutch cargo, or fishing
vessel, propelled by oars and sails. He had entered the
Hudson River, traded with the Indians. When ready for
his return voyage with a cargo of furs, fire broke out,
the ship flamed, burned to the water's edge. The crew
escaped.
    Blok set about to build another boat. He cut down
trees, laid a keel, beached the Tiger's hull. In the
spring the new ship was ready. It was 38 feet on the
keel, 44 1/2 feet overall, 11 feet on the beam. 16
tons. He called it the Onrust, meaning, "the restless."
She was launched on the Hudson River, 1614-1615.
    With the Onrust, Blok explored the coast. He found
the island, Long Island, which he named. He sailed
through the strait to the east of the island, named it
Hellegate, "hell passage." He kept on exploring to

strengthen Dutch claim. He made maps, charts. On
their basis a charter was granted to the United New
Netherlands Company for a colony to be called New
Netherlands. After mapping and charting he sailed for
Holland with a cargo of furs.

OREGON   (Steamboat)
    It is said that this is the first steamboat to enter San
    Diego Bay. She was owned by the Pacific Mail in 1849.

OREGON   (Steamboat)
    The first vessel to bring the news that California had
    been admitted to the Union.

ORETO   (Cruiser)
    The first Confederate cruiser was built in England. The
    vessel left Liverpool for the Bahamas on 22 March 1862.
    Captain John Newland Maffitt became commodore. The
    stores and guns came in a ship that followed the Oreto.

ORIENT   (Brigatine)
    The first ship to be sent out by Marblehead to the West
    Indies. The master, Edmund Bray, brought a cargo of
    cottons, gunny sacks, ginger, sugar, cigars, carpets,
    cords, blinds, bandanas from Calcutta, arriving at home
    port in 1806. 187 tons. In 1801 custom's duties at
    Marblehead amounted to $22,300. In 1807 they rose to
    $156,000.

ORIENTAL   (Clipper)
    The first American clipper to land a cargo of tea at the
    West Indies docks, London, after the repeal of the Navi-
    gation Laws. Alleged to be the first American clipper
    in London. This 1003 ton clipper was built in 1849 by
    Jacob Bell at New York, for $70 a ton. She was owned
    by A. A. Low & Brothers of N.Y.

ORLEANS   (Steamboat)
    The first steamboat on the Ohio River. She had a speed
    of eight miles per hour. A new era of river transporta-
    tion was ushered in with her coming.

ORUKTER AMPHIBOLOS   (Steam Scow)
    The first steam propelled vehicle in the United States
    was a dredging scow. In 1803-4 the Board of Health of
    Philadelphia, Pa., ordered Oliver Evans, an American
    inventor from Newport, Delaware, to construct a dredg-

ing machine for raising mud from the harbor. Evans
designed it; built it; owned it. The flat scow-type hulled
vessel had a high pressure boiler and a small engine to
work the machinery. The scow was mounted on four
large iron wheels to propel it from Evans' workshop to
the Schuylkill River. It had a paddle wheel at the stern
that moved the scow when in water. It was used as a
dredge to deepen the harbor at Philadelphia.

OTTER (Ship)
The first American ship to touch a California port when
it sailed into Monterey from Boston, Mass. In 1796
Captain Ebenezer Dorr anchored his ship to get wood and
water. The vessel had six guns and 26 men. Surrepti-
tiously he landed 10 men and a woman on Carmel beach
at night, forcing them from the rowboat at the point of
a gun. The sailors were English, the woman a convict
from Botany Bay. The men had to work as carpenters
and blacksmiths at 19 cents a day. Later Royal orders
transferred them to Spain.

PATAPSCO (Yacht)
The first trip abroad in a pleasure yacht was made in
this vessel. An American gentleman, Silas E. Burrows,
went to the USSR to appeal to the Czar for repayment
of expenses occurred when his ship rescued 200 officers
and men from the wreck of a Russian man-of-war. He
left New York 30 June 1848, carrying dispatches for the
American Minister to Russia.

PATOKA, U.S.S. (Ship)
The first ship built with a masthead sea anchorage for
a dirigible. The ZPI Shenandoah attached itself to this
masthead on 15 August 1925, off Newport News, Virginia.
Then she was towed in 20 miles.

PATRICK HENRY (Ship)
The first liberty ship in WW II. It's first voyage was
made to Alexandria, Egypt, with Captain Richard Gallow
Ellis as commander. The vessel was launched 27 September 1941 at Baltimore, Maryland, and delivered 30
December 1941 to U.S. Maritime Commission, who
transferred the ship to the Lykes Brothers Steamship
Company in New Orleans. She had a single-screw
steam reciprocating propulsion and made 11.19 knots.

9146 tonnage.

PEACOCK (Ship)
The first Americans to occupy a prison in San Diego
were four men who went ashore from this vessel to pro-
cure provisions. Captain Kimball had anchored off San
Juan Capistrano in April 1806. He sent the men ashore
in a boat. The men were sent to San Diego to be put in
prison, and when the vessel arrived they escaped, but
could not reach the ship. They were sent back to the
Presidio, later to San Blas.

PEGGY (Ship)
This vessel brought the first cargo of Bombay cotton in-
to Massachusetts Bay for Salem. This was an Elias
Haskett Derby ship.

PENNSYLVANIA (Warship)
Once was known as the largest wooden warship in the
world. It was launched 18 July 1837. 120 guns.

PEORIA (Steamboat)
The first steamboat to come up the Illinois River, which
may have been seen at Peoria. 1828.

PHOENIX (Steamboat)
This vessel was the first gold dredger plying the Sacramento River. It was not a successful venture, for its
dredging machinery was faulty.

PHOENIX (Steamboat)
The first steamboat to travel on the ocean when taking
the trip from Sandy Hook to Cape Henlopen is also the
first paddle steamer. Colonel John Stevens built the
vessel at Hoboken, New Jersey, in 1808. New features
were invented for her. She had American-made engines,
boxed-in machinery, a sturdy hull.
The Clermont was built by Robert Fulton and began
operating several days before the Phoenix. Fulton got
the sole right to operate steamers on all New York inland waterways, so the Phoenix was taken to Delaware
Bay. At Philadelphia she operated from that point to
Trenton for a number of years. Captain Moses Rogers
was her commander and took her out on the ocean in
June or July of 1809.

PILGRIM (Steamboat)
It is alleged that this steamboat is the first to be lighted
by electricity, although City of Worcester had it two
years earlier. She was the first to be fireproofed seriously. Her double bottom iron hull was an innovation.
She operated on Long Island Sound in 1883 and was
called one of the queens of the Sound. She was an elite
vessel with orchestra, seated 1000 passengers at one
time in the salon. Light came from 1000 incandescent
electric bulbs, equal to 12,000 candles. There were box
stalls for 42 horses.

PINTA (Gunboat)
The first gunboat built for the U.S. Navy was the fastest
vessel in the Navy. This fourth class gunboat, built in
1864, saw regular service at the Alaska station. She
had a part in bringing news to the United States concern-
ing the Virginius affair in the fall of 1873.
The Virginius, of American registry, was carrying
arms to the Cuban rebels when a Spanish gunboat captured the boat 5 November 1873. The captain and his 36
men were executed as "pirates" by the Governor of Santiago. Resentment in America was high when the Pinta
brought the news. It was later discovered that the
Virginius was actually owned by Cubans, however the
American government asked that the Virginius be restored to the United States. She was surrendered in December 1873.

PIONEER (Steam Whaler)
The first steam whaler. Captain Ebenezer Morgan's
voyage as commander, the second voyage of the vessel,
was the first time this Captain had made a voyage on a
steam vessel.
The vessel was built at Charlestown, Massachusetts,
as a government transport. She was converted to a
whaler in 1855, later rebuilt with auxiliary steam in
1866 at New London. As a whaler she profited $151,000
on a single voyage. She was sold during the Civil War
at a price four times her cost. In 1867 the Pioneer was
crushed in the ice.

POINT COUNTERPOINT (Barge)
The first performance of one of the works of Sir Arthur
Bliss of London was performed on this barge. The barge
moved down historic rivers, giving twilight concerts
twice a week. A towboat took the vessel to the river

towns, where she tied up for a performance, in 1959.
The barge was specially designed for concerts and replaced a makeshift barge tied up at the Alleghany River
bank. Later, in 1960, fine art shows, new compositions
and classical symphonies were added to the repertoire.
The orchestra was flown to England for concerts on the
Thames. Abroad and in America it played to a third of
a million people in 1961.

POLIAS   (Ship)
    The first concrete ship built for the U.S. Shipping Board
    Emergency Fleet Corporation was launched 22 May
    1919 and delivered 23 October 1919. The Atlantus was
    the first concrete ship launched, 4 December 1918.

PRAIRIE   (Steamboat)
    The first stateroom boat to call at the levee of St. Louis.

PRESIDENT   (Frigate)
    This 44-gun vessel fired the first shots of the War of
    1812 when it engaged the 36-gun British frigate Belvidera,
    on the evening of 23 June 1812. The Belvidera limped
    away, badly damaged, throwing fresh water, gear, an-
    chor, boats overboard to lighten the weight. On the
    President a gun burst that killed and wounded 16 men.
    Its Captain Rodgers fractured a leg. The President
    chased the Belvidera, but gave up. It was an unsatis-
    factory engagement. The President was with the squad-
    ron that consisted of the United States, Congress, Argus
    and Hornet.

PRESIDENT   (Steamboat)
    The first all steel passenger steamboat on the Mississip-
    pi River running between New Orleans and St. Paul.

PRESIDENT ADAMS   (Galley)
    The first galley of the United States Navy was launched
    19 May 1798.

PRESIDENT HARRISON   (Steamboat)
    The first steamboat to give round-the-world service
    regularly. She sailed from San Francisco, California,
    in February 1934. Other steamers began to make the
    trip once a year.

PRINCE OF WALES   (Ship)
    For the first time Archibald Menzies, botanist and sur-

geon of the Vancouver Expedition (1791-95) brought plants
from the Paccbast of North America to the notice of the
world. The botanist sailed on this vessel on his first
voyage, in 1786. It was commanded by Captain Colnett.
They arrived at Nootka, July 1787.

PRINCETON   (Screw Warship)
    First steam propellor sloop-of-war, ordered by and built
    for the U.S. Navy. Also the first war vessel in the
    world with a screw propellor.
    This 31-gun vessel of 673 tonnage was ordered in
    1839; designed by John Ericsson in 1841; launched 10
    December 1843 at Philadelphia, Pa., at a cost of
    $212,000. Its wood hull was built in the United States
    at the Navy Yard. The machinery was built by Merrick
    & Towne, Philadelphia, Pa. She carried two long 225
    pounders, twelve 42-pound carronades and wrought iron
    guns. The Princeton is an historic vessel, pioneering
    in steam propulsion, taking part in the Mexican War.

PRISCELLA   (Steamboat)
    The largest steamboat of the 19th century. In 1893 she
    was one of the three Queens of the Sound. Built at a
    cost of $1,500,000 she ran between New York and Bos-
    ton. There was a concert hall that could seat 1000 peo-
    ple. It could accommodate 1500 people with sleeping
    berths. It was decorated in plush and velvet and had a
    restaurant. It ran 23 miles an hour.

PROBUS   (Ship)
    The first American ship to establish a new record in
    the tea trade in 1841. This 647-ton vessel was built at
    Medford, Massachusetts, by J. Stetson for Parker of
    Boston. On her maiden voyage her round trip took 8
    months 15 days including discharging and reloading at
    Macao. At the time it was the fastest, finest ship ever
    in the China trade.

QUERO   (Schooner)
    This 62-ton vessel was the first to carry to England the
    news of the Lexington skirmish ahead of the King's mes-
    senger. Captain Richard Derby, Jr. a Salem shipmaster,
    made the voyage in 29 days, and beat the Royal Express
    packet Sukey which had left Boston four days before.
    The Quero left in the night, stealing out of the harbor,

with the idea of keeping the deposition, letters and papers she carried a secret. The Sukey brought General Gage's reports before the 2nd week of June. By then the news had already been made public in England by Benjamin Franklin in the Essex Gazette of Salem in 28 May issue. Reprints spread through the British Isles a day later. Derby left England as quietly as he had arrived, before he could be questioned. He let it be known to some that he had gone to Spain to purchase arms and ammunition. Others thought he was taking a cargo of fish, and still others thought he had said that he was going for a load of mules. He carried home to America the first tiding of peace in 1783 when he arrived from France in the Astrea with the message that a treaty had been signed. See also ASTREA I.

RAINBOW (Extreme Clipper)
The first extreme clipper ship ever built; and the first true clipper. Designed by John W. Griffiths, a pioneer who studied shipbuilding as a science; built with care; launched January 1845.
This clipper ushered in the golden age of the clippers. Captain John Land claimed she was the fastest ship in the world. She became a pattern, for many similar vessels were constructed. She brought great fortune to her owners. On her last voyage (fifth) bound from New York to Valparaiso in 1848, she went missing under the command of Captain Hayes.

RAJAH (Schooner)
This vessel, with the Cadet with which it sailed, claims first in direct importation of a cargo of bulk pepper brought to Salem from Sumatra in 1779 by Jonathan Carnes. Captain Carnes heard of pepper growing wild on the northern coast of Sumatra. He took 10 men, four guns, and acquired pepper in bulk. Salem became the center of the pepper trade for years. Salem seamen were energetic in tracing eastern spices to their sources, so brought wealth to individuals and the city of Salem. See also CADET.

RAJO (Tuna Clipper)
The first tuna clipper with a raised deck.

RANDOLPH (Frigate)
>   The first all-American frigate to go to sea. It was con-
>   structed by Wharton and Humphreys, in Philadelphia,
>   Pa. 32 guns. Of the 13 new warships ordered by the
>   Continental Congress in December 1775, this vessel was
>   the first home-built frigate to sail for the U.S. Navy.
>   She sailed from the Revolutionary Capital in February
>   1777 with Captain Nicholas Biddle as commander. She
>   reached the ocean, the only one of the four frigates to
>   escape the blockade. The Washington, Effingham, and
>   Delaware never made it.

RANGER (Aircraft Carrier)
>   The Ranger is the first aircraft carrier built as such.
>   She was built by the Newport News Shipbuilding and Dry-
>   lock Company, Newport News, Va. The keel was laid
>   26 September 1931; launched 25 February 1933; delivered
>   4 June 1934. Her first commander was Captain Arthur
>   Leroy Bristol.

RANGER (Man-of-War)
>   The first man-of-war to receive a foreign salute was
>   made when John Paul Jones received nine salutes from
>   the French fleet, commanded by La Mott Picquet inside
>   Quiberon Bay, 14 February 1778. The official American
>   flag with alternate red and white stripes, 13 white stars
>   in a blue canton, was hoisted 4 July 1777, personally
>   raised by John Paul Jones on this vessel. The story is
>   told that a group of ladies made the flag out of cloth
>   taken from their own and their mothers' gowns, then
>   they presented it to Captain John Paul Jones.
>   The ship was built by James Hackett in 114 days at
>   Portsmouth, New Hampshire in 1777; launched May 1777.
>   John Paul Jones never was pleased with the Ranger for
>   he said it sailed too slow, and "is of trifling force."
>   With this vessel he carried the war to England's shores;
>   captured Charleston, South Carolina when the British
>   took the fort, 12 May 1780. See also ALFRED.

REBECCA SIMS (Whaler)
>   First recording of a vessel encountering a sea serpent
>   when Alonzo Sampson, crew member, wrote of his ex-
>   periences with it in "Three Times Around the World."
>   The 400-ton vessel was built in 1801; refitted in 1807 at
>   Philadelphia. Alonzo Sampson was sailing with the
>   Monongahela at the time of the sighting. Both vessels
>   stood on either side of the serpent, whose head was like

an alligator's, 10 feet long, it is said. The harpoon
was thrust into the middle of the serpent first. The
men in both vessels continued to harpoon the animal.
It was captured.

RECOVERY (Ship)
One of the first merchant ships to go off the usual trade
routes, adventuring to Mocha to bring back the first full
cargo of coffee berries to Salem, Mass. in 1801. She
was the first American vessel to enter the Red Sea.
Captain Joseph Ropes opened trade in 1798 getting a re-
ception equal to that of Columbus.

RED DRAGON   (British East Indiaman)
This vessel was the first to voyage for the East India
Company merchants. It was the flagship and largest of
the fleet of four. On 13 February 1601, under the command of Captain James Lancaster, the fleet sailed to
establish advance bases for trading. The men were put
ashore to start a "factory," or establish trading quarters,
as offices, storerooms, living quarters. The East India
Company was one of the richest and longest lived of
trading companies, existing from 1601-1858. Indirectly
it influenced American affairs as it had a persuasive
policy on the colonial policy of Great Britain.

RED JACKET   (Extreme Clipper)
First in many things. The fastest in the world, the
fastest of the big wood clippers, fastest of her day, best
of clipper ships, handsomest of the large clipper vessels, known for the delicate beauty of her graceful lines.
This Rockland, Maine, built ship of 2305 tonnage, constructed by Deacon George Thomas was launched 2 November 1853. Her figurehead was a full-length carving
of Sagoyewatha, an Indian chief of the Wolf Clan of the
Senecas, who because of his friendliness toward Great
Britain during the American Revolution had been given a
red coat by a British officer.
She took the speed laurels away from the Memnon in
1854 when she left New York 10 January 1854 and anchored in Liverpool on 23 January, in 13 days, 1 hour,
25 minutes, with Captain Asa Eldridge, commanding.
On the passage she met hail, snow and rain, high seas,
and on 21 January terrific squalls, gales, strong winds.
She was sold to the Liverpool White Star British-Aus-
tralian Packet Line. Her days ended in the Quebec
lumber trade.

RED ROVER, U.S.S.   (Hospital Ship)
The first hospital ship of the U.S. Navy. The vessel was
captured from the Confederate forces 20 September 1862.
On 26 December it was converted into a hospital ship.
It saw service until 12 August 1865. See also SOLACE,
U.S.S.; SANCTUARY, U.S.S.

REINDEER   (Steamboat)
The first time this vessel, or any American vessel,
transported the famous Swedish singer, Jenny Lind. She
voyaged from Castle Garden to Albany on it in 1851, as
crowds cheered her on the banks. The vessel was a
champion racer on the Hudson River. A boiler exploded
at Bristol Landing, September 1851, and the boat was
consumed in flames.

RELIEF, U.S.S.   (Ambulance Ship)
First ship designed and built as a hospital for the transportation of the ill and wounded naval men.
Her keel was laid 4 July 1917; launched 23 December
1919. The ship contained 515 beds in 14 wards, as well
as 15 officers' rooms. Speed 16 knots, 9750 tons displacement. See also SOLACE, U.S.S.; SANCTUARY,
U.S.S.

REPRISAL   (Brig)
The first American built warship to enter European
waters occurred 4 December 1776. The first capture by
the American Colonies of a ship in enemy waters was
carried out by this vessel when in the Bay of Biscay she
captured two vessels, one the King's Packet. On the
way over two other vessels were captured.
It was the first attempt to block and destroy English
commerce in English waters. She carried Benjamin
Franklin travelling incognito to France when he sought
French assistance. The vessel, which was a 16-gun converted merchant-man was commanded by Captain Lambert
Wickes.

REPUBLIC   (Ship)
The first time wireless was used in a shipwreck was on
23 January 1909 when this White Star Liner rammed the
Italian Florida. The ships collided in a fog off the
shoals at Nantucket. Two passengers on the Republic
were lost. Jack Binns was the radio operator who
flashed the distress signal.

RESOLUTION (Collier)
 The first vessel to find the archipelego of small islands
 in Polynesia, New Zealand, which were called Cook Islands, during Captain Cook's second voyage. First to
 sail around New Zealand and discover that North and
 South Islands were insular. They had been believed to
 be a part of the Southern continent.
 First to find island of New Georgeo. First to cross
 Antarctic Circle, middle of January 1773. They found
 gales and heavy seas, fog, icebergs, pack-ice, and the
 decks and rigging coated with ice. On this collier Cook
 left Plymouth, England, 13 July 1772, returned to England in 1775. The purpose of the voyage was to settle
 the question of a southern continent. See also EN-
 DEAVOUR BARK.

RIO HUDSON (Ship)
 The first merchant ship to be formally blessed at a
 launching ceremony occurred on 27 November 1940 at
 the yards of the Sun Shipbuilding and Drydock Company
 in Pa. She carried 197 passengers.

ROANOKE, U.S.S. (Frigate)
 This vessel was the first turreted frigate in the U.S.
 Navy. Originally it was a wooden screw steam frigate
 built at the Norfolk Navy Yard, launched 13 December
 1855. Her maiden voyage was made in 1857. She was
 made an ironclad in 1862-3 by the Novelty Iron Works
 of New York. She had three revolving turrets, two
 pilot houses, and a battery of two 15-inch guns, two
 11-inch and two 150-pounder rifle guns. The hull could
 not stand the weight, so she was sold in 1883.

ROBERT FULTON (Steamboat)
 This vessel is the world's first large ocean-going full-
 powered steamer. She was constructed at New York in
 1819 by Henry Eckford, for David Dunham. She was
 twice the size of the Savannah. She was built of oak,
 cedar, locust, Georgia pine and copper fastened. She
 was designed to carry mail, passengers and light freight.
 Under Captain Inott she sailed with the Swallow Tail
 Line for four or five years, performing admirably, but
 she didn't pay. So she was withdrawn and converted
 into a sloop-of-war, sold to Brazil.

ROBERT F. STOCKTON (Ship)
 This ship is the first iron vessel to cross the Atlantic

Ocean. The Robert F. Stockton introduced the screw
propellor in America 35 years after John Stevens, Jr.
of Hoboken, New Jersey, used the screw with some success in driving a steamboat. 64 years later David Bushnell used the screw propellor successfully in a submarine.

ROGER STUART   (Ship)
The first sailing vessel to bring the first foreign circus
to America. Cooke's Royal Circus, owned by Thomas
Taplin Cooke, came to the United States with 130 per-
formers, 42 horses and 14 ponies, servants and helpers.
It was the first completely equipped and organized circus
company to come to America.
Cooke built an amphitheatre in New York which seated
2000. Then fire blazed through the theater, and everything except the horses was lost. He constructed another
amphitheater in Baltimore, this building also burning.
Bad luck continued to pursue Cooke. He went back to
England and took part in hippodramatic performances
there.

ROOSEVELT   (Ship)
Robert Edwin Peary was the first to plant the American
flag at the North Pole, 6 April 1900 voyaging in this
specially constructed vessel.

ROSCINO   (Packet)
First Atlantic liner built to measure over 1000 tons. A
three-masted packet built in New York in 1838, she made
the Atlantic passage, New York to Liverpool, in less
than two weeks. She was called "Queen of Ships"; the
forebear of the clipper ships to come.

ROYAL WILLIAM   (Ship)
The first ship to cross the Atlantic Ocean by steam
alone, occurring in 1833, from Quebec to London in 25
days. See also SAVANNAH.

RUFUS KING   (Steamboat)
First steam tugboat built in America, by Smith and
Dimon in 1825, for the New York Dry Dock Company
to tow vessels back and forth from their railway in New
York City.

SAGINAW (Steamboat)
The first steamboat built on the Pacific Coast for the U.S. government. This 453-ton vessel was built by Peter M. Donahue at the Union Iron Works, San Francisco, California, in 1860. On 29 October 1870, it was wrecked at Ocean Island in the Pacific Ocean.

ST. CLAIR (Brig)
The first square-rigged vessel built on the Ohio River. This 104-ton ship was built by Stephen Devol at Marietta, Ohio, in 1800; launched in 1801. Captain Abraham Whipple, 70 years old, brought it down the Ohio River on its maiden voyage. She went to New Orleans, then to Havana with a cargo of pork and flour; then to Philadelphia with sugar, in 1803.

ST. JOHN (British Schooner)
The first British schooner, or vessel, of the British armed fleet to enforce the payment of duties during the 10 years previous to the American Revolution. First British vessel stationed in Rhode Island waters. The vessel had been ordered to examine every trading vessel in the waters, see that the cargos were legitimate; levy prescribed fines. Sometimes with this action American seamen were impressed into the British Navy. An entire crew of a brig would be removed.
Captain Hill of the St. John waited until a brig arrived in port, discharged its cargo, reloaded. When the American vessel got to sea, she followed her, caused her return as a suspected smuggler. The captain found the cargo regular. But time had been lost, greater expense incurred which aroused indignation. In this way Captain Hill deliberately planned to annoy the colonists. So the colonists planned to destroy or take the St. John, and armed a sloop. They captured a boat of the Maidstone, a British man-of-war at the wharf, dragged it to the commons, burned it.

ST. JOHN (Steamboat)
The first Hudson River palatial steamer. At the time it was built it was the largest steamboat in the world; larger than anything except the Great Western, England's ocean steamship. She was built by "Deacon" Daniel Drew; launched in 1862, at a cost of $600,000. The beautiful staircase was carved mahogany inlaid with white holly.

ST. LOUIS (Gunboat)
   The world's first ironclad gunboat was one of four iron-
clads. James Eads constructed this vessel in 1861, in
five weeks, at his ironworks at the edge of St. Louis.
Others were built at Mound City near Cairo, Illinois.
These powerful vessels won Fort Donelson and Fort
Henry for the Union.

ST. MARY (Steamboat)
   The first steamboat known to be built from lottery
money. Sam Gaty won $40,000 in a Havana, Cuba, lot-
tery; then he built the St. Mary which he sold to Captain
Joseph La Barge.

ST. NICHOLAS (Ship)
   It is recorded that this vessel is the first to be wrecked
on the coast of Washington. This Russian ship was in
command of Captain Nikolai Bulagin when she left Sitka,
Alaska, 8 September 1808 on an exploring voyage along
the Pacific Coast to chart and trade. The vessel was
carried by the current into the sharp rocks near Destruction Island during a dead calm. There she hung up.
The passengers and crew saved food and usable goods,
and clambered ashore. They set up tents. Then hostile
Indians appeared. The Russians held them off temporar-
ily with their arms and ammunition.
   Gradually the St. Nicholas was pounded to pieces, so
Bulagin decided to walk overland to Gray's Harbor where
the Kodiak was at anchor. The crew made the cannon
unusable by dumping it into the ocean. Then with only
the essentials they started out. Arriving at a river,
they tried to ferry across, but in the middle of the
stream, the Indians pulled the plug out of the canoe,
leaving them at the mercy of spears raining around them.
Bulagin's wife had been kidnapped by this time.
   When the party ran into the hostile Guilentes, the
captain tried to ransom her. He wouldn't give up their
muskets and ammunition so he had to go on without her.
Then Bulagin became the prize of a chief. His wife,
he discovered, had also been owned by a chief and had
soon died in captivity. Months later Bulagin died. The
American brig Lydia freed some of the prisoners in
1811. The Mercury crew freed a crew member later.
13 of the St. Nicholas crew were ransomed; seven died
in captivity.

ST. PETER (Ship)
Vitus Jonassen Bering was the first to discover Bering
Strait, voyaging on this vessel, although fogs prevented
him from verifying his guess. Czar Peter the Great
commissioned Bering, a Danish sea captain, to discover
whether America and Asia were divided. He left St.
Petersburg 5 February 1725, crossed overland to the
Kamchatka River and built his ships, St. Peter and St.
Paul, on the shore, fitted them out.
      He discovered the Strait in 1728; the Saint Lawrence
and Diomede Islands, 4 June 1741. He sailed from Kamchatka, which he founded in 1740, in command of his two
vessels. The ships got separated. He sighted Mt. Saint
Elias, sailed past Kodiak Island. On returning to Kamchatka, because of illness and storms, he was cast on
an island near Kamchatka, where he died.

SAN AGUSTIN (Galleon)
The first shipwreck recorded on the Pacific Coast occurred north of the Mexican border in 1595. This
Spanish vessel with Captain Sebastian Cermenon, charted
all harbors on its way back to Spain. The vessel anchored in Drake's Bay while a charting boat was built
ashore. These workers could not get back to their ship
as a flash southwester struck the coast. A few were
aboard the vessel. The storm blew intensely, dragged
the vessel toward the rocks.
      Finally she lay over a rock reef, twisted, torn, the
bottom gone. The cargo of beeswax, porcelain and
precious silks was lost. The captain and his men, in
the open survey boat, departed for Mexico. The crew
told their story, listing their discovery of San Francisco Bay at 38 degrees.

SAN ANTONIO (Ship)
The largest of Magellan's fleet of five vessels, this
120-ton ship was commanded by Juan de Cartagena.
It deserted the fleet in the south Atlantic, before it was
to proceed through the straits (of Magellan) at the bottom
of South America. First known vessel to enter San
Diego harbor.

SAN CARLOS (Ship)
This vessel made the first entry into San Francisco Bay
in midsummer of 1775. This small vessel was buffeted
by winds and currents from the time it appeared off the
Heads. It had difficulty sailing through the Golden Gate.
She was commanded by Captain Juan Manuel de Ayala.

It has been called the <u>Mayflower</u> of Alta California for it brought the first colonists.

SANCTUARY, U.S.S. (Hospital Ship)
For the first time in American Naval History, both men and women will see active duty aboard this vessel. During November 1972 two of the 70 officers and 60 of the 460 enlisted personnel will be women when the ship leaves port at San Francisco for training exercises and sea trials. Women have served as nurses on medical staffs of hospital ships but not as crew members. Russian merchant ships have sailed with women crew members for a long time. Captain Thomas A. Rogers of Philadelphia is the commanding officer. Captain Alezander C. Hering of Baltimore will be in charge of the hospital.

SAVANNAH (Ship)
The first ship to be powered by nuclear power. This vessel was built in 1956 as an experiment by the U.S. government. Its nuclear reactor heats water to make steam for ordinary turbines. She attains a speed of 20 knots.

SAVANNAH (Steamboat)
The first steamboat built in America usually credited with being the first steam vessel to cross the Atlantic Ocean. This 350-ton vessel was a full-rigged ship with steam machinery. Designed by Daniel Dod of Elizabeth, N.J.: constructed by Francis Fickett and Crocker at their yards at Corlear's Hook, N.Y., at a cost of $50,000. She was launched 22 August 1818. The vessel had large collapsible paddle wheels which could be brought in on deck in 30 minutes; a 90-horsepower engine. The wheel boxes had an iron framework covered with canvas. There were 32 staterooms, two cabins.

The vessel left Savannah, Georgia, without any passengers. She had sailed there on a trial run from New York, on 22 May 1819 and arrived at Liverpool, England, 20 June 1819. In 29 days and 11 hours after leaving Savannah she arrived at Liverpool. The ship carried 75 tons of coal, 25 cords of wood, all of which were used by the time the ship reached the Thames when it operated on steam again. The fuel had given out half way over, yet steam had been used only in calm weather. Some recorders say that the engines were run during only 80 hours of the 648 hour voyage.

As the Savannah was bound for St. Petersburg, Russia, to sell the vessel as a steamer to the Czar, she
headed for Stockholm, then on to St. Petersburg. The
captain invited the royal family and Russian nobles
aboard. He received valuable gifts from royalty wherever
he anchored. The king of Sweden presented him with a
stove and muller. The Emperor of Russia gave him two
iron chairs, a large gold watch. Upon his return he was
given a silver urn in America. For some reason the
Czar didn't want the vessel. Eventually the engines were
removed. She ended her days as a sailing vessel and
smashed on the rocks off Long Island. She paved the
way for giant ocean liners. See also ROYAL WILLIAM;
MISSOURI, U.S.S.

SCHOONER (Schooner)
The first schooner built in America, she was built in the
spring of 1714 at Cape Ann, Gloucester, Mass., by a
man named Robinson. Sources say Andrew, Adam, or
Henry, in Robinson's shipyard. This vessel is fore-and-
aft rigged, small (50-100 ton) with two masts, designed
for speed, seaworthiness and the coasting trade.
A spectator watching the launching cried "see how she
schoons." "Schoon," or "scoon" is a Yankee word de-
scribing the action of skipping a flat stone across the
water, thus the name "schooner." The schooner de-
veloped in the 1880's and 1890's to vessels of 2000 or
3000 tons, having four, five and even six masts used in
foreign trade. Only one seven-master was built of 5200
tons (Thomas Lawson, which see), in 1901-2.

SCORPION (Schooner)
The first vessel of Elliott's squadron to fire the first
shot on Lake Erie in the War of 1812. She was built
in 1813 by Noah Brown on Lake Erie. 2 guns.

SCOTT (Ship)
The first ship to make a successful trip to the Falls of
the Ohio River. She was built in 1805 by Jonas Spoir
on the Kentucky River, 20 miles above Frankfurt. After
the Louisiana purchase in 1803, men in the East sent
mechanics to build ships on the Ohio River. The Scott
waited several months for the river to rise to allow it
to float over the Falls.

SCRIMSHAW
This is the art of carving or scratching bone, ivory,

steel, or wood, made by sailors in their leisure time,
and to fill the long hours at sea. The whalemen de-
veloped their own tools with which they etched on the
teeth of the sperm whale, or on whalebone. They inlaid
the designs with mother-of-pearl, tortoise shell, bits of
ivory. Out of the whalebone they made jagging or crimp-
ing wheels, work boxes, rolling pins, napkin rings, spool
holders, knitting needles, clothespins, coat racks, dip-
pers, and many other things.

SEA GULL (Steamboat)
A little steamer from the Connecticut River used as a
flagship of the West Indian Squadron in its fight against
pirates was one of two such "firsts." See also DEMO-
LOGOS.

SEA OTTER (British Ship)
This British trading ship was Oregon's first recorded
shipwreck, occurring 22 August 1808. A vessel of 1120
tons, she ventured into the North Pacific for furs, especially otter, to help supply the world market demand.
Captain Niles, commander.
At the mouth of the Umpqua River, in stormy weather,
the Sea Otter met her doom. Six of the crew survived
to make the end of their journey on foot through Indian
country where there were no settlements. They trav-
eled to the Red River, La., enduring indescribable hardships of weather--wind, rain, snow, desert heat, the
mountains.

SEAMAN'S BRIDE (Clipper)
One of the first two clippers to carry moon sails. The
other was the Hurricane. This diminutive clipper was
built at Baltimore. Only a few clippers carried moon
sails--Seaman's Bride, built in 1851; the Hurrican, built
in 1851; Phoenix, built in 1853; the James Baines in
1854. The Seaman's Bride carried three moon sails
above the sky sails. The Hurricane carried a moon sail
on her main.

SEATRAIN
The first seatrain went into service between New Orleans,
Louisiana, and Havana, Cuba. It was built in 1928 for
the Seatrain Lines, Inc., by the Sun Shipbuilding Company, Chester, Pa. They began operating 12 January
1929. Loaded freight cars are hoisted on the seatrain,
which can transport 95 railroad cars. Seatrains are

named after the cities they serve, as <u>New Orleans.</u>

SELANDIA   (Danish Ship)
  This vessel is alleged to be the first diesel ship fitted
  with sails for emergency use in case the engines broke
  down.

SENATOR   (Steamboat)
  The first steamboat to round Cape Horn and be the
  earliest respectable steamer in California. It is alleged she earned more money than any other steamboat
  in history.
  This sidewheeler of 750 tons was built at New York in
  1848 by William H. Brown for the run between Boston
  and St. John, New Brunswick. Then the whisper of gold
  reached the east coast and the vessel was taken to the
  west coast, leaving New York 10 March 1849 on its
  17,000 mile voyage to San Francisco. At Panama the
  vessel picked up 200 gold seekers at $500 per person.
  Arriving at San Francisco the vessel immediately went
  on the run from that city to the gold diggings, 100 miles
  up the Sacramento River, which it covered in eight or
  nine hours.
  Almost immediately it displaced all small craft,
  scows that took two weeks to make the trip. Tickets
  were sold for $45 to $60, depending on how much you
  ate and if you wanted a berth. Freight cost $40 to $80
  a ton. Sometimes at capacity, she garnered $50,000 on
  a one-way trip. Although she monopolized the trade,
  she was not the first steamboat on the Sacramento River.
  She spent from 1849-1854 in this trade. After that she
  went coastwise to San Diego, alternating with river trade.
  In 1884 her engines were removed. She was rigged as
  a barkentine, made a voyage to New Zealand where she
  was converted to a coal barge.

SENECA CHIEF   (Packet)
  The first in a long line of vessels at Buffalo to lead the
  parade through the Erie Canal on 26 October 1825.

SHASTA   (Steamboat)
  The first steamboat built on the West Coast. This 120-
  ton side-wheeler was built at the Rincon Yard of Little-
  ton and Co.; launched in 1853 by a private concern. The
  vessel was built for the upper reaches of the rivers for
  she drew 18 inches. In 1868 she was disposed of.

SHOOTING STAR (Clipper)
    First of the Medford, Massachusetts, clippers. This
    903-ton clipper was built by J. O. Curtis, designed by
    Capt. John Wade for S. G. Reed & Co., Boston, Mass.,
    in 1851.
    One of the best contests of 1852 was the race between
    the Staffordshire (McKay's) and the Shooting Star, with
    Captain Judah P. Baker, commanding. The two vessels
    left Boston for San Francisco 3 April 1852. At the Horn
    the Staffordshire passed out through heavy gales into the
    Pacific ahead of the Shooting Star. The Shooting Star
    kept coming at a remarkable pace, but the Staffordshire
    kept the lead, passed the Golden Gate 13 August 1852,
    101 days out, and four days later the Shooting Star came
    in. It was the second time for both vessels around the
    Horn; both had been overhauled and re-rigged for the run.
    The Shooting Star was sold to a merchant of Siam in
    1862. In 1867 she was wrecked on the coast of Formosa.

SHOSHONE (Steamboat)
    This large stern-wheeler was the first steamboat to try
    going down the river from the Upper Snake River to the
    Columbia River. She was built above Snake Canyon at
    old Fort Boise at great expense.
    On her first voyage in 1866 she reached the Boise
    River mouth. It was planned she carry miners to the
    Boise Diggings. But before she was built, the miners
    found a shorter route. So she was beached two years
    on the Upper Snake. It was decided to bring her down,
    or wreck her in trying. So in March 1870 when this was
    begun, it was discovered that her wood was brittle, her
    seams had opened. There was nothing to caulk her with;
    no time to do it.

SHOWBOAT (Barge)
    The first unquestioned, unnamed floating palace showboat
    was that of the Chapmans launched at Pittsburgh, Pa.,
    in 1831 by Chapman and family. Chapman purchased a
    barge 100 feet by 16 feet on the top of which he put a
    crude barn. There was a shallow stage with muslin cur-
    tains. Its footlights were candles. The bow was devoted
    to the family living quarters. Between it and the stage
    on deck, were fastened down benches, without backs or
    pillows. In the center of the area hung a hogshead hoop
    chandelier dripping candle wax over the audience. Shake-
    speare was acted most of the time.
    The barge drifted down the Ohio, Mississippi Rivers

to New Orleans, giving one night performances wherever they could get an audience. They hired, at each stop, the local town crier to advertize the performances. He blew a trumpet and tacked up posters, hand-printed by one of the women of the cast, showing that the admission price was 50 cents, half for Negroes and children. Often potatoes, fruit, bacon were accepted for the price of a ticket.

Chapman went down the rivers to New Orleans, making one night stands. There in New Orleans he sold the barge, took a steamer back to Pittsburgh, built a new barge in the spring. He continued this routine of selling and built new showboats for four years. See also NOAH'S ARK; FLOATING CIRCUS PALACE.

SILVIE DE GRACE (Packet)
This vessel is considered the first vessel of major importance to be shipwrecked near Astoria. She also was the first vessel to bring the news of the French Revolution to America. She was stranded on a rock near Astoria in 1849.

SIRIUS (English Packet)
The first transatlantic English steam packet (700 tons) to cross the Atlantic entirely under steam, reaching an American port. She made the passage from Cork to New York in 17 days in 1838. When she reached Sandy Hook, she ran out of coal, so all spars were chopped and burned to keep up the steam so that she could be brought in on steam only. While throwing clouds of black smoke with cannon saluting church bells tolling, 1000 people shouted, waved at the first English steam packet to enter port.

SITKA (Steamboat)
The first California river steamboat. This 40-ton side-wheeler moved by a miniature engine was 37 feet long. The tiny steam launch was built in Sitka by an American as a pleasure boat for the officers of the Russian Fur Company. Then William A. Leidesdorff bought it from the Russians and took it down to San Francisco Bay in October 1847. In Sitka it became known as the Little Sitka. It was taken to San Francisco and lashed to the deck of the bark Naslednich intended for use in collecting furs and hides.

She made a trial trip to Santa Clara, then Sonoma 15 November 1847. Then she took a dozen passengers to

Sacramento. The voyage took six days and seven hours.
Down river the Sitka was beaten by an ox team by four
days. When the Sitka returned to Yerba Buena (San
Francisco) she was wrecked at anchorage in a gale. She
was raised; her engines removed and put into a schooner
called the Rainbow which ran on the Sacramento River
after the discovery of gold. Two years after inland
steam navigation began the Sitka became a sailing vessel.
The Little Sitka was the forerunner in California of a
great age of steam navigation.

SMELTER (Steamboat)
This vessel provided for the first "fashionable tour, " an
excursion trip up the Mississippi River to Fort Snelling
where the passengers got off to gaze at the wonders of
the Minnehaha Falls. It came up from Cincinnati decorated with evergreens. Launched in 1837; owned by the
Harris Brothers. It was equipped with private state
rooms. It made a record 5-day run from Cincinnati to
Dubuque, Iowa. It ran all the way to Minnesota.

SOCONY 200 (Barge)
This barge is the first reinforced steel concrete barge
for carrying bulk oil. She was built by the Fougner
Shipbuilding Company, Flushing Bay, N.Y.; launched 27
July 1918.

SOLACE, U.S.S. (Ambulance Ship)
This vessel was the first ambulance ship to carry the
Geneva Cross flag. She was used for transporting and
caring for the sick. 5700 tons; in service 14 April
1898. She was once the S.S. Creole and had been used
in naval warfare in the war against Spain. See also
RELIEF, U.S.S.; RED ROVER, U.S.S.

SOUTHERN (Steamboat)
The first passenger steamer lost on the shores of Washington. The wreck occurred in 1847 when this side-
wheeler, just after all its passengers were off, swept
into the coast, buffeted by breaker after breaker. Finally
it lay at rest, as the tide ebbed, a battered wreck. All
hands left the vessel before the next rise of the sea.
The sea came in again. The breakers rose higher and
higher, pounding on the vessel relentlessly as her passengers watched her cave in, leaving only splinters of
wood.

SOVEREIGN OF THE SEAS (Clipper)
  For the first time in history, up to this time, a ship
sailed more than 424 nautical miles in 24 hours; a new
speed record.   This 2421-ton clipper was built by Donald
McKay at East Boston; launched 15 November 1852.   No
expense was spared and she was famed for her splendor,
magnificence.   The crew consisted of 105 men and boys.
Her commander was Captain Lauchlan McKay.
  The figurehead was a sea-god--half man, half fish--
with a conch shell raised to his mouth, as if blowing it.
In 1852 she sailed through furious snows, rain and gales
on her only voyage to San Francisco.   She was partly
dismasted in the South Pacific.   She was rigged again;
and at sea in 14 days.   She made port in 103 days, a
record for that season of the year.
  Lieut. Maury brought her from New York to the Sandwich Islands in 82 days, breaking all records of the time.
She proceeded to lower the record from New York to
Liverpool in June when the weather was usually unfavor-
able for fast passages, in 13 days 23 hours.   Donald
McKay was the only shipbuilder whose clippers were un-
iformly successful.   He had a name synonymous with the
finest in men and ships.   The vessel was sold to a Ham-
burg firm, then was wrecked on the treacherous Pyramid
Shoal in the Malacca Straits, 6 August 1859, a total loss.
She is called "the immortal among clipper ships."

SPARROW HAWK (Ketch)
  This vessel became the first wreck of an emigrant vessel
bringing Pilgrims to the Plymouth Colony.   The Sparrow
Hawk was one-masted with a single spar.   It was 28
feet by 10 feet long on keel; 40 feet long overall; 12 feet
10 inches beam; 9 feet 7 1/2 inches deep.   She was
built of English oak with outside planking two inches
thick.   She had a square stern; a raking sternpost four
inches to a foot.   She brought 40 passengers including
the crew.   Historians think she was similar to Blessing
of the Bay.
  The six-weeks' voyage was rough.   The master had
scurvy.   There were only a few gallons of wine left
when they anchored off the shallow entrance to Pleasant
Bay.   A storm blew the vessel high up onto the shore,
battering it, until it was a total loss.   The passengers
were taken in by the Plymouth families.   For a long
time the timbers of the vessel lay buried in the sand
when one day a storm brought them to light.   The hull
was tiny, smaller than that of the Mayflower.   It was

about the burden of the Little James. The pieces of the
vessel were carefully assembled and may be seen at Plymouth Hall, Plymouth. See also BLESSING OF THE BAY.

THE SPRAY (Sloop)
    The first vessel to circumnavigate the globe with only
    one in the crew. This nine-ton sloop was built in Fair-
    haven, Massachusetts, at a cost of $550. It was 36 feet
    9 inches long; 14 feet 2 inches wide and 4 feet 2 inches
    deep. Captain Joshua Slocum sailed from Boston, Massa-
    chusetts, 24 April 1895, returning 3 July 1898, a trip of
    46,000 miles.

SQUIRREL (Frigate)
    The first British attempt to plant a colony in the New
    World on the shore of Newfoundland was made by Sir
    Humphrey Gilbert. The vessel went down off the Azores
    in a tempest in 1583.

STAG HOUND (Extreme Clipper)
    This extreme clipper was Donald McKay's first real ex-
    treme clipper. She was built by McKay for Upton of
    Boston; launched 7 December 1850. 1534 tons. Her
    maiden voyage was made to California arriving at San
    Francisco 25 May 1851 having left New York 1 February
    1851, a 113-day passage.

STATES (Whaler)
    This vessel collected the first cargo of seal skins in the
    Falkland islands. The ship was launched at Boston in
    1783; owned by Lady Haley of Boston. She was fitted
    out and sent to the Falklands in search of sea elephant
    oil, fur and seal. The vessel brought in 13,000 skins
    which sold in Canton for $65,000. She opened the market
    for these skins from these Islands.

STURDY BEGGAR (Schooner)
    This ship was the first armed merchant-man of Richard
    and Elias H. Derby during the American Revolution.
    This 90-ton vessel of Salem had six carriage guns; used
    a crew of 25. It was built by the Derbys as a merchant-
    man with Captain Peter Lander in command. It was
    their first vessel to make reprisals on the enemies of
    the Colonies.
        Derby was a peaceful merchant who had three of his
    ships seized by the British in 1776 while voyaging to
    Salem from Jamaica. So he decided to arm his ships,

and either trade with letter-of-marque vessels, or cruise
with out-and-out privateers. So it became a privateer
brig with Captain George Williams in command. From
1776 to 1782 the Derbys armed 23 privateers and 16
other vessels bearing letters-of-marque. Sturdy Beggar
was captured by the British. See also NANCY.

SUHAILI   (Ketch)
The first non-stop circumnavigation of the globe to date
was finished by Robin Knox-Johnston in 312 days.

SULLIVANS, THE   (Destroyer)
The first naval ship with a plural name. It was launched
at San Francisco 4 April 1943. The ship was named for
five brothers of Waterloo, Iowa, who had enlisted 3 January 1942 and were lost when the cruiser Juneau sank off
Guadalcanal in the Solomon Islands 15 November 1942.

SUMTER   (Cruiser)
The first confederate cruiser to raid Union commerce.
She was constructed at Philadelphia, a steamer with bark
rig, five small guns. She was fitted out in New Orleans
in 1861. The ship became a Confederate raider during
the Civil War. Captain Raphael Semmes, more than any
other man, with the Sumter and Alabama paralyzed the
ocean-carrying trade of the nation, from 3 July 1861 to
18 January 1862. The first capture of the Sumter was
the clipper Golden Rocket; and it was the first prize of
the Civil War.

SURPRISE   (Schooner)
The first steam schooner to be built in California. In
1884 Charles G. White constructed this schooner at San
Francisco.

SUSAN CONSTANT   (Flagship)
One of the first three, and the largest (100 tons, 71 or
more crew) of the vessels, to carry the first permanent
colonists from England to Virginia in the sixth attempt
to colonize. The three ships left Blackwell, England, on
19 December 1606: The Discovery, a pinnace of 20 tons,
and the Godspeed of 40 tons, with Captain Christopher
Newport commanding, were the other two. There were
stores, ammunitions, arms, tools, trading trinkets
aboard. Everyone slept on the deck on which had been
lashed a dismantled shallop for exploring shallow shore
waters. The three ships carried 104.

On 23 March 1607 the vessel anchored off the coast of the West Indies and sited the new land (Virginia) on 26 April 1607. The colonists to found Jamestown came off the ship after Captain Christopher Newport, who carried a sealed mystery box. It had been given to him by the Council of the Virginia Company of London, which firm financed the expedition. In the box were the papers on which they found the names of the governing council of the new colony. They were: Gosnold, Ratcliffe, Capt. John Smith, Newport, Wingfield, Martin and Kendall. After the names were revealed the colonists began to build their fort. See also GODSPEED; DISCOVERY.

TECUMSEH (Ironclad)
The first of Admiral David Glasgow Farragut's ironclads. The vessel was constructed at Bath, Maine, in 1889. It sank when it struck a torpedo in Mobile Bay. See also ADMIRAL.

TERROR, U.S.S. (Minelayer)
The first U.S. Navy vessel built as a minelayer. The keel was laid 3 September 1940; launched 6 June 1941 at Philadelphia, Pa. She cruised at 20 knots; mounted four 5-inch 38 caliber dual purpose guns and two twin-40-millimeter anti-aircraft guns.

THOMAS W. LAWSON (Schooner)
The first seven-masted steel schooner built. Construction began at Quincy, Massachusetts, 1 November 1901 by the Fore River Ship & Engine Co., of Boston; launched 10 July 1902. The masts alone weighed about 17 tons each. There were three steel decks, six cargo hatches.
This mammoth, impractical craft was cumbersome, unwieldy and slow. It was unsuitable for the deep sea; too large for coastwise trade. It did operate between Gulf ports and the Delaware River and carried cargo to Europe. It was wrecked at St. Agnes, the Scilly Islands, England. The commander, Captain George Dow and the engineer were saved but 16 of the crew drowned.

TILLIE E. STARBUCK (Ship)
The first American built full-rigged iron ship, built in 1883; tonnage 2033.

TOPAZ (Whaler)
The captain of the Topaz, Mayhew Folger, was the first
person to solve the mystery of the fate of the H.M.
Bounty. The vessel was built at Wanton, Massachusetts,
in 1805. It was 6 February 1808 when the Topaz arrived at Pitcairn Island, saw smoke on the island which
was supposed to be uninhabited. He found Alexander
Smith, sole survivor, living on it.

TRAVELLER (Ship)
The first cargo of grain to be exported from California
in an American vessel was shipped in the Traveller. In
March 1817 Captain James Smith Wilcox in this vessel
came from the North where he had sold cloth to the
Presidio; bringing the share assigned to San Diego.
When he left, he took the cargo of grain to Loreto. The
vessel traded up and down the coast during the month of
June 1817.

TRINIDAD (Flagship)
Her captain, Ferdinand Magellan was the first European
to discover the Straits of Magellan at Cape Horn. He
was the first to name the western sea discovered by
Balboa, Mar Pacifico, or "calm sea."

TRIUMPH OF THE CROSS, THE (Ship)
The first ship built in California. The vessel was built
in September 1719 on the banks of the river Mulegé by
Father Juan Ugarti and skilled workers. In September
1719 Father Ugarti nailed a cross on the bowsprit;
christened it; launched it, calling it El Triunfo de la
Cruz.
The Indians told Father Ugarti that large straight
trees were to be found 200 miles to the northwest of
Loreto. So he secured a shipwright from across the
Gulf, took soldiers, several Indians and went to the
mountains of Guadalupe where he found the trees in the
most inaccessible place. The shipwright said it was impractical but Father Ugarti was determined. With axes,
the soldiers and Indians set to work felling trees for
planks. They cleared and built a road from the place to
Santa Rosalia, 30 leagues away. Oxen and mules from
the mission were used to bring down the finished planks.
Father Ugarti superintended and labored and finally
saw the vessel rise from keel to bulwarks. The ship
was large and strong. She made her first voyage to
found the new mission at La Paz. This was 80 leagues

from Loreto. The vessel carried Father Jayme Bravo
and his assistants with Father Ugarti as commander,
leaving Loreto on 15 May 1721 with 20 people. Later
it carried 60 people. A pinnace went with it. This
vessel served the missionaries for years.

TRUELOVE   (Ship)
This ship is America's oldest wood ship, having served
110 years. She was built in Philadelphia in 1764. The
Truelove spent the first 20 years of her life as a merchantman and privateer before the British captured her.
They operated her as a whaler for 84 years. It is
alleged she captured 500 whales. Then she became a
general trader until broken up in England in 1874, at
the age of 110. She seems to have the best record for
the longevity of a ship. Some think the Charles W. Morgan may be the second oldest ship, as it was 100 years
old when taken to Mystic, Connecticut. See under Part
IV, CHARLES W. MORGAN.

TUGBOAT   (Tugboat)
The first diesel electric tugboat went into operation in
1929. It is owned by the Tennessee Coal Iron and R.R.
Co. and operates on the Warrior River, Alabama. Its
tow is limited to seven barges.

TURTLE   (Submarine)
The first practical submarine in history and the first to
be used in actual warfare. This vessel was invented by
David Bushnell of Saybrook, Connecticut, in 1776, and
held one man. It was the first to use piston pumps to
fill and empty ballast tanks. It was designed and built
for war purposes. Sergeant Ezra Lee of Lyme, Connecticut and the Continental Army made an attempt to
sink the British frigate Eagle of 50 guns which failed.
     Thirty pounds of gunpowder was to be attached to the
bottom of the enemy vessel, then exploded by a fuse.
The Turtle was in position but couldn't attach the powder
to the hull. Later Lee let the torpedo float into the
East River where it exploded as he tried to escape British soldiers on Governor's Island. In 1776 when it was
ferried across the river on a surface craft, it sank. It
was recovered but it was never put back in working
order.

UMATILLA (Steamboat)
This sternwheeler is said to have been the first to go
through the gorges and rapids at Celilo and run Tumwater Falls. It was built at Celilo in 1908 on the Colorado River. At Celilo are a series of narrow, rocky
gorges and rapids, headed by Tumwater Falls. Steamboats ran them, though the Umatilla was first.

UNITED STATES (Frigate)
One of the first frigates built for the U.S. Navy. It
was built at Philadelphia by Joshua Humphreys in the
same year as the Constitution: authorized in 1794, it
was launched 10 May 1797. 44 guns. 1576 tons.
Commodore John Barry was the first captain.
She was scuttled when Federal forces abandoned Norfolk Navy Yard 20 April 1861 at the outset of the Civil
War.

VANDALIA (Steamboat)
The first steamboat engine built in America for a screw-
propelled boat was put in this vessel. She was the first
screw-propelled vessel on the Great Lakes. Designed
by John Ericsson; built by Captain Sylvester Doolittle;
launched 1 December 1841. 138 tons displacement.

VICTORIA (Ship)
The first vessel (85 tons) to circumnavigate the globe,
under Captain Sebastian del Cano, sent by Spain as part
of Magellan's historic five-ship fleet. People desired
spices to make food exciting. This caused many to open
their purses, finance navigators and explorers in finding
a new trade route to the land of spice and gold--the
Indies.
So Ferdinand Magellan [Fernão da Magalhães] (1480-
1521), Portuguese navigator renounced his citizenship
and went to the King of Spain telling him that he could
find a route to the Malaccas. Financed by Spain, Magellan sailed from San Lucar de Barrameda on 20 September 1519 to seek a western route in command of five
vessels: Trinidad (the flagship); Victoria, Concepción,
San Antonio, and Santiago. Many hardships caused the
captains to mutiny and to seize three ships, leaving Magellan his flagship and the small Santiago. When the
captain of the Victoria was killed the ship was recap-
tured. Due to bad weather the Santiago was lost before

entering the Straits.   Captain Gomez quietly headed the
San Antonio back to Spain.   The other three vessels
worked their way through the turbulent Straits.   They
sailed into the calm Pacific and Magellan called the
Great South Sea, "El Mar Pacifico" for its gentle, favorable breezes and calm water.

On 6 March 1521 they reached the Ladrones, which
Magellan named for the natives who were such thieves.
There they obtained fresh fruit and other foods.   Nine-
teen of the crew died of scurvy and the rest were ill
with it.   At the Malaccas the Concepión was dismasted
and burned.   The other two ships were loaded up with
spices.   The Trinidad sprang a leak; the Victoria set
sail toward the west over the Cape of Good Hope route.
The Trinidad was repaired and headed for Panama.   For
months adverse winds baffled it and finally turned it back
to the Malaccas, having lost 35 of the crew due to
scurvy and starvation, so that there were only 19 survivors.   On a Pacific island Magellan was killed in a
war with the natives of Matan.   The natives killed the
crew.

The Victoria had a bad time.   It started across the
Indian Ocean.   The men were starving.   They could
hardly man the sails, they were so weak.   Fortunately,
the King of Portugal sent a man-of-war to intercept
them; so after three years and 29 days of sailing they
anchored at Seville.   Only 18 men of the original crew
of 230 survived the voyage.

Magellan discovered that America was not a series
of islands, but a new continent; the southwest passage
through to the Great South Sea; that the Great South
Sea was vast, of great magnitude; that the Spice Islands
lay in a part of the world that had been given to Portugal; that the kingdoms of the Great Khan did not lie westward across the Atlantic.   See also TRINIDAD.

VIGILANT   (Revenue Cutter)
One of the first U.S. revenue cutters, forerunner of the
present Coast Guard fleet.   It was built in 1791 by Ebenezer Young.

VINCENNES   (Warship)
The first warship to circumnavigate the globe.   She left
New York 31 August 1826 for the Pacific via Cape Horn,
returning in 1829 via Cape of Good Hope arriving at New
York 8 June 1830.   Her commanding officer was Captain
William Bolton Finch.

VINDEX (Yacht)
The first iron sloop yacht. The yacht was built at
Chester, Pennsylvania, by Reany Son & Company in
1871. 54 tons. The first owner was Robert Center.
She was abandoned 30 June 1898.

VIRGINIA (Pinnace)
The first ship to be built in the colonies of America.
She was built at the Sagadahoc (Kennebec) River by
Thomas Digby, a Londoner. She was 40 feet long, 14
feet beam, 9 feet deep; 30 tons burthen. Moss was
used for caulking; shirts for sails. Authorities vary as
to measurements. Her hull was partly decked over to
protect the cargo. There seems to have been one mast,
a sizeable sprit sail, probably one square sail and a
foresail, or jib. There were oars for confined waters
and calms. She was launched in the fall of 1607.
She was built for coastwise trade with the Indians and
deep-sea voyages. She made several voyages across the
Atlantic Ocean and up and down the coast of Virginia.
It is recorded that she went along the coast to obtain furs
to take to England. She carried a cargo of salt cod south
of Jamestown. On her first voyage home to England she
carried sassafras root and furs, with some of the returning colonists.
The vessel took home the disheartened. In 1609 it
was part of a fleet bringing settlers to Jamestown and
Virginia. She is recorded as plying between England and
Virginia for 20 years until wrecked on the Irish coast
with a cargo of tobacco. Another source claims she
ended her days with Englishmen chained to it, among the
Barbary pirates.

VIRGINIA (Steamboat)
The first vessel to tow an American man-of-war, the
Congress. This 289-ton vessel was built at Baltimore
in 1817. In December 1817 she towed the frigate from
Ready Island to Hampton Roads at the rate of four miles
an hour facing strong winds and tides. Later she became the Temple of the Muses.

VIRGINIA (Steamboat)
The first steamboat to go up the upper Mississippi River.
She made the trip in 1823, carrying produce, a family,
a missionary to the Indians, Great Eagle, and an Indian
agent on the expedition to find the source of the river.

WALK-IN-THE-WATER   (Steamboat)
The first steamboat on the Great Lakes. She was built at Black Rock, Buffalo, New York, for McIntyre and Stewart. Launched 4 April 1818, 338 tons. She was a brig-rigged paddle-wheel steamboat. On the first voyage she took with her 100 passengers bound for Detroit, Michigan. She carried emigrants from Buffalo to Detroit. She lasted three seasons. She had to be helped against the current of the Niagara River, so eight yoke of oxen were used. She was wrecked in a gale in Buffalo Harbor.

WALLAMET   (Steamboat)
This side wheeler was the first steamboat on the upper Willamette River. It then went on the Portland-Astoria run. It was sold; towed to California. It lasted only a short time.

WAR EAGLE II   (Steamboat)
This vessel headed the first parade of steamboats on the great excursion to celebrate the laying of the last span of railroad on the river bank at Rock Island. This span linked the Atlantic coast with the Mississippi by rail. Captain Harris was in command. Captain Harris built the second War Eagle in Cincinnati, in 1854. He made the elegant boat famous on the Upper Mississippi River.
In the grand parade the steamboats following the War Eagle were: the G. W. Sparhawk, Lady Franklin, Galena, Jenny Lind, Blackhawk and Golden Era. On deck were cows to provide fresh milk; tubs of iced oysters, clams, lobsters; crates of uneasy turkeys and chickens destined for the sumptuous banquet tables. Fireworks glowed, bells and whistles resounded intermittently with the band music as the excursion progressed.
At midnight a thunder storm vied with the fireworks. Jagged lightning speared the sky. Thunder crashed, wind rushed through the atmosphere, and rain drove the sightseers into their cabins. The next morning the parade led up Fever River to the blaring of whistles. There it and the others tied up at the cobblestone wharf of Galena, famous and picturesque lead mining town. The passengers viewed the old Fort on its rocky perch, and the colonnaded market house. There were wagonloads of food and drink everywhere.
Then on up the river. On Lake Pepin the parade stopped. Four steamboats lashed themselves together. The passengers danced to the music of the band from

the War Eagle. Then on up to St. Paul where a thousand
hailed greetings. For years the War Eagle carried
miners, immigrants, sawmills, pipe organs, mules,
reapers, fire engines, barrels of wheat, cranberries up
and down the upper river. Then in 1870 it burned at La
Crosse.

WARSHIP FLEET
The first warship fleet to circumnavigate the globe. The
fleet, consisting of 16 warships and some auxiliaries,
left Hampton Roads, Virginia, on 16 December 1907.
Rear Admiral Robley Dunglison Evans was in command.
On its return, the fleet left San Francisco 7 July 1908
and arrived back at Hampton Roads 22 February 1909.

WASHINGTON   (Ship)
The first American ship to adopt the iron chain for the
lower shrouds. Eventually wire rope was used for this
purpose.

WASHINGTON   (Steamboat)
The first two decker steamboat on western waters. There
was a cabin between decks. For the first time the boilers were placed on deck, where before they had been in
the hold. The first steamboat explosion occurred on this
vessel. She revolutionized steamboat design. A new era
of the paddle wheeler began. It was discovered she was
speedier; more dependable than the barge.
    She was the ninth steamboat in the central west. She
was constructed by Captain Henry M. Shreve at Wheeling;
launched 4 June 1816. The engines were built at Browns-
ville, Pa.; the hull was built at Wheeling, W. Va. Her timbers came from the old bastion Fort Henry.
    Shreve was the first, not Livingston, not Roosevelt,
to solve the problem of western river navigation. In
1817 he invented and demonstrated the practicality of,
the stern-wheel, high powered, beamy, wide and high,
shallow-draft river steam boat--a shallow draft boat that
sailed on the water not in it. She rubbed over the
shoals. The banner flying from her flagstaff showed
fame blowing a trumpet. She left Wheeling, West Virginia,
on 4 June 1816. Below Marietta, Ohio, she ran aground.
She left Marietta on Monday afternoon after freeing herself, the 7th, and upon arriving off Point Harmar anchored until Wednesday morning. Fires were kindled,
she made ready for resuming her journey down the Ohio
River.

The boat was being carried by force of currents to
the Virginia shore and Captain Shreve found it difficult
to get her in proper position to start the machinery. A
kedge anchor was thrown out at the stern. While the
men were doing this, the end of the cylinder nearest the
stern was blown off. Scalding water spouted over everyone. Some inhaled it. Some were killed immediately.
The crew was badly injured. The Captain and others
were thrown overboard. All but one was rescued. The
cause was the disarrangement of the safety valve which
became immovable.

There is a story that a man told a cabin boy he would
give him all his money if the boy would knock him out,
put him out of his misery. There is no record of whether the cabin boy did as he was asked. The Shreve steamboat ran from New Orleans to Louisville in 21 days.
She made an historic run up the Mississippi River from
New Orleans to Louisville in 1816 against the spring current.

WASHINGTON   (Steamboat)
With this vessel the Ocean Stream and Navigation Company flew an American flag on each of its vessels between United States and European ports. She left New
York City with 120 passengers on 1 June 1847 bound for
Bremen, Germany. Her figurehead was a full length
effigy of George Washington.

WASHINGTON   (Whaler)
Captain George Bunker in this ship was the first to
fly the American flag at Callao, Peru. This city was
a rendezvous for the South Seas whalers of New England.

WESTERN ENGINEER   (Flagship)
The first steamboat to be built for exploring and surveying the head waters of the Missouri River. It was built
in 1819 with three other boats: the Thomas Jefferson,
Expedition, and R. M. Johnson. The steamboat looked
like a huge serpent, black and scaly, rising out of the
water under the boat. The head was pushed forward and
out of its mouth came smoke. The huge animal seemed
to be carrying the steamboat on its back. All the machinery was hidden to make it look like a sea-serpent
moving through the water.

It was intended to frighten the Indians. The Indians
said the white man was keeping a great spirit chained to
the boat, making it build fire to move the vessel. It

was called Long's dragon. The sternwheel was protected
from snags. Three brass cannon, also to frighten the
Plains Indians, were placed on it. The expedition took
along a cargo of presents to appease the natives. The
banner it flew was that of a white man and an Indian
shaking hands, one holding a sword, the other the peace
pipe. The boat was to be taken apart at the source of
the Missouri, carried five miles over mountains, and
reassembled for a run to the Pacific Ocean. The expedition failed to reach even halfway to the Yellowstone River
where the men intended to build a fort at its mouth. The
Western Engineer got as far as Fort Lisa now Omaha,
Nebraska.

The Thomas Jefferson snagged in Osage Chute and
was the first wreck on the river. The R. M. Johnson
and the Expedition got to Atchison, Kansas, when winter
closed in on them. The latter vessel delivered 163,000
silver dollars to the Bank of Missouri. Because of the
delay and expense of the Yellowstone Expedition, Congress
became disinterested, refused further funds. However
Major Stephen H. Long, leader, went on to make a scientific exploration to the Rocky Mountains, adding much
to the knowledge of Indian lore of the Plains Indians,
zoology, botany and geology.

WIDE WEST (Steamboat)
    First locally built "floating palace" on the Colorado
    River. This stern-wheeler was built at Portland, Ore-
    gon, in 1877 for passenger service. It was luxurious,
    fast. Good meals were served.

WILLIAM J. WHITE (Schooner)
    First four-masted schooner to be built. It was launched
    in June 1880 at Bath, Maine.

WILLIAM P. FRYE (Ship)
    First American ship lost in WW I. This 3374 ton, steel
    sailing vessel was built in 1901. The German cruiser
    Prinz Eitel Friedrich sunk her.

WILLIAMSBURG (Ferry)
    This steam ferry established a record of 52 trips in a
    single day, across the East River. Its average time was
    seven minutes for the 1 1/2 mile run, in 1820. Later,
    larger ferries could not surpass this record.

WORDEN, U.S.S. (Ship)
The first gyro stabilizer to be installed on an American vessel was put on this ship by the Sperry Gyroscope Company, Brooklyn, New York, in April 1913.

YELLOWSTONE   (Steamboat)
The first cargo of Indian trade goods was taken on this boat. The first steamboat to be taken by George Catlin when he left St. Louis in his eight years of travel among the tribes of Indians in North America--1832-1839.
She was built by Pierre Chouteau, Jr., of the American Fur Company in 1830, especially for Missouri River navigation. A high wheel house was added to view snags better. It was a small boat with but one engine, a wood-burner. Poles were provided to propel her if the engine failed. For 30 years to 1830, keelboats carried the fur trade on the rivers. Then in 1831 on 15 April, the Yellowstone with Pierre Chouteau, Jr. aboard, ascended the Missouri River. It went to Fort Tecumseh and returned to St. Louis having to lighten her cargo at the mouth of the Niobrara where she was stopped by low water.
The second trip was made in the spring of 1833 when it ran to the new post of Ft. Union at the mouth of the Yellowstone. On it voyaged George Catlin, a young, self-taught artist who was to sketch some 600 Indian portraits, scenes of native life, and landscapes, all of which may be seen at the Smithsonian Institute, and in journals reporting his voyage. This trip the Yellowstone ran aground at the mouth of the Grand River.

YORKSHIRE   (Packet)
On this vessel the midget, General Tom Thumb, made his first trip to Europe. Captain Bailey was in command of this ship which had the reputation for speed. On it P. T. Barnum engaged five staterooms for the use of the little General and the attendants. On this vessel, after a highly successful career in America, at Barnum's American Museum in New York, the midget was going to meet Queen Victoria and perform for the English. On board he dressed as a sailor, sang his song, "The deep, deep sea" to the delight of all the passengers and crew. Barnum placed him on the dining table. He hopped around the food and plates, then took a seat on a cut glass tumbler.

At one time, 31 May 1846 the reporters of the New
York Herald met the <u>Yorkshire</u> on a pilot to get the
news of the Corn Laws report.   This vessel was the
first to bring the news.   The reporter asked for a horse
at a farm house to ride to the Greenport railway depot.
At Greenport he put the horse in a stable, took a loco-
motive, arrived at the Brooklyn Ferry to get the news
in the hands of the Herald editor.

YUKON   (Steamboat)
The first steamboat on the Yukon River.   This sternwheeler was built in San Francisco in 1819 for the
Alaska Fur Company.   Sometimes the vessel went
aground when herds of moose swam in the Yukon River.

ZEBULON M. PIKE   (Steamboat)
The first steamboat to reach St. Louis in August 1817.
She was built in Henderson, Kentucky.   Her engine was
low pressure.   The vessel went up to St. Louis in 1817.
The crew pushed using setting poles because of the engine's inability to push against the current.   All the
town came out to see the steamboat, the first to dock at
its wharf.   She spent a year plying the river between St.
Louis and Louisville; then she went into the Red River
trade.   There she snagged; sank.

III. U.S. SHIP NAMING POLICY

AIRCRAFT CARRIERS (CVA and CVS)
>are named for famous historical fighting ships of the United States, or for important battles and engagements.

AIRCRAFT FERRIES (AKV)
>are named for sounds, bodies of water.

AMMUNITION SHIPS (AE)
>are named for volcanoes, also words suggesting fire or explosives are used.

BATTLESHIPS (BB)
>are named for the states.

CARGO SHIPS (AK)
>are named for the heavenly bodies and for the counties of the United States.

CARGO SHIPS, Attack (AKA)
>are named for the heavenly bodies and for the counties of the United States.

CRUISERS, Heavy and Light (CA and CL)
>are named for the cities of the United States.

CRUISERS, Large (CB)
>are named for the territories and insular possessions of the United States.

DESTROYERS (DD)
>are named for: (1) deceased Navy, Marine and Coast Guard officers who served their country with exceptional bravery and distinction; (2) inventors; (3) members of Congress closely identified with naval affairs; and (4) outstanding Secretaries, or Assistant Secretaries of the U.S. Navy.

DESTROYER ESCORTS (DE)
>are named for the personnel of the U.S. Navy, Marine and Coast Guard killed in action in WW II, who served their country with exceptional bravery or distinction; also, outstanding Secretaries of the U.S. Navy.

DESTROYER TENDERS (AD)
    are named for the localities and areas of the U.S.--
    example: Prairie and Dixie.

FLAGSHIPS, AMPHIBIOUS FORCE (AGC)
    are named for mountains and mountain ranges.

FRIGATES
    are named for noted and outstanding U.S. admirals.

HOSPITAL SHIPS (AH)
    are named with words that suggest their mission, such
    as Sanctuary, Consolation, Repose, Relief.

ICEBREAKERS (AGB)
    are named for bays, islands, territories and posses-
    sions of the U.S.

LANDING SHIPS (LS)
    are named for places of historic interest in the U.S.

LANDING SHIPS, DOCK (LSD)
    are named for historical places in the U.S., especially
    the homes of former Presidents.

LANDING SHIPS, TANK (LST)
    are named for the counties of the U.S. with the word
    county as part of the name, such as Cook County,
    King County.

MINESWEEPERS
    are named after birds or logical words, such as Bold,
    Dash, Recruit.

NET LAYING SHIPS (AN)
    are named for trees and the monitors of the Old Navy
    of the U.S.

OCEAN RADAR STATION SHIPS (AGR)
    are named with words that indicate their job such as,
    Guardian, Sky Watcher.

OCEANOGRAPHY RESEARCH SHIPS (AGOR)
    are named for mathematicians, oceanographers, and
    officer scientists.

OILERS (AO)
    are given names of rivers with Indian names.

REPAIR SHIPS (AR, ARC, ARL)
    are named for characters in ancient mythology and
    overseas islands.

RESCUE ESCORTS
    are named for the cities of the U.S. with a population
    from 2500 to 10,000.

SALVAGE LIFTING VESSELS (ARSD)
    are named with words that indicate their jobs, or
    equipment.

SALVAGE SHIPS (ARS)
    are named with words that indicate their jobs, or
    equipment.

SEAPLANE TENDERS (AV)
    are named for men who pioneered in aviation and for
    sounds, as Salisbury Sound.

SEAPLANE TENDERS, Small (AVP)
    are named after the bays, inlets, islands, sounds, and
    straits, of the United States and its possessions.

STORE SHIPS (AF)
    are named after the heavenly bodies.

STORES ISSUE SHIPS, GENERAL (AKS)
    are named after the heavenly bodies.

SUBMARINE RESCUE VESSELS (ASR)
    are named after birds.

SUBMARINE TENDERS (AS)
    are named after characters in mythology and men who
    are noted in the submarine development.

SUBMARINES (SS)
    are named after fish, and other sea creatures, famous
    Americans, such as George Washington, and states.

SUBMARINES, FLEET BALLISTIC MISSILE
    are named after famous Americans, statesmen and
    leaders.

SURVEYING SHIPS (AGS)
> are given the names of oceanographers, officer scientists.

TANKERS, GASOLINE (AOG)
> are named for rivers with Indian names.

TRANSPORTS (APS)
> are named after Army and Marine generals.

TRANSPORTS, ATTACK (APA)
> are named after American patriots, and counties of the U.S.

TUGS, FLEET OCEAN (ATF)
> are named after Indian tribes.

TUGS, LARGE HARBOR (YTB)
> are named after noted Indians and given Indian words.

IV. ENSHRINED SHIPS

ALABAMA, U.S.S.   (Battleship)
Enshrined at Mobile, Alabama, in Memorial Park.
The Alabama was:
        launched 16 February 1942
        at Norfolk Navy Yard.
        First Captain: Captain G. B. Wilson.
        Commissioned 16 August 1942.
She served:
        in the North Atlantic and the Pacific areas.
        Protected, with the British Home Fleet, convoys
        to Britain and Russia during the year 1943.
        Provided fire support and anti-aircraft screening.
She earned:
        9 battle stars for World War II service.

ALBACORE   (Submarine)
Enshrined at Submarine Memorial, Submarine Base,
Pearl Harbor, Hawaii.   One of 52 submarines lost
during World War II.

ALASKA, U.S.S.   (Cruiser)
Artifacts from the Alaska are on display at Juneau,
Alaska.
The Alaska was:
        launched 15 August 1943 by the N.Y. Shipbuilding
        Corp., Camden, N.J., commissioned 17 June 1944.
        First Captain: Captain P. K. Fischler.
She served:
        by joining the Pacific Fleet at Pearl Harbor on
        13 January 1945.   Placed out of commission, on
        reserve at Bayonne, N.J., 17 February 1947.
She earned:
        3 battle stars for service in World War II.

ALMA   (Scow Schooner)
Enshrined at San Francisco Maritime State Historic
Park, Hyde Street, San Francisco, Cal.
The Alma was:
        built by Fred Siemer in 1891 at Hunter's point.
        The scow schooner, called "hay scow," was a
        local development.   It had a heavy, flat bottom
        making it inexpensive to build.   It was used for
        kedging, pushing, sailing, poling into backwater,

creeks and tide flat. Hay was carried more than
any other produce.
The three in the crew loaded and unloaded their
cargoes.

AMBERJACK (Submarine)
    Enshrined at Submarine Memorial, Submarine Base,
    Pearl Harbor, Hawaii. One of 52 submarines lost
    during World War II.

AMBROSE (Lightship)
    Enshrined at South Street Seaport Museum, New York.

ARGONAUT (Submarine)
    Enshrined at Submarine Memorial, Submarine Base,
    Pearl Harbor, Hawaii. One of 52 submarines lost
    during World War II.

ARIZONA, U.S.S. (Battleship)
    Enshrined at Pearl Harbor, Hawaii, partially submerged.
    The bells of the Arizona hang in the Student Union
    tower at the University of Arizona. The relics of the
    Arizona are in the museum near the ship.
    The Arizona was:
        launched 19 June 1915 by the New York Navy Yard.
        Commissioned 17 October 1916.
        First Captain: Captain J. D. McDonald.
    She served:
        by joining the Atlantic Fleet 18 November 1918,
        sailing from Hampton Roads, Va., to join Naval
        forces in British waters.
        On 12 December 1918 she assisted in escorting
        the George Washington, carrying President Wood-
        row Wilson to Brest, France.
        In 1930 she carried President Herbert Hoover to
        the West Indies.
        She was wrecked by explosion from a bomb pene-
        trating the powder magazine during the Japanese
        attack on Pearl Harbor. She took hits from one
        torpedo and 8 bombs. She sank 7 December
        1941 with 1104 personnel.

ARKANSAS, C.S.S. (Ironclad)
    A citizen's group in Baton Rouge, La., is interested
    in raising the ironclad's remains.
    The Arkansas defended Vicksburg with Issac Newton
    Brown commanding the vessel. It was a single-handed

engagement with the flotillas of Farragut and Davis, in the Mississippi River, on 15 July 1862.

AUSTRALIA   (Schooner)
Enshrined at Mystic Seaport, Connecticut.

BALAO, U.S.S.   (Submarine)
Conning tower on display at Admiral Willard Park, outside the U.S. Navy Memorial Museum, Navy Yard, 8th and M. Streets, S.E., Washington, D.C.
The Balao was:
launched 27 October 1942 by the Portsmouth Navy Yard.
Commissioned 4 February 1943.
First Commander: R. H. Crane.
She served:
with the Pacific Fleet 25 July 1943 to 27 August 1945. Recommissioned on 4 March 1952; assigned to the Atlantic Fleet.
Earned:
9 battle stars in 10 patrols sinking half a dozen Japanese merchantmen.

BALCLUTHA   (Merchantman)
This squarerigger is docked at pier 43 on the Embarcadero near the San Francisco Maritime Museum.
The Balclutha was:
launched on the Clyde River at Glasgow, Scotland, by builder Charles Connell and Sons, 27 December 1886.
Given a Gaelic name which means, "bastion, rock, or town" on the "Clutha," or Clyde. It is an ancient name for Dumbarton where the ship's first owner lived.
She served:
As Star of Alaska she accommodated the salmon and fisherman. As Pacific Queen, she was "an ark of nautical monstrosities," with a steam calliope that could be heard 20 miles away, hitched to a donkey boiler. A dummy pirate hung from her fore yard arm. Her figurehead is a lady, a queen with a crown. She flew the "Red Duster," as the British merchant flag is known, in her deepwater days. Then she loaded the San Joaquin Valley wheat for Western Europe. Wine and spirits came from London when she returned. She carried a million and a half board feet of

lumber to Australia; coming back she brought
coal for the sugar refineries in Honolulu, for
the railway locomotives in California. She made
17 voyages around Cape Stiff, as Cape Horn is
called sometimes.

BALTIMORE   (Clipper Schooner)
An 1812 ship is planned for display at Portsmouth, N.Y.

BARBEL   (Submarine)
Enshrined at Submarine Memorial, Submarine Base,
Pearl Harbor, Hawaii. One of 52 submarines lost
during World War II.

BARNEGAT   (Lightship)
Enshrined at Chesapeake Bay Maritime Museum, St.
Michaels, Maryland. The vessel was built in 1904.

BILOXI, U.S.S.
A memorial is being erected at Biloxi, Mississippi, by
Mobile Construction Battalion 121.
The Biloxi was:
     launched 23 February 1943 by the Newport News
     Shipbuilding and Drydock Co., Newport News,
     Va., commissioned on 31 August 1943.
     First Commander: Captain D. M. McCurl.
She served:
     in the Pacific Fleet.
She earned:
     9 battle stars in World War II service.

BONEFISH   (Submarine)
Enshrined at the Submarine Memorial Submarine Base,
Pearl Harbor, Hawaii. One of the 52 submarines lost
during World War II.

BOUNTY, H.M.S.   (Ship)
The MGM film company's Bounty used in the movie
Mutiny on the Bounty is exhibited at Vinoy Basin, St.
Petersburg, Florida, restored in every detail following
the original blueprints on file at the British Museum.
She served as a trader. England had equipped her to
obtain breadfruit tree plants in the South Seas for
transplanting in the West Indies. She left Spithead 23
December 1787 for Otaheite (Tahiti), with Commander
Lieutenant William Bligh, whose disciplinary measures
and violent temper led to a mutiny by part of the crew

on 28 April 1789. The leader, Fletcher Christian, set
Bligh and 18 of his supporters adrift in a small boat
with scanty supplies. Christian left all but 8 of the
remaining crew at Tahiti. He and his followers headed
for Pitcairn Island in 1790 where they lived undiscover-
ed until 1808, when only one survivor remained. Bligh
returned home safely in 1790. The men who had been
left on Tahiti were treated as deserters by the Navy,
returned to England in irons, convicted, and hanged.
See also under Part II, CHARLES DOGGETT.

BOWDOIN, U.S.S. (Schooner)
Enshrined at Camden, Maine, after removal from
Mystic Seaport, Connecticut.

BRILLIANT (Schooner)
Enshrined at Mystic Seaport, Connecticut.

BULLHEAD (Submarine)
Enshrined at Submarine Memorial, Submarine Base,
Pearl Harbor, Hawaii. One of 52 submarines lost
during World War II.

C.A. THAYER (Schooner)
Enshrined at San Francisco Maritime State Historic
Park, San Francisco, Cal.
The C.A. Thayer was:
        built on Humboldt Bay near Eureka, California,
        in 1895 by Hans Bendixsen, a Danish-born ship-
        builder.
        a three-masted sailing vessel.
She served:
        as an Alaskan fishing vessel.
        as a lumber carrier for 17 years. She voyaged
        to the Hawaiian Islands, California and Australia
        until the faster steam schooners came along to
        take her place.

CABRILLA, U.S.S. (Submarine)
will be displayed at San Jacinta Battleground, Houston,
Texas, near the battleship Texas.
The Cabrilla was:
        launched 24 December 1942.
        by Portsmouth Navy Yard.
        commissioned 24 May 1943.
        her first commander was: D. T. Hammond.

She served:
>with the Pacific Fleet.
>She sank 38,767 tons of shipping.
>She was placed out of commission 7 August 1946.

She earned:
>6 battle stars in World War II service.

CAIRO, U.S.S.   (Ironclad Gunboat)
After restoration she will be placed in the Vicksburg Museum.

The Cairo was:
>built by James B. Eads of Mound City, Illinois, under an Army contract.
>commissioned as an Army ship 25 January 1862.
>first commander: Lieutenant James M. Prichett.
>known as a "Pook Turtle" for its designer and because it was ungainly.

It served:
>to spearhead the Union thrust into the South along the Mississippi River and its tributaries.
>On 12 December 1862 while clearing mines from the Yazoo River, preparatory to an attack on Haines Bluff, Mississippi, she struck a torpedo (mine); sank. She was salvaged the summer of 1956. A gun was raised in 1960. She was restored at Pascagoula, Mississippi.

CAPELIN   (Submarine)
Enshrined at Submarine Memorial, Submarine Base, Pearl Harbor, Hawaii. One of 52 submarines lost during World War II.

CAVIARE   (Schooner)
A wood fishing schooner to be on display, South Street, Seaport, N.Y.C., a waterfront construction of the 1800's.

CERO, U.S.S.   (Submarine)
Enshrined at East St. Louis, Illinois.

The Cero was:
>launched 4 April 1943 by the Electric Boat Co., Groton, Connecticut.
>commissioned 4 July 1943.
>First commander: D. C. White.

She served:
>in Pacific waters beginning 17 August 1943. She sank 18,159 tons of enemy shipping.

Decommissioned and in reserve at New London, 23 December 1953.
She earned:
7 battle stars for World War II service.

CHAMPIGNY see GREAT BRITAIN

CHARLES W. (Schooner)
The massive stern is on exhibit at the San Francisco Maritime Museum at Foot of Polk Street, San Francisco.
She served:
as a scow schooner.

CHARLES W. MORGAN (Bark)
Enshrined at Mystic Seaport, Connecticut.
The Charles W. Morgan was:
built in 1841.
a whaler that 6 September 1841 set out for an 80 year active life on the sea.
she was constructed of live oak, copper fastened; designed like the crack packets of the 1820's.
she had artificial gunports, pierced in her sides so that pirates wouldn't challenge her.
She served:
she put out at New Bedford and made 37 voyages whale killing in the South Atlantic and the South Pacific. She caught more whales; made more money than any other all-sail whaling vessel ever sent to sea. She brought back oil for lubricating our machinery; oil to light our lamps and lighthouses.
Once she was gone 5 years and sailed all the oceans of the globe. She was never seriously damaged though she was in two hurricanes, frozen by the winter gales of the Arctic regions, ran ashore on coral reefs, sailed under blistering tropical suns. She operated after whale oil was not needed; made New Bedford a great whaling port.
In 1921 she gave up whaling.

CHARON, H.M.S. (British Frigate)
The reconstructed gun deck, captain's cabin, and cannon tubes are displayed at Yorktown, Virginia.
The Charon was:
sunk during the Battle of Yorktown, during the

siege of fire from the French gun batteries in
1781.

CHATTAHOOCHEE, C.S.S.   (Gunboat)
Plans are being made to raise and restore this steam
gunboat.
The Chattahoochee was:
        a wooden twin screw bark with three masts, one
        yard on foremast, one on mainmast; a black hull;
        bowsprit.
She served:
        on the Apalachicola River. Her boilers blew up
        27 May 1863, and she sank. She was raised and
        the boilers, salvaged from the CSS Raleigh, were
        to be installed in her. Then in December 1864
        she was deliberately destroyed by the Confederates
        to prevent her capture. Sledge hammers were
        used to disable the power plant.

CISCO   (Submarine)
        Enshrined at Submarine Memorial, Submarine Base,
        Pearl Harbor, Hawaii. One of 52 submarines lost
        during World War II.

COLUMBIA   (Lightship)
        Enshrined at the Museum in Astoria, Oregon.
        The Columbia was:
                built in 1908 at Quincy, Massachusetts.
        She served:
                Her service ended at the mouth of the Columbia
                River in 1961.

COMMERCE   (Schooner)
        Her bow and trailboards are on display at the San
        Francisco Maritime Museum, San Francisco, Cal.
        She served as a lumber schooner.

CONNECTICUT, U.S.S.   (Battleship)
        Her figurehead is on exhibit at Hartford, Connecticut.

CONSTELLATION, U.S.S.   (Frigate)
        Enshrined at downtown Baltimore Harbor at Fort
        McHenry. One of her 6000 pound anchors is at the
        Naval Station in New Port, R.I.
        The Constellation was:
                authorized 27 March 1794.
                designed by J. Humphreys and J. Fox.

built by D. Stodder, who altered plans.
at the Sterrett Shipyard, Baltimore, Md.
launched 7 September 1797, second of the U.S.
frigates to go down the ways.
She served:
brilliantly under Commodore Thomas Truxton
during the naval war with France. Victorious
over L'Insurgente, (1799) and La Vengeance
(1800). She is the symbol of victory, high
standards set for the new national navy. She
was called "Yankee Race Horse." On 1 December 1917 she was renamed "Old Constellation" to
permit her name to be given a new battle cruiser.
She served as a training vessel for naval cadets
in her last active years, at Newport, R.I.

CONSTITUTION, U.S.S. (Frigate)
She ship is enshrined at Boston Naval Shipyard, close
to Bunker Hill. Blocks, used to hoist sail on ship,
are at Bremerton Naval Shipyard Museum, Bremerton,
Washington.
The Constitution was:
approved 27 March 1794.
designed by Joshua Humphreys.
built at Hartt's Shipyard, Boston, Mass.
launched on 21 October 1797, at Charlestown.
christened by Captain James Sever.
First commander: Captain Samuel Nicholson.
Her timbers came from states ranging from
Maine to Georgia. Her copper bolts and spikes
were supplied by Paul Revere.
She served:
putting to sea 22 July 1798.
The first important naval battle of the War of
1812 occurred between the Constitution and the
H.M.S. Guerrière on 19 August 1812 in which
under Captain Issac Hull, she captured the
Guerrière. The name "Old Ironsides" was
acquired while in this combat when a seaman of
the Guerrière saw the British fire fall away from
her iron hull, and gave her the name. She was
renamed "Old Constitution" to give her name to a
battle cruiser. On 1 July 1931 she was recommissioned with 21 gun salutes. The following day
she sailed on a tour of the U.S. ports along the
Atlantic, Pacific, Gulf Coasts. On 7 March 1934
she returned to Boston. She remains in commis-

sion the oldest ship on the Navy list.
She earned:
> The ship was chosen by the Post Office as one of
> the three symbols of our heritage--along with the
> Eagle and the Liberty Bell, which appeared on a
> 4 cent blue stamped envelope.

CORVINA   (Submarine)
> Enshrined at Submarine Memorial, Submarine Base,
> Pearl Harbor, Hawaii. One of 52 submarines lost
> during World War II.

CUMBERLAND, U.S.S.   (Warship)
> Her anchor chain is on display in the garden of the
> White House of the Confederacy at Richmond, Virginia.
> An outdoor exhibit at Hamptom Roads, the Sidney E.
> King oil paintings of the 8 March 1862 battle when the
> CSS Virginia (Merrimack) destroyed the U.S.S. Cumber-
> land and Congress, of the Hampton Roads blockading
> fleet. The second scene, the 9th of March four-hour
> battle, is on display at Monitor-Merrimack Overlook,
> near the mouth of Salters Creek.
> The Mariners Museum, Newport News, has a diorama
> battle display.
> The Navy Memorial Museum, U.S. Navy Historical
> Display Center, Navy Yard, Washington, D.C., has
> another diorama.

DARTER   (Submarine)
> Enshrined at Submarine Memorial, Submarine Base,
> Pearl Harbor, Hawaii. One of 52 submarines lost
> during World War II.

DAUNTLESS   (Steam Yacht)
> Enshrined as a training ship and displayed at the Lande-
> berg-Maryland Seamanship School, Piney Point, Md.
> The Dauntless was:
> > built as the Delphine in 1921.
> > by the Great Lakes Engine Works, Ecorse,
> > Michigan.
> > acquired by the Navy 21 January 1942.
> > commissioned 11 May 1942.
> > First commander: C. F. Grisham.
> She served:
> > when departed on 27 May 1942 for Washington,
> > D.C., arriving on 16 June. She relieved the
> > Vixen as Admiral King's WW II Flagship. De-

commissioned 17 May 1946. Transferred to Maritime Commission 10 June 1946 for disposal.

DELAWARE, U.S.S. (Frigate)
The figurehead is enshrined at the U.S. Naval Academy
Museum, Annapolis, Maryland.

DORADO (Submarine)
Enshrined at the Submarine Memorial, Submarine Base,
Pearl Harbor, Hawaii. One of 52 submarines lost
during World War II.

DOROTHY A PARSONS (Schooner)
Enshrined at Mystic Seaport, Connecticut.

DRUM, U.S.S. (Battleship)
will be displayed at Mobile, Alabama, near the battle-
ship Alabama.
The Drum was:
      launched 12 May 1941, by the Portsmouth Navy
      Yard.
      commissioned 1 November 1941.
      First commander: Lieut. Comm. R. H. Rice.
She served:
      at Pearl Harbor 1 April 1942; then went on war
      patrol.
      Decommissioned 16 February 1946.
      On 18 March 1947 whe began service at Washing-
      ton, D.C., to members of the Naval Reserve in
      the Potomac River Naval command which continued
      through 1962.
She earned:
      12 battle stars for World War II service. She
      sank 15 ships and 80,580 tons enemy shipping.

EAGLE, USCGC (Bark)
Enshrined at the Coast Guard Academy at New London,
Conn.
The Eagle was:
      a training bark for the German Navy.
      built in 1936 as the Horst Wessel.
      acquired by the U.S. in 1946 as war reparations.
      commissioned as a sail training ship for U.S.
      Coast Guard Academy.
      There is a Diesel engine for auxiliary power;
      sails allow her speed to go to 18 knots.

ELFIN, U.S.S.   (Gunboat)
Will be enshrined possibly near or at Johnsonville, on
the Tennessee River.
The Elfin was:
        a light draft boat.
        purchased as the W.C. Mann by Admiral D. D.
        Porter at Ancum, 23 February 1864.
        First commander: Master A. F. Thompson.
She served:
        assigned to the Mississippi Squadron.
        4 November 1864 began operating with the U.S.S.
        Tawah and U.S.S. Key West, in the Tennessee
        and Cumberland Rivers.   There were several
        hours of heavy Confederate shore batteries rid-
        dling the vessel.   It was impossible to save her
        so she was burned to prevent capture, after the
        destruction of Johnsonville Base on 4 November
        1864.   See also KEY WEST.

ENTERPRISE, U.S.S.   (Schooner)
Enshrined at Little Curaçāo Island, West Indies.
The Enterprise was:
        built by Henry Spencer of Baltimore in 1799 to
        deal with the French Privateers in the West Indies.
        First commander: Lieutenant John Shaw.
        12 gun; later converted into a brig.
She served:
        departed 17 December 1799 from the Delaware
        Capes for the Caribbean to protect U.S. mer-
        chantmen from depredations of French privateers
        during the quasi-war with the French.
        She captured eight privateers and liberated 11
        American vessels from captivity, achievements
        which insured her inclusion in the 14 ships re-
        tained in the Navy after the Quasi-War.
        She had a long and brilliant career.   So she has
        become known as "Lucky Little Enterprise."
        This career ended 9 July 1823 when she stranded
        and broke up on Little Curaçāo Island in the West
        Indies without injury to the crew.   The Dutch
        government assisted in searching for the wreck.

EPPLETON HALL   (Tug)
Enshrined at San Francisco Maritime Museum Associa-
tion, San Francisco, California.
The Eppleton Hall was:
        a paddle wheel that steamed from England to San

Francisco in 1969-70. She was presented to the
Maritime Museum by her commander Captain
Scott Newhall after a six-month voyage.

ESCOLAR   (Submarine)
Enshrined at the Submarine Memorial Base, Pearl
Harbor, Hawaii.   One of 52 submarines lost during
World War II.

EUREKA   (Ferry Steamer)
Enshrined at the San Francisco Maritime State Historic
Park, San Francisco, Cal.
The Eureka was:
   built in 1890, originally called Ukiah.
She served:
      as a ferry steamer from Marin County, then Oak-
      land, across San Francisco Bay.
      She is the last paddle wheel, walking-beam en-
      gineered ferry to operate in the Bay, making her
      last trip in 1957.
      As the Ukiah she carried passengers and railroad
      cars between Tiburon and San Francisco for years.
      She was at one time the largest, fasted double-
      ended ferry in the world, churning the water at
      18 knots.   She was called Eureka in 1922.

FALLS OF CLYDE   (Iron Ship)
May be preserved at Honolulu, Hawaii.
The Falls of Clyde:
   was built in 1878.
   is a full-rigged; four-masted vessel.

FENIAN RAM   (Submarine)
On display in West Side Park in Paterson, New Jersey,
northwest of George Washington Bridge (N.Y.)
The Fenian Ram was:
   built for three men, in 1881.   It is a forerunner
   of the 54 foot U.S.S. Holland.

FLASHER, U.S.S.   (Submarine)
The conning tower, bridge, shears and periscope are
on exhibit at the U.S. Naval Submarine Base, New
London, Conn.
The Flasher was:
      launched 20 June 1943, by the Electric Boat Co.,
      Groton, Conn.
      commissioned 25 September 1943.

First commander: Captain R. T. Whitaker.
She served:
        she sailed for her first war patrol 6 January 1944.
She earned:
        she received the Presidential Citation for her bril-
        liant third, fourth, and fifth war patrols. For
        her six war patrols, each successful, she re-
        ceived 6 battle stars. 100,231 tons of Japanese
        shipping were sunk. This was two percent of
        the enemy's tonnage destroyed by U.S. submarines.

FLIER (Submarine)
        Enshrined at Submarine Memorial, Submarine Base,
        Pearl Harbor, Hawaii. One of 52 submarines lost
        during World War II.

FORESTER (Schooner)
        The wheel pumps, the fife rail, and section of mizzen
        mast are enshrined at San Francisco Maritime Museum,
        San Francisco, Calif. She was a four-masted schooner.

FRANKLIN, U.S.S. (Carrier)
        Her navigation bridge is to be enshrined at the city of
        Norfolk, Virginia.
The Franklin was:
        commissioned 31 January 1944.
        First commander: Captain Leslie E. Gehres.
She served:
        in the Pacific and on 19 March 1945 she maneu-
        vered closer to the Japanese Coast than any other
        carrier during World War II. Her planes struck
        Honshu, the Japanese home island, Kobe Harbor.
        Direct hits from a semi-armor Japanese plane
        caused her to lay dead in water 50 miles from
        Japan's coast at a 13 degree list. Burning from
        exploding munitions, Lieut. Leslie E. Gehres
        maneuvered the vessel to minimize fires, fought
        them tenaciously. 724 were killed; 265 wounded.
        The Pittsburgh took the Franklin in tow until she
        got up speed to 14 knots. She sailed under her
        own power to Brooklyn, N.Y.
        Decommissioned in 1947. In 1966 she was sold
        for scrip.
She earned:
        Captain Leslie E. Gehres was awarded the Navy
        Cross for saving the ship. Lieut. Comdr. J. T.
        O'Callaham and Lieut. Donald Gary received

Medals of Honor.

GAZELA PRIMERO   (Barkentine)
On view at Pier 15 North, Philadelphia Maritime
Museum, Philadelphia, Pa.
The Gazela Primero was:
>built at Cacilhas, of stone pine, maritime pines,
with a copper sheathed hull. Speed 6 knots.
built in Portugal in 1883. Held 701,053 pounds
of fish.
She served:
>This Portuguese square-rigged fishing vessel
sailed from Portugal to the Grand Banks--the cod
fishing area off Newfoundland.
Each year for over a century she sailed. Each
fisherman in his single dory caught up to 1000
pounds of cod fish a day. A 12-hour day ended
only after additional time was given to cleaning
the cod, put down in salt in the hold. He might
have only four hours of sleep. They fished five
to six months, every day, in fog and rain. They
last sailed the Grand Banks in 1969.
In 1970 she was acquired by the Philadelphia
Maritime Museum. In 1971 a volunteer crew
sailed her from Lisbon to Philadelphia.

GEORGE M. VERITY   (Steamboat)
is located at the George M. Verity Museum, Keokuk,
Iowa.
The George M. Verity was:
>built by the Dubuque Boat and Boiler Works in
1927 as a sternwheel towboat, to be used on the
Upper Mississippi River for the Barge Line Company. She had a steel hull; shipped a crew of 17.
Her original name was S.S. Thorpe after a barge
line sponsor.
She served:
>as the S.S. Thorpe she plied the upper and lower
Mississippi Rivers for Inland Waterways until
1940. Armco Steel Corp. purchased her; renamed
her the George M. Verity. She went into service
on the Ohio River, towing coal barges.
In 1960 she was retired; given to the city of
Keokuk for a museum. Her last journey of 1000
miles was made to her final home where she tied
up for the winter. Then she was fitted out as a
museum of upper Mississippi River history.

She earned:
>   the honor of being the tow boat to inaugurate
>   modern barge service to the Mississippi River.

GERMAN MIDGET SUBMARINES
>   are exhibited at U.S. Naval Submarine Base, New
>   London, Connecticut (e.g., Seehund II HU75); at
>   Mariners Museum, Newport News, Va. (a German one-
>   man torpedo carrying Marder type submarine), and at
>   Admiral Williard Park Navy Yard, Washington, D.C.,
>   as part of the U.S. Naval Historical Display Center.

GJOA (Ship)
>   is exhibited at Golden Gate Park, San Francisco, Cal.
>   The Gjoa is a famous Norwegian ship that took the
>   Northwest Passage route in 1903-06 under Captain
>   Roald Amundsen.

GOLDEN DOUBLOON   (Galleon)
>   a replica is displayed by Treasure Ship, Inc., Fort
>   Lauderdale, Florida.   The Golden Doubloon was a
>   Spanish galleon of 1680.

GOLET (Submarine)
>   Enshrined at Submarine Memorial, Submarine Base,
>   Pearl Harbor, Hawaii.   One of 52 submarines lost
>   during World War II.

GRAMPUS (Submarine)
>   Enshrined at Submarine Memorial, Submarine Base,
>   Pearl Harbor, Hawaii.   One of 52 submarines lost
>   during World War II.

GRAYBACK (Submarine)
>   Enshrined at Submarine Memorial, Submarine Base,
>   Pearl Harbor, Hawaii.   One of 52 submarines lost
>   during World War II.

GRAYLING (Submarine)
>   Enshrined at Submarine Memorial, Submarine Base,
>   Pearl Harbor, Hawaii.   One of 52 submarines lost
>   during World War II.

GREAT BRITAIN (Ship)
>   to be towed from the Falkland Islands, with the
>   Champigny to the "Gold Rush" Pier at San Francisco.
>   These ships are square-rigged.

GRENADIER   (Submarine)
   Enshrined at Submarine Memorial, Submarine Base,
   Pearl Harbor, Hawaii.   One of 52 submarines lost
   during World War II.

GROWLER   (Submarine)
   Enshrined at Submarine Memorial, Submarine Base,
   Pearl Harbor, Hawaii.   One of 52 submarines lost
   during World War II.

GRUNION   (Submarine)
   Enshrined at Submarine Memorial, Submarine Base,
   Pearl Harbor, Hawaii.   One of 52 submarines lost
   during World War II.

GUDGEON   (Submarine)
   Enshrined at Submarine Memorial, Submarine Base,
   Pearl Harbor, Hawaii.   One of 52 submarines lost
   during World War II.

GUNDEL   (Ketch)
   Enshrined at the Mystic Seaport village, Mystic, Conn.

HARDER   (Submarine)
   Enshrined at Submarine Memorial, Submarine Base,
   Pearl Harbor, Hawaii.   One of 52 submarines lost
   during World War II.

HARTFORD, U.S.S.   (Sloop-of-War)
   A ship bell is displayed at the Constitution Plaza,
   Hartford, Connecticut.   An anchor at the University
   of Hartford, Hartford, Connecticut.   An anchor at the
   entrance to Mystic Seaport's yacht basin at Mystic,
   Connecticut.   An anchor, a ship bell, and a bowsprit
   arrow, or "cock of the walk spur" are at the Navy
   Memorial Museum.   The skylight rests near the
   Secretary of Navy's office in the Pentagon.   Bilge
   pump, the gilded billethead, the fife rail, a stanchion
   are at the Mariners Museum, in Newport News, Va.
   An anchor is on exhibit at Fort Gaines on Dauphin Island in Mobile Bay, the scene of the actions in which
   the Hartford participated.
   The Hartford was:
         launched 22 November 1858, at the Boston Navy
         Yard.
         commissioned 27 May 1859.
         First commander: Captain Charles Lowndes.

She served:
> by relieving the Mississippi as flagship in the
> Orient.   Then at the outbreak of the Civil War
> she was ordered home to help preserve the Union.
> She left the Straits of Sundu with the Dacotah 30
> August 1861.   She arrived at Philadelphia 2 De-
> cember to be fitted out for war-time service.
> The screw sloop-of-war left the Delaware Capes
> 28 January as flagship of Flag Officer David G.
> Farragut, commander of the newly created West
> Gult Blockading Squadron.   See also under Part
> II, ADMIRAL.

HARVEST MOON, U.S.S.   (Flagship)
> to be viewed when the State of South Carolina and
> patriotic groups raise her and preserve her as a Civil
> War monument.

The Harvest Moon was:
> the flagship of Rear Admiral John A. Dahlgren,
> ordnance expert and commander of the South At-
> lantic Blockading Squadron.

She served:
> in the Civil War; sank in Winyah Bay, near
> Georgetown, South Carolina, 1 March 1865 by a
> Confederate "torpedo, " or mine.

HERRING   (Submarine)
> Enshrined at Submarine Memorial, Submarine Base,
> Pearl Harbor, Hawaii.   One of 52 submarines lost
> during World War II.

HOLLAND, U.S.S.   (Submarine)
> the first Holland product is on exhibit in the Paterson
> Museum, Paterson, New Jersey, a few miles north-
> west of New York's George Washington Bridge.

The Holland was:
> John Philip Holland's first submarine.   It was 14
> feet long, was a steam-powered midget, prototype
> of the vessel bought by the United States on 11
> April 1900, which was 54 feet long, to inaugurate
> the "Silent Service. "   The first Holland was
> raised from the Passaic River in 1927.   The
> U.S.S. Holland was the first submarine to have
> power to run submerged for any considerable
> distance.   The U.S. Navy purchased her, ordered
> six more.
> launched at Crescent Shipyards, Elizabeth, New

Jersey, 17 May 1897.
Commissioned 12 October 1900 at Newport, R.I.
First commander: Capt. Harry H. Caldwell.
She served:
    Under tow of the tug Leyden on 16 October 1900,
    she was taken to Annapolis where she trained
    cadets at the Naval Academy. She finished her
    career at Norfolk, sold as scrap to Henry A.
    Hitner and Sons, Philadelphia, 18 June 1913.

INAUGURAL, U.S.S. (Minesweeper)
    This may be preserved at St. Louis, Missouri, by the
    Fighting Ships, Inc.

INDIANA, U.S.S. (Battleship)
    Her mainmast and two twin-mount 40mm guns are
    erected at the University of Indiana at Bloomington.
    An anchor is displayed at Fort Wayne, Indiana. 210
    tons of her 12-inch armorplate form a lead-lined
    laboratory for radiation research under the lawn of
    Salt Lake City's Medical Center in Utah. 65 tons of
    her armor plate serve the same purpose at the VA
    Hospital, Hines, Illinois.
    The Indiana was:
        launched by Newport News Shipbuilding & Dry
        Dock Co., Newport News, Va., on 21 November
        1941.
        commissioned 30 April 1942 flying the battle flag
        of the first Indiana, 1898, which fought in the
        Battle of Santiago.
        First Commander: Captain A. S. Merrill.
    She served:
        in the Pacific Area during the early months of
        World War II as a unit in Vice Admiral J. F.
        Shafroth's Task Group in July 1945. She was
        effective on targets on Honshu, Japanese island.
        She was stricken from the Navy list 1 June 1962
        and sold for scrap.
    She earned:
        9 battle stars for World War II service.

INTELLIGENT WHALE (Submarine)
    Enshrined at the Navy Memorial Museum, Naval His-
    torical Display Center, Washington Navy Yard.
    The Intelligent Whale was:
        an experimental hand-cranked 30-foot submarine
        built on the design of Scovel S. Meriam, 1863,

by Augustus Price and Cornelius S. Bushnell.
sold to the Navy Department 29 October 1869.
manned by 6 to 13 persons; could submerge
several hours; make 4 knots underwater.
The vessel was unsuccessful so it was abandoned. It
was the last official attempt to develop a submarine
until the 20th century made submarines practical.

IOWA, U.S.S. (Battleship)
The steel plates are enshrined at Bremerton Museum,
Bremerton, Washington.
The served in the Blockade and Battle of Santiago 19
May 1898 with four other battleships and two armored
cruisers. During the Spanish American War shells
pierced the plates.

ISAAC H. EVANS (Schooner)
This 1886 coastal vessel may be seen at the Bath
Marine Museum, Bath, Maine.

ITALIAN MIDGET SUBMARINES
Two submarines are displayed at Newport News, Vir-
ginia.
They were:
One was a two-man submarine called a "Pig."
Its type penetrated the harbor at Alexander,
Egypt, 19 December 1941, sank the battleships
Queen Elizabeth, Valiant, and an oil tanker.
The other type was used in World War II to
attach warheads to the keel of a ship to be
destroyed. Their operators wore diving equip-
ment that had breathing apparatus, and they rode
in the open cockpit.

J. T. LEONARD (Sloop)
Enshrined at Chesapeake Bay Museum, St. Michaels,
Md.
The J. T. Leonard was:
built on Taylor's Island, Maryland, in 1882.
a round-bottom topmast sloop.
She served:
as carrier for farm cargoes to and from tide-
water towns of the Chesapeake until steamers took
over this trade and then she joined the oyster
fleet, operating until Spring of 1966.

JAPANESE MIDGET SUBMARINES
Two are enshrined at the U.S. Naval Submarine Base,
New London, Conn.
Others are on display at the Admiral Willard Park as
part of the U.S. Naval Historical Display Center in the
Navy Yard, Washington, D.C.
at Lighthouse Museum, Key West Art Historical Society
in Florida.
at Submarine Base, Pearl Harbor, Hawaii.
at Mariners Museum, Newport News, Virginia.
One of the two-man Japanese midget submarines is in-
tact, recovered off Cape Esperance in 1943. One with
sides cut away was used for instruction at the Submarine School, Yokosuka. One is a diverging boat
used for salvage work, another Japanese type. The
latter craft was built in 1935 for gathering coral, but
were unsuccessful. (A full-scale model is found at
Kure, Japan.)

JOSEPH CONRAD
A training ship enshrined at Mystic Seaport, Mystic,
Conn.

JULIUS C. WILKIE (Steamboat)
Enshrined at Julius C. Wilkie Steamboat Museum,
Levee Park, Winona, Minnesota.

KAIULANI (Barge)
is being restored at Subic Bay by the Maritime Historical Society of the District of Columbia, assisted by
the Republic of the Philippines Navy. She is the sole
survivor of 17,000 square-rigged merchant ships built
in America over three centuries.
The Kaiulani was:
   built at Sewall Yard, Bath, Maine, the last
   American built merchant square-rigger.
She served:
   hauling mahogany logs among the Philippine Islands since World War II.
   sailed as Star of Finland in 1913.
When she is restored, she will sail with a volunteer
crew across the Pacific Ocean around the Horn, up the
Potomac River to the new Maine avenue waterfront in
Washington, D.C.

KETE (Submarine)
Enshrined at the Submarine Memorial, Submarine Base,

Pearl Harbor, Hawaii.   One of 52 submarines lost during World War II.

KEY WEST, U.S.S.   (Gunboat)
This will be enshrined possibly in the vicinity of Johnsonville on the Tennessee River.
The Key West was:
a wooden steam wheeler built at California, Pa. for W. S. Evans at Cairo, Illinois, on 16 April 1863.
commissioned 26 May 1863.
First commander: Master E. M. King.
She served:
on patrol duty in the Tennessee River, supporting the Army and protecting Federal positions in the Tennessee Valley from Confederate Calvary raids. she assisted the Tawah in capturing the Venus, taken by the Confederates 30 October 1863.   On 4 November 1863, the Key West, Tawah, Elfin were caught in the narrow shallow section of the river, near Johnsville by Confederate forces under General Nathan B. Forrest.   The three Union vessels were riddled, and almost without ammunition were set afire; scuttled to avoid capture by the Confederates.   See also ELFIN; TAWAH.

L. A. DUNTON
A Gloucester fisherman's boat enshrined at Mystic Seaport, Mystic, Connecticut.

LANCASTER, U.S.S.   (Frigate)
Enshrined at Mariners Museum, Newport News, Va., is a large hand-carved eagle; the figurehead from the Lancaster.

LIGHTHOUSE (1842)
On view at Stonington Point, Borough of Stonington, Stonington, Connecticut.

LOGARTO (Submarine)
Enshrined at Submarine Memorial, Submarine Base, Pearl Harbor, Hawaii.   One of the 52 submarines lost during World War II.

LUCY EVELYN (Schooner)
is enshrined as a gift shop and Marine Museum at Beach Haven, New Jersey.

She is a three-masted ship, built in Harrington, Maine.
She served as a commercial sailing vessel until 1848.

MACEDONIAN, U.S.S.   (Frigate)
The monument and figurehead are enshrined on Stribling
Walk, U.S. Naval Academy, Annapolis, Maryland.

MAINE, U.S.S.   (Battleship)
The mainmast is in Arlington National Cemetary, D.C.
The foremast is near the sea wall of the U.S. Naval
Academy, Annapolis, Md.   One anchor is enshrined on
Penn's Commons, Reading, Pa.   A plaque cast from
the metal of the Maine is on display at the Commis-
sioned officers Mess at Naval Station, Brooklyn, N.Y.
A capstan is at Charleston, S.C., and a turret sight
hood is at Key West, Florida.
The Maine was:
    launched 18 November 1889.
    commissioned 17 September 1895.
    First commander: Captain Arent S. Crowinshield.
She served:
    cruising the Atlantic Coast from Maine to Key
    West, arriving at Havana 25 January 1898.   Her
    mission was to protect American interests during
    the Cuban revolt against Spain.
    15 February 1898, while she was moored to a
    buoy in Havana Harbor, she was torn in half by
    two explosions and sank in minutes.   Her sinking
    precipitated the Spanish-American War.
    On 2 February 1912 her hulk was floated; towed
    to sea; sunk in deep water in the gulf of Mexico
    with ceremony and military honors, 16 March
    1912.   See also under Part II, MAINE.

MANITOU   (Steamship)
An old brass binnacle, compass, wheel from this ship
is enshrined at the Manistee County Historical Society,
Inc., Manistee, Michigan.

MARYLAND, U.S.S.   (Battleship)
The bell of this ship is enshrined on the grounds of the
State House, Annapolis, Maryland.
She served in the Pacific Fleet, and while anchored at
Pearl Harbor, Hawaii, was damaged by bombs during
the Japanese raid on the fleet that brought about World
War II.

MASSACHUSETTS, U.S.S.   (Battleship)
    Enshrined at State Pier, Fall River, Mass., on 14
    August, 1965.
    The Massachusetts was:
        laid down 20 July 1939 by the Bethlehem Steel Co.,
        Quincy, Massachusetts.
        launched 23 September 1941.
        commissioned 12 May 1942.
        First commander: Captain Francis E. M. Whiting.
    She served:
        as the flagship for Admiral H. Kent Hewitt. On
        24 October 1942 she made rendevouz with the
        western Naval Task Force for the invasion of
        North Africa. She played a part in the Casa-
        blanca action 8 November, 1942.
        She helped power the Pacific Fleet from the
        Gilbert Islands to Japan. She fired on industrial
        plants along the coast of Honshu.
        Her last assignment was upon arriving at Norfolk
        in 1946, when her crew manned the rail for
        President Harry S Truman, embarked in the new
        carrier Franklin D. Roosevelt.
        She is affectionately known to her crew and others
        as the "Big Mamie."

MAYFLOWER II
    An enshrined replica of the first Mayflower may be
    seen moored permanently at Plymouth, Massachusetts.
    A memorial to the first Mayflower that brought Pil-
    grims to New England 350 years ago.
    The Mayflower II was:
        built in Great Britain.
        given to the Americans as a token of friendship.
        fifty-three days sailing the Atlantic with a volun-
        teer crew of 33, in 1957.

MERMAID (Ship)
    Enshrined at Aquatic Park, San Francisco Maritime
    Museum, San Francisco, California.
    Kenichi Horie voyaged in this tiny vessel from Japan
    to San Francisco in 1962; donated the vessel to the
    museum.

MICHIGAN, U.S.S.   (Man-of-War)
    Enshrined bow and cutwater are to be found at the foot
    of State Street, Erie, Pa. The mainmast is in Fair-
    port Marine Museum, Fairport Harbor, Ohio.

The Michigan was:
        designed by Samuel Hart.
        fabricated parts were made in Pittsburgh during
        last half of 1842.
        carried overland of Erie, Pa., where she was
        assembled.
        launched 5 December 1843. As she slipped down
        the ways her 50-foot hull stuck before reaching
        water. Prodding her was useless. As night had
        descended and it was too dark to see, the men
        went home to bed. When they got up in the
        morning they found her riding in the water.
She served:
        Captain William Inman in command, built her for
        defense of Lake Erie. For over a century she
        was on the Great Lakes--1844-1849. Most of the
        time she was the only ship-of-war on these inland
        waters.
        In 1905 she was renamed "Wolverine." World
        War I sailors trained on her. In 1927 she was
        loaned to Erie as a relic, scrapped in 1949. In
        1950 her bow and cutwater were erected as a
        monument near the shipyard where she was built.
        See under Part II, MICHIGAN.

MISSOURI, U.S.S. (Battleship)
        Enshrined at Bremerton Museum, Bremerton, Washing-
        ton. A bronze surrender plaque is embedded in her
        deck. This plaque designates the end of World War II
        with names of countries and participants. The iron
        mess table used for signing the Japanese surrender is
        preserved at the U.S. Naval Academy in Annapolis,
        Maryland. The flag that flew on the ship on VJ Day
        was placed by General MacArthur on the American Em-
        bassy in Tokyo.
The Missouri was:
        laid down 6 January 1941 by New York Naval
        Shipyard.
        launched 29 January 1941.
        commissioned 11 June 1944.
        First commander: Captain William M. Callaghan.
She served:
        at Iwo Jima and Okinawa; first with the task force
        58, then as flagship of Admiral William F. Hal-
        sey.
        in 1948 the "Big Mo," or "Mighty Mo" as she is
        nicknamed, was the only battleship in commission

in the U.S. Navy.
She earned:
> 5 battle stars for Korea; 3 battle stars for World
> War II service.
> She was a symbol of American seapower in the
> eastern Mediterranean; and of VJ Day.
> Now she is part of the U.S. Navy's Reserve Fleet
> at Bremerton, Washington, where 100,000 visit
> her each day.

MONITOR-MERRIMAC   (Ironclads)
On view is an outdoor painting of the 9 March 1862
battle between the Monitor and Merrimac at the Chris-
topher Newport Park, Newport News, Va.
At Monitor-Merrimac Overlook near mouth of Salters
Creek is the second scene of that 9th of March.
A diorama is at Mariners Museum, Newport News, Va.
Another diorama may be seen at Navy Memorial Muse-
um, United States Navy Historical Display Center,
Navy Yard, Washington, D.C.
The Monitor was:
> contracted on 4 October 1861.
> designed by John Ericsson.
> her hull was made at the Continental Iron Works,
> Green Point, L.I.
> the engines by Delamater & Co., New York.
> the turret by Novelty Ironworks, N.Y.C.
> she had a low freeboard, one or more revolving
> turrets of iron, each containing one or more
> large 11-inch Dahlgren guns.
> launched 30 January 1862.
> commissioned 25 February 1862.
> First commander: Lieut. John L. Worden.

She served:
> leaving New York 27 February 1862. Her steering
> failed; she returned 6 March towed by the Seth
> Low, headed for the Virginia Capes, and Hampton
> Roads to meet the Merrimac.

The Merrimac was:
> reconstructed by the Confederates from the hull
> of the U.S. Frigate Merrimack, which had been
> sunk when the Union forces abandoned the Norfolk
> Navy Yard. The Confederates raised her, re-
> named her Virginia, and Merrimac. She was the
> first Confederate Ironclad warship. She was ready
> one day before the Monitor to go to the scene of
> battle.

She was:
     designed by a board of three appointed by the
     Confederate Navy Dept. 23 June 1861.
     equipped with two 7-inch rifles, two 6-inch
     rifles, six 9-inch smooth-bores.
     The Merrimac on 8 March 1862, at noon, a day ahead
of the Monitor with two gunboats, the Raleigh and the Beau-
fort, each one gun, came out of the Elizabeth River into
Hampton Roads and stood toward the Union Fleet off Newport
News and Fort Monroe. The steam frigates of the Union,
Minnesota, Congress, Roanoke, each with 50 guns, the sail-
ing-frigate St. Lawrence, 12 guns and the sloop Cumberland
with 24 guns, all with the heaviest armament the U.S. government could assemble.
     The Merrimac rammed the Cumberland; she sank flag
flying. The burning Congress surrendered. The Minnesota
had grounded to where the Merrimac couldn't reach her.
After some hours of trying to reach the Minnesota the Merrimac finally gave up, turned back to Norfolk. On the next
day, the 9 March, the Monitor entered the battle, having
hurried to the battle scene without being accepted by the
government or without a trial run. In the five-hour battle
the shells bounced off both ironclads. Ramming, running
down each other was no use. Neither won a clear victory.
     The battle revolutionized warship design and gunnery.
Wooden ships were no longer practical. The success of the
ironclads led to the construction of many others of the same
type. After the evacuation of Norfolk on 9 May, the Merrimac was destroyed by the Confederates. The Monitor
foundered in a storm off Cape Hatteras after midnight with
four officers and 12 men lost. Her hulk was never located.

MUSCOGEE [or JACKSON], C.S.S. (Ironclad)
     Enshrined remains preserved and restored by the
     Georgia Historical Commission at the Confederate
     Naval Museum in Columbus.
     The Muscogee was:
         until recently thought to be a centerwheel ironclad
         steamer. Evidence now points to twin-screw
         machinery.
         launched December 1864 at Columbus, Georgia.
     She was:
         captured and burned before commissioning by
         Federal troops during Wilson's cavalry raid on
         Columbus, Georgia, 17 April 1865.

NARWAHL (Submarine)
Two 6-inch deck guns are enshrined at the Naval Submarine Base, New London, Gròton, Conn.
The Narwahl was:
laid down at Portsmouth Navy Yard, New Hampshire, 10 May 1927.
launched 17 December 1929.
commissioned 15 May 1930.
She served:
cruised to the West Indies on 11 August 1930.
trained in New England waters until 31 January 1931.
her first war patrol began 2 February 1942.
She was one of the oldest submarines in the Navy in World War II.
She sank seven Japanese ships and a river gunboat.
She was a troop and cargo submarine. She carried provisions and ammunition to guerilla forces.
a carrier for covert landins.
she made 13 war patrols.
she was one of the five submarines docked at Pearl Harbor when the Japanese aerial raiders struck 7 December 1944.
She earned:
15 battle stars for World War II service.
She was struck from the Navy list 19 May 1945; sold for scrap.

NEUSE, C.S.S. (Ram)
Her hull is displayed at the Governor Richard Caswell Memorial site two miles west of Kinston, N.C.
The Neuse was:
a flat-bottomed shallow draft ship used in sounds and rivers along the North Carolinas. She was a twin screw steamer; 376 tons; carried 150 officers and men.
She served:
until the Confederates burned her; then sank her in March 1865 when General Sherman marched to Georgia. She lay on the bottom of the Neuse River for 100 years.

NEW YORK, U.S.S. (Cruiser)
Anchors are enshrined outside of the U.S. Naval Academy Museum, Annapolis, Maryland.

NIAGARA   (Brig)
    Enshrined at the foot of State Street, Erie, Pa.
    The Niagara was:
        built at Presque Isle (Erie), Pa., by Adam and
        Noah Brown under supervision of Sailing Master
        Daniel Dobbins and Oliver H. Perry.
        110 feet in length; 20 guns.
        launched in summer of 1813.
    She served:
        on Lake Erie to win and end the battle between
        the British and United States.
        as relief flagship of Commodore Oliver Hazard
        Perry in the Battle of Lake Erie, 10 September
        1813.   To this ship Perry transferred the flag
        with the words, "Don't Give up the Ship," from
        the Lawrence and went on to victory.
        The ship was raised from Misery Bay near Erie;
        reconstructed by Pennsylvania Commonwealth
        from the remains.   See also under Part II,
        NIAGARA.

NORTH CAROLINA   (Battleship)
    Enshrined off the Channel of the west bank of Cape
    Fear River, in view of downtown Wilmington, N.C.
    The North Carolina was:
        laid down 27 October 1937 by the New York Naval
        Shipyard.
        launched 13 June 1940.
        first commissioned of U.S. Navy's modern battle-
        ships at New York, 9 April 1941.
        First commander: Captain Olaf M. Hustvedt.
    She served:
        40 months in the Pacific in combat, veteran of
        every major Pacific campaign of World War II
        from the Guadalcanal landings in 1942 to the
        signing of the peace treaty September 1945.
    She earned:
        12 battle stars for World War II service.
        She was called "The Showboat."
        Six times "Tokyo Rose" reported her sunk.

OHIO, U.S.S.   (Ship-of-the-Line)
    Enshrined since 1954 the figurehead of Hercules is at
    the Village Green in Stonybrook, Long Island, New
    York.   It was first exhibited by the owners of Canoe
    Place Inn, Long Island, N.Y.

The Ohio was:
  authorized in 1816.
  designed by Henry Eckford.
  laid down by New York Navy Yard in 1817.
  launched 30 May 1820.
  The vessel decayed badly, was refitted in 1838.
She served:
  as the flagship for Commodore Isaac Hull for two
  years.
  policed the newly acquired California territory
  during the Gold Rush.
  in 1850 she went to Boston and went into ordinary.
  in 1851 she became a receiving ship at the navy
  yards.
  in 1875 she went into ordinary again.
  she was sold at Boston to J. L. Snow of Rockland,
  Maine, 27 September 1883 for scrapping.
  Before she could be put in warfare, the intro-
  duction of armor plate, steam and explosive shells
  made her almost obsolete.

OKLAHOMA, U.S.S.   (Battleship)
  Her anchor is on display at Oklahoma City, Oklahoma.
  The Oklahoma was:
    laid down 26 October 1912 by the New York Ship-
    building Corp., Camden, New Jersey.
    launched 23 March 1914.
    commissioned at Philadelphia, Pa., 2 May 1916.
    First commander: Captain Roger Welles.
  She served:
    with the Atlantic fleet for two years; then joined
    part of the Pacific fleet operations, based at
    Pearl Harbor when the Japanese attacked.   Then
    she was sunk, bottom up.
    Decommissioned 1 September 1944.
    Sold 5 December 1946 to Moore Drydock Co.,
    Oakland, Cal.   She sank 540 miles out from
    Pearl Harbor 17 May 1947.
  She earned:
    1 battle star for World War II service.

OLYMPIA, U.S.S.   (Cruiser)
  This vessel is enshrined in the Delaware River at the
  foot of Race Street in Philadelphia, Pa.
  The Olympia was:
    laid down 17 June 1881 by the Union Iron Works,
    San Francisco, Cal.

launched 5 November 1892.
commissioned 5 February 1895.
First commander: Captain John J. Read.
She served:
> as flagship for Commodore George Dewey when
> she joined the Asiatic fleet from 25 August 1895
> to 3 January 1898. She led the Squadron past the
> batteries on Corregidor into Manilla Bay 1 May
> 1898, at daybreak. By 12:40 there was no longer
> a Spanish fleet in the Philippine Islands.
> Decommissioned 9 December 1922.
> She is the U.S. Navy's oldest steel ship still
> afloat.

OREGON, U.S.S.   (Battleship)
Her mast and bow plate are enshrined in a special
park on the Willamette River. Silver service, pennant,
other relics are preserved by the Oregon Historical
Society.
The Oregon was:
> laid down 19 November 1891 by the Union Iron
> Works, San Francisco, Cal.
> launched 26 October 1893.
> commissioned 15 July 1896.
> First commander: Captain Henry L. Howison.
She served:
> in a crisis due to impending war with Spain (1898).
> She sailed around South America at astonishing
> speed beginning at San Francisco 19 March to
> Key West 26 May to participate in the blockade
> of Santiago. In the action there Spanish Admiral
> Cervera's fleet was destroyed.
> on duty as escort for transports of the Siberian
> Expedition in 1918 ended her commissioned service.
> During World War II she served as a floating am-
> munition depot at Guam. In 1956 she was sold;
> towed to Japan for scrap.

PERCH   (Submarine)
Enshrined at Submarine Memorial, Submarine Base,
Pearl Harbor, Hawaii. One of 52 submarines lost
during World War II.

PHILADELPHIA   (Gondola)
This small gunboat is enshrined at the Smithsonian In-
stitution (U.S. National Museum), in Washington, D.C.
The hull, ship equipment and shot that may have sank

sank her, are also at the Smithsonian.

The Philadelphia was:

    constructed by General Benedict Arnold on Lake
    Champlain at Skenesboro, New York.

    laid down July 1776.

    launched August 1776.

    First commander: Captain Rice.

    Crew: 45.

She served:

    as a part of Benedict Arnold's flotilla to check
    the expected British invasion being launched from
    Montreal by the Royal Governor of Canada.

    She fought in the Battle of Valcour Island on Lake
    Champlain, 11 October 1776. This action had
    great influence on America's achieving a victory
    at Saratoga.

    From 1776 to 1935 she remained on the bottom
    of Lake Champlain. She may be our oldest ship
    extant.

PICKEREL   (Submarine)

    Enshrined at Submarine Memorial, Submarine Base,
    Pearl Harbor, Hawaii.   One of 52 submarines lost
    during World War II.

PIONEER, C.S.S.   (Submarine)

    This submarine is on display at Presbytere Arcade,
    Louisiana State Museum, New Orleans, La.

The Pioneer was:

    a two-man Confederate privateer.

    built in 1861-1862

    out of the riveted iron plates cut from old boilers.

She served:

    as a patrol in Lake Pontchartrain.

    in making descents into the Lake, she destroyed
    practice targets; including a schooner.

    Before she could attack, Flag Officer David Far-
    ragut surprised New Orleans, drove a wedge up
    the Mississippi River.

    She was scuttled; lay at the bottom for years.

    After the war was over, this submarine was
    raised and placed in Jackson Square in front of
    the Cabildo, New Orleans, until it was removed
    to its present place.

POINT FERMIN   (Lighthouse)

A national historic site at Point Fermin Park, 807

Paseo, Del Mar, San Pedro, California, is to be re-
stored.
The lighthouse was:
    built in 1874
    by Phineas Banning at the headlands of the Palos
    Verdes Peninsula.
She serves:
    with a remote-controlled beacon that provides
    clear warning for ships near the rocks.
    It is one of the last survivors of 19th-century
    lighthouses on the Pacific Coast.

POMPANO (Submarine)
    Enshrined at Submarine Memorial, Submarine Base,
    Pearl Harbor, Hawaii.   One of the 52 submarines lost
    during World War II.

PORTLAND, U.S.S.   (Cruiser)
    mast, open bridge, bell are enshrined at Portland,
    Maine, in Fort Allen Park.
    The Portland was:
        laid down 17 February 1930 by the Bethlehem
        Steel Co., Shipbuilding Division, Quincy, Mas-
        sachusetts.
        launched 21 May 1932.
        commissioned 23 February 1933.
        First commander: Captain H. F. Leary.
    She served:
        Two months later she was the first ship at the
        scene of the Akron airship disaster.   On 3 April
        1933, the Akron had been forced down in a violent
        storm, fell into the water, cracked up.   Toll: 73.
        served through 24 major Pacific actions.
    She earned:
        a Navy Unit Commendation for heroic naval
        actions in the Solomons.
        She won 16 battle stars for World War II service.
        She was called the "Sweet Pea."

PORTSMOUTH (Lightship)
    Enshrined on the Elizabeth River at London slip and
    Water Street in downtown Portsmouth.   It serves as a
    Coast Guard Museum.

QUEEN MARY, R.M.S.
    Enshrined at the end of the Long Beach Freeway, Long
    Beach, California.

The Queen Mary was:
> built by John Brown & Co., Ltd., Clydebank,
> Scotland.
> her keel was laid 1 December 1930.
> highest speed: 31.7 knots.

She served:
> on war duty March 1940 to September 1946.
> carried wounded returning U.S. prisoners to
> camps in the United States.
> carried 12,886 GI brides and children.
> carried Winston Churchill to three conferences in
> the United States.
> Last great cruise was to Long Beach, 31 October
> 1967 to 9 December 1967, just after being retired
> 19 September 1967.
> removed from the British registry, turned over
> officially to the City of Long Beach, 11 December
> 1967.
> she is serving as the Queen Mary Museum and
> features a Queen Mary Tour.
> she houses Captain Jacques-Yves Cousteau's
> Living Sea.
> The Queen Mary has been variously named "Queen
> of the Atlantic," and "Gray Ghost."

R-12   (Submarine)
> Enshrined at Submarine Memorial, Submarine Base,
> Pearl Harbor, Hawaii.   One of 52 submarines lost
> during World War II.

RALEIGH   (Frigate)
> A replica of the Continental Frigate Raleigh is planned
> for display at Portsmouth, New Hampshire.

RAVEN   (Landfinder)
> Replica of a Viking ship is enshrined in Lincoln Park,
> Chicago, Illinois.

The Raven was:
> donated by the Norwegian people, 6 November
> 1920.

She served:
> she sailed from Norway by way of the Erie Canal
> and the Great Lakes to the Chicago World's Fair
> of 1893, taking 44 days.

REDFIN, U.S.S.   (Submarine)
> to be enshrined by the Submarine Veterans of World

War II at Manitowoc, Wisconsin.

REGINA M.   (Schooner)
Enshrined at Mystic Seaport, Mystic, Connecticut.

ROBALO   (Submarine)
Enshrined at Submarine Memorial, Submarine Base,
Pearl Harbor, Hawaii.   One of 52 submarines lost
during World War II.

RUNNER   (Submarine)
Enshrined at Submarine Memorial, Submarine Base,
Pearl Harbor, Hawaii.   One of 52 submarines lost
during World War II.

S26, S27, S28, S36, S39, S44   (Submarines)
Enshrined at Submarine Memorial, Submarine Base,
Pearl Harbor, Hawaii.   Six of 52 submarines lost
during World War II.

SAGINAW, U.S.S.   (Gig)
Enshrined at Saginaw Museum, 1126 North Michigan
Ave., Saginaw, Michigan, is the Saginaw Gig.
The Saginaw was:
    shipwrecked off Ocean Island in 1871.   Survivors
    of the wreck sailed in this gig, 1500 miles, to
    get aid.

SAN FRANCISCO, U.S.S.   (Cruiser)
The navigation bridge of this vessel is built into a
memorial on "Land's End," a 450-foot cliff, overlooking
the Golden Gate, San Francisco, California.
The San Francisco was:
    commissioned at Mare Island in 1934.
She served:
    in the naval Battle of Guadalcanal, 12-15 November
    1942.
She earned:
    the U.S. and Philippines Republic presidential unit
    citations.
    17 battle stars for World War II service.
She was scrapped in 1960.

SANTA MARIA   (Ship)
This replica of Columbus' ship is at pier 3 in Washing-
ton, D.C.   Plans are being made to remove it to St.
Louis.

The <u>Santa Maria</u> replica was:
constructed in Spain 500 years after Columbus
made his voyage. Tools and methods of the 15th
century were used in building it. She was brought
to the United States from Spain and was viewed
in New York at the 1964-1965 World's Fair.

SCAMP   (Submarine)
Enshrined at the Submarine Memorial, Submarine Base,
Pearl Harbor, Hawaii. One of the 52 submarines lost
during World War II.

SCORPION   (Submarine)
Enshrined at the Submarine Memorial, Submarine Base,
Pearl Harbor, Hawaii. One of the 52 submarines lost
during World War II.

SCOTLAND   (Lightship)
This ship will be displayed at South Street, Seaport,
N.Y.C. in an exhibit to include waterfront construction
of the 1800's.

SCULPIN   (Submarine)
Enshrined at the Submarine Memorial, Submarine Base,
Pearl Harbor, Hawaii. One of the 52 submarines lost
during World War II.

SEA DOG, U.S.S.   (Submarine)
will be enshrined at the head of navigation on the
Arkansas River in Oklahoma.

SEALION   (Submarine)
Enshrined at the Submarine Memorial, Submarine Base,
Pearl Harbor, Hawaii. One of 52 submarines lost
during World War II.

SEAWOLF, U.S.S.   (Submarine)
A monument to this famous submarine, crew and passengers is a full size torpedo, flanked by three-inch
guns, located beside the U.S.S. <u>Texas</u> at the San
Jacinto Battleground.
The <u>Seawolf</u> served:
15 war patrols; sank more enemy tonnage than
any other American ship to that time.
In 1944 she went on a special mission carrying
30 Army commandos to the Japanese held
Philippines. It was sunk.

SEMMES, ADMIRAL RAPHAEL
His cap, pistol, and telescope may be seen at the
Museum of the Confederacy, Richmond, Virginia.

SHARK   (Submarine)
Two vessels of this name are enshrined at the Subma-
rine Memorial, Submarine Base, Pearl Harbor, Hawaii.
Two of 52 submarines lost during World War II.

SNOOK   (Submarine)
Enshrined at Submarine Memorial, Submarine Base,
Pearl Harbor, Hawaii.   One of 52 submarines lost
during World War II.

SOUTH DAKOTA, U.S.S.   (Battleship)
Propellor of this ship is on display at the Mariners
Museum, Newport News, Va.   Another propellor may
be seen at the U.S. Navy Memorial Museum, Washing-
ton, D.C.   A memorial is planned for North Sheraton
Park, Sioux Falls, South Dakota.
The South Dakota was:
    built at Camden, New Jersey, 1939-1942, first
    of the new class of battleships.
She served:
    in Pacific waters, off Guadalcanal as "Battleship
    X."
She earned:
    13 battle stars and a unit of commendation on her
    record.
    She was scrapped 21 years after building.

SOUTHGATE   (Ship)
A square-rigger to be displayed at South Street, Newport, N.Y.C., in a waterfront reconstruction of the
1800's.

SPRAGUE   (Steamboat)
Enshrined at Mississippi River Museum, City Water-
front, Vicksburg, Massachusetts.
The Sprague was:
    a paddlewheel boat known widely for nearly half
    a century on the Mississippi and Ohio Rivers.
    She was designed to tow 49 barges.   She carried
    a crew of 55.
The Sprague has been claimed to be the world's largest
steamwheeler.

SQUALUS, U.S.S.   (Submarine)
Conning tower is displayed at Portsmouth Naval Shipyard, Portsmouth, N.H.
The Squalus was:
reconstructed when on 23 May 1939 she was
raised in the Isles of Shoals off New Hampshire.
26 men were lost in her diving mishap.
she was recommissioned Sailfish.
She served:
in the Pacific Area; sank the Japanese escort
carrier Chuyo.

STAR OF INDIA   (Merchantman)
Enshrined at Maritime Museum Association of San
Diego, San Diego, California.
The Star of India is:
an iron hulled windjammer, built as a square-
rigger, was built on the Clyde River, Scotland,
to carry a crew of 16.
She served:
Several years in the Indian trade;
became an emigrant ship; sailing to New Zealand
and Australia.   Originally named Euterpe, as a
British ship.
After flying the Hawaiian flag, she became an
American ship in an Alaska packer's fleet.
In 1926 she was towed to San Diego; restored.

SUSAN CONSTANT   (Ship)
Replicas of the three full-rigged ships, Susan Constant,
Godspeed and Discovery may be seen moored at Cen-
tennial Park, Jamestown, Virginia.
The Susan Constant was:
with the other ships, built in West Norfolk, Virginia, in 1956.
She served:
the original three ships brought the first permanent
English settlers to America at Jamestown, Virginia, in 1607.   They brought wheat seed, barley
oats; beer and wine.   See also under Part II,
DISCOVERY; GODSPEED; SUSAN CONSTANT.

SUWANEE   (Steamboat)
This replica of the paddlewheel boat may be seen at
Greenfield Village, Dearborn, Michigan.
The Suwanee was:
an 1880 steamboat which in 1920 sank on Lake

Okechobee, Florida. The engines were raised;
installed in the replica.
She serves:
as a pleasure boat.

SWORDFISH (Submarine)
A torpedo from this submarine is displayed in St. Paul,
Minnesota.
This ship served:
in the Pacific Area during World War II. It was
lost off Okinawa, January 1945.
she sunk a dozen Japanese supply ships.

TANG (Submarine)
Enshrined at the Submarine Memorial, Submarine Base,
Pearl Harbor, Hawaii. One of 52 submarines lost
during World War II.

TARAWA (Aircraft Carrier)
Relics of this carrier are to be seen at Hartford, Conn.
The Tarawa was adopted by Connecticut as the state's
ship in 1951.

TAWAH see ELFIN; KEY WEST

TECUMSEH, U.S.S. (Ironclad)
The bronze deck ventilator recovered in July 1967 has
been preserved, and is on display at Mobile Bay. The
ironclad has been located and identified in Mobile Bay
where she sank during the Civil War.
She served:
in the Civil War at the Battle of Mobile Bay with
Captain T. A. M. Craven as commander. She
fired the first shot of the battle. Less than a
hour later, she struck a mine, sank on 5 August
1864. Craven and almost all of the crew were
lost. See also under Part II, ADMIRAL.

TEXAS, U.S.S. (Battleship)
is on exhibit, permanently berthed, off Houston Ship
Channel, Houston, Texas.
The Texas was:
commissioned at Norfolk, 1914.
April 1944 was assigned to the invasion forces;
took part in assault on Cherbourg, June 22, 1944.
She served:
in two World Wars.

in Mexican waters to uphold America's rights
against the brutality of General Victoriano Huerto.
joined the task force 1 September 1939, helping
land troops in North Africa.
bombarded munition dumps.
in World War II bombarded Iwo Jima and Okinawa
in the Pacific Area.
joined on Magic Carpet duty after the surrender
of Japan.
in 1948 voyaged from Norfolk to Galveston, Texas.
she sank 38,767 tons of enemy shipping.

TICONDEROGA, U.S.S.   (Schooner)
This side-wheeler gradually deteriorated and then sank
in the East Bay where she was moored.   Then she was
raised in 1958; remains are seen near Skenesborough
Museum, Shelburne, Vt.
The Ticonderoga was:
    built, fitted out on Lake Champlain.
    laid up in 1815.
    sold at Whitehall, N.Y., 19 July 1825.
She served:
    with the Flotilla of Commodore Macdonough,
    which defeated and captured the British Fleet and
    so controlled the lake.   The British withdrew.

TRIGGER   (Submarine)
Enshrined at Submarine Memorial, Submarine Base,
Pearl Harbor, Hawaii.   One of the 52 submarines lost
during World War II.

TRITON   (Submarine)
Enshrined at Submarine Memorial, Submarine Base,
Pearl Harbor, Hawaii.   One of the 52 submarines lost
during World War II.

TROUT, U.S.S.   (Submarine)
Memorial to this submarine is alongside the Cape Cod
Canal not far from Bournedale, Mass.
The Trout was:
    a submarine of Massachusetts, lost in action 29
    February 1944.
She served:
    Took gold and securities from Corregidor,
    January 1942; after having taken ammunition to
    supply defense.

Sank a dozen Japanese ships.
She earned:
The Presidential Unit Citation.

TULLIBEE   (Submarine)
Enshrined at Submarine Memorial, Submarine Base,
Pearl Harbor, Hawaii.   One of 52 submarines lost
during World War II.

U-505   (German U-Boat)
is exhibited on dry land outside the Museum of Science
and Industry on the lake front at Lake Shore Drive and
E. 57th St., Chicago, Illinois.
She served:
Off Cape Blanco, France, West Africa in 1944,
where she was captured 4 June by Admiral D. V.
Gallery's Task Force.
The U-505 was towed from Portsmouth, New
Hampshire, to Chicago, then overland.

UTAH, U.S.S.   (Battleship)
The bell is displayed in Salt Lake City at the Utah
Historical Society.   Another bell is found at Naval
Supply Depot, Clearfield, Utah.
She served:
in the Vera Cruz Expedition when it was organized.
V. Huerta seized the Mexican presidency in 1913.
The U.S. refused to recognize him.   Some U.S.
marines were arrested at Tampico when it was
under martial law.   They were soon released, but
President Woodrow Wilson asked for a 21-gun
salute to the Stars and Stripes which was not
forthcoming.   Therefore troops landed 21 April
1914 and with bombardment, the city was taken.
she was on Atlantic convoy duty in World War I.
transferred to a mobile target; anti-aircraft
training ship in 1931.
served over 30 years.
wrecked at Pearl Harbor, where part of her can
be seen.

VIRGINIA, C.S.S.   (Ironclad)
This ship's bell is to be seen at the Museum of the
Confederacy, Richmond, Virginia.   See also MONITOR-
MERRIMAC.

W. P. SNYDER   (Steamboat)
Enshrined at the River Museum of the Campus Martius
State Memorial at Marietta, Ohio.
The W. P. Snyder was:
a sternwheel towboat that was a coal carrier.

WAHOO, U.S.S.   (Submarine)
A plaque on a torpedo is displayed in the court-house
yard at Wahoo, Nebraska.
She served:
in seven patrols; sank 20 Japanese vessels.
active a little more than a year.
She earned:
the Presidential Unit Citation.

WAPAMA   (Schooner)
is enshrined at San Francisco Maritime State Historic
Park, San Francisco, California.
The Wapama was:
a wooden steam schooner to replace the sailing
lumber schooners of the Pacific coast.
built in 1915 in St. Helens, Oregon.
launched 19 January 1915 by Charles R. McCor-
mick Lumber Co.
She served:
carried lumber and passengers between California ports and Pacific Northwest.
carried nearly one million board feet of lumber.
sold to the White Flyer Line and transported
freight and passengers between San Francisco and
Southern California ports.
worked for Alaska Transportation Company, plying
between Puget Sound and Alaskan ports, until
1947. Laid up, sold for scrap in 1947. But she
was not scrapped and the State of California
bought her in 1957.

WASHINGTON, U.S.S.   (Battleship)
Bell, wheel are exhibited in the State Capital, Olympia,
Washington.
The Washington was:
commissioned May 1941.
She served:
Murmansk to Okinawa in the Pacific area;
sank the Kirishima, the Japanese battleship.
It is said of her, "the ship that was always
there."

she earned:
13 battle stars for World War II service.

WAVERTREE   (Ship)
The hull of this rigged ship is displayed at South Street
Seaport Museum, 16 Fulton St., N.Y.C.

WAWONA   (Schooner)
Restoration is being undergone at Seattle, Washington.
She was:
a three-masted schooner.
She served:
carrying redwood lumber to San Francisco.

WELCOME   (Ship)
A replica of William Penn's vessel will be displayed on
the waterfront at Philadelphia, Pa.

WEST VIRGINIA, U.S.S.   (Super-Dreadnaught)
Mast is on display at Morgantown at the University of
West Virginia.   Flagstaff is on Main Street side of
court-house yard at Clarksburg, West Virginia.
The West Virginia was:
commissioned in December 1923.
She served:
in the Pacific Area.
she was sunk at Pearl Harbor; raised 30 May
1942; went back to the Pacific War in October
1944.
She earned:
5 battle stars.

WHITE PLAINS, U.S.S.   (Cruiser)
Bell, flag enshrined at White Plains, Westchester
County, New York.
The White Plains was:
christened November 1943 at Vancouver, Washing-
ton.
She earned:
5 battle stars in World War II service.
Philippines Republic and Presidential Unit Cita-
tions.

I must go down to the seas again to the vagrant
  gypsy life,
To the gull's way and the whale's way where the
  wind's like a whetted knife;
And all I ask is a merry yarn from a laughing
  fellow-rover,
And quiet sleep and a sweet dream when the long
  trick's over.

"Sea Fever"
last stanza

SOURCES

Abbott, Carlisle S.
    Recollections of a California Pioneer. New York:
    Neale Publishing Co., c1917.

Adams, James T.
    Dictionary of American Biography. New York: Scrib-
    ner, 1944. 6 vols.

Adams, Samuel Hopkins
    The Erie Canal. New York: Random House, c1953.

Albion, Robert Greenhalgh
    Square-Riggers on Schedule. Princeton, N.J.:
    Princeton University Press, 1938.

Arthur, William
    An Etymological Dictionary of Family and Christian
    Names. Sheldon, Blakeman & Co., 1857.

Baldwin, Leland D.
    The Keelboat Age on Western Waters. Pittsburgh:
    University of Pittsburgh, c1941.

Bancroft, Hubert Howe
    Works of Hubert Howe Bancroft. University of Cali-
    fornia Press, vol. 2, 1801-1824.

Bauer, Helen
    Hawaii: The Aloha State. New York: Doubleday,
    1960.

Best, Gerald M.
    Ships and Narrow Gauge Rails: Story of the Pacific
    Coast Company. Berkeley, Calif.: Howell-North, 1964.

The Bible.

Brown, Giles T.
Ships That Sail no More; Marine Transportation from
San Diego to Puget Sound, 1910-1940. Lexington,
Ky.: University of Kentucky Press, 1966.

Buehr, Walter
Ships of the Great Lakes. New York: Putnam, c1956.

Campbell, Marjorie Wilkins
The Saskatchewan. (Rivers of America.) New York:
Rinehart, c1950.

Canby, Henry Seidel
The Brandywine. New York: Farrar & Rinehart,
1941.

Carmer, Carl
The Hudson. New York: Farrar & Rinehart, c1939.

Carruth, Gorlon & Associates
Encyclopedia of American Facts and Dates. 3rd ed.
New York: Crowell, c1962.

Carter, Hodding
Lower Mississippi. New York: Farrar & Rinehart,
c1942.

Catlin, George
North American Indians. 2 vols. Philadelphia:
Leary, Stuart and Co., c1913.

Chapman, Charles E.
History of California: Spanish Period. New York:
Macmillan, c1921.

Chase, Mary Ellen
Donald McKay and the Clipper Ships. Boston:
Houghton Mifflin, c1959.

Christensen, Jack Shields, comp., pub.
(co-ed. by F. K. Meinecke). Instant Hawaiian.
Kalakaua, Hon. District of Pacific Film Corp., c1967.

Chu, Daniel and Samuel Chu
Passage to the Golden Gate. New York: Doubleday,
c1967.

Church, Albert Cook
Whale Ships and Whaling. New York: Norton, c1938.

Clark, Arthur H.
The Clipper Ship Era, 1843-1869. New York: Putnam, c1920.

Clark, J. G.
Lights and Shadows of Sailor Life. Boston, c1848.

Clark, Sydney
All the Best in Hawaii. New York: Dodd, Mead, c1961.

Cleland, Robert Glass
From Wilderness to Empire: A History of California, 1542-1900. New York: Knopf, c1944.

Cleveland, Richard J.
In the Forecastle; or, 25 Years a Sailor. New York: Hurst and Co., [n.d.].

Coffin, Robert P. Tristram
Kennebec: Cradle of Americans. New York: Farrar & Rinehart, c1937.

Colum, Padraic
Legends of Hawaii. New Haven, Conn.: Yale University Press, c1937.

Compere, Tom, ed.
The Navy Blue Book. New York: Military Publishing Institute, c1960.

Concise Dictionary of American History.
New York: Scribners, c1962.

Cosgrave, J. O'H. II
America Sails the Seas. Boston: Houghton Mifflin, c1962.

Culver, Henry B.
Book of Old Ships. Garden City, New York, c1924.

Cutler, Carl C.
500 Sailing Records of American Built Ships. Marine Historical Assoc., March 1952.

Cutler, Carl C.
    Greyhounds of the Sea: The Story of the American
    Clipper Ship. U.S. Naval Institute, c1930.

Cutler, Carl C.
    Queens of the Western Ocean; Story of America's
    Mail and Passenger Sailing Lines. Maryland, U.S.
    Naval Institute, c1961.

Dana, Julian
    The Sacramento. New York: Rinehart, c1939.

Davis, Clyde Brion
    The Arkansas. New York: Farrar & Rinehart,
    c1940.

Davis, Julia
    The Shenandoah. New York: Farrar & Rinehart,
    c1945.

de Borhegyi, Suzanne
    Ships, Shoals and Amphoras. New York: Holt,
    Rinehart and Winston, c1961.

Dillon, Richard H.
    Embarcadero. New York: Coward McCann, c1959.

Donovan, Frank
    River Boats of America. New York: Crowell, c1966.

Eldredge, Zoeth Skinner
    History of California. New York: Century History
    Co., [n.d.].

Emmons, Lieut. George F.
    The Navy of the U.S. from the Commencement 1775
    to 1853; with a Brief History of Each Vessel's Service
    and Fate as Appears on Record.... Washington,
    printed by Gideon & Co., 1853.

Fairburn, William Armstrong
    Merchant Sail. 6 vols. Maine, Fairburn Marine
    Educational Foundation, c1945-1955.

Flexner, James Thomas
    Steamboats Come True. New York: Viking, c1944.

Frere-Cook, Gervis, ed.
    The Decorative Arts of the Mariner. New York:
    Little Brown, c1966.

Friel, Kent
    Hawaii: Its Physical Aspects and Science Experiences.
    New York: Fearon Pub., c1960.

Gibbs, James A.
    Shipwrecks of the Pacific Coast. Oregon: Binfords
    and Morts, c1962.

Gray, James
    The Illinois. New York: Rinehart, c1940.

Guerber, H. A.
    Myths of Northern Lands. New York: American Book
    Co., c1895.

Havighurst, Walter
    Upper Mississippi. New York: Farrar & Rinehart,
    c1937.

Havighurst, Walter
    Voices of the River. New York: Macmillan, c1964.

The Hawaii Book. Pub. by J. G. Ferguson Publishing Co.
    [n.d.].

Here's Hawaii. Honolulu: Tongg Pub. Co. [n.d.].

Hillinger, Charles
    The California Islands. Los Angeles, Calif.:
    Academy Publishers, c1958.

Hinkle, George and Bliss
    Sierra-Nevada Lakes. New York: Bobbs-Merrill,
    c1949.

Historic Ship Exhibits in U.S.
    Washington, D.C.: Naval History Division, c1969.

Hittell, Theodore H.
  History of California, 1885-97. 4 vols. San Francisco: N.J. Stone & Co., c1898.

Hittell, Theodore H.
  El Triunfo de la Cruz ... (California Historical Society Special Collection #38). San Francisco: California Historical Society, 1963.

Holbrook, Stewart H.
  The Columbia. New York: Rinehart and Co., c1956.

Horgan, Paul
  Great River; The Rio Grande. New York: Holt, Rinehart, Winston, c1954.

Hults, Dorothy Niebrugge
  New Amsterdam Days and Ways. New York: Harcourt, c1963.

Hurd, Edith T.
  Sailors, Whalers and Steamers. Menlo Park, Calif.: Lane Book Co. [n.d.].

Jennings, John
  Clipper Ship Days. New York: Random, c1952.

Judd, Henry P.
  Hawaiian Language: Complete Grammar. Hon. Hawaiian Service. [n.d.].

Karraker, Cyrus H.
  Piracy was a Business. New Hampshire, Richard R. Smith, publisher, c1953.

Kirkwood, G. M.
  A Short Guide to Classical Mythology. New York: Rinehart, Inc., c1959.

Kroeber, A. L.
  Handbook of the Indians of California. Berkeley: California Book Co., c1953.

La Grange, Jacques
Clipper Ships of America and Great Britain, 1833-1869. New York: Putnam, c1936.

Laing, Alexander
Clipper Ships and Their Makers. New York: Putnam, c1966.

Lambert, R. A.
The World's Most Daring Explorers. New York: Sterling Pub. Co., c1956.

Lubbock, Basil
Romance of the Clipper Ships. Locke, c1949.

McKenney, Thomas L. and James Hall
The Indian Tribes of North America. 3 vols. Edinburgh: John Grant, c1933.

MacMullen, Jerry
Paddle Wheel Days in California. Palo Alto, Cal.: Stanford University Press, c1944.

MacMullen, Jerry
They Came by Sea; Pictorial History of San Diego Bay, c1969. Los Angeles: W. Ritchie Press, c1969.

Matschat, Cecile Hulse
Swannee River; Strange Green Land. New York: Literary Guild, c1939.

Mellen, K. D.
In a Hawaiian Valley. New York: Hastings House [n.d.].

Meyers, William H.
Naval Sketches of the War in California.... New York: Random House, c1939.

Mills, Randall V.
Stern Wheelers up the Columbia. Pacific Books, c1947.

Minter, John Easter
The Chagres: River of Westward Passage. New York: Rinehart, c1948.

Morison, Samuel Eliot
    Builders of the Bay Colony. Boston: Houghton Mifflin, c1930.

Morison, Samuel Eliot
    The Maritime History of Massachusetts, 1783-1860. Boston: Houghton Mifflin, c1921.

Morison, Samuel Eliot
    Story of the "Old Colony" of New Plymouth, 1620-1692. New York: Alfred A. Knopf, 1956.

Naval History Division, Navy Department
    Dictionary of American Naval Fighting Ships. 5 vols. Washington, D.C.: Navy Dept. Office of Chief of Naval Operations, Naval History Division, 1969. illus. (v. 6 in preparation-Q-Z).

Niles, Blair
    The James. New York: Farrar & Rinehart, c1939.

Norton, Dan S. and Peters, Rushton
    Classical Myths in English Literature. New York: Holt, Rinehart and Winston, Inc., c1952.

Osbun, Albert G.
    To California and the South Seas; Diary of Albert G. Osbun, 1849-1851. San Marino, Cal.: Huntington Library, c1966.

Paine, Ralph D.
    The Old Merchant Marine: A Chronicle of American Ships and Sailors. New Haven, Conn.: Yale University Press, c1919.

A Pocket Guide to Hawaii
    Office of Armed Forces Information and Education, Department of Defense. Washington, D.C.: Department of Defense, [n.d.].

Pratt, Fletcher
    Civil War in Pictures. New York: Garden City Books, c1955.

Pratt, Fletcher and Hartley E. Howe
The Compact History of the U.S. Navy. New York:
Hawthorn Books, 1957, 61, 62.

Pratt, Helen Gay
The Hawaiians. New York: Scribner, c1941.

Quadflieg, Josef
The Saints and Your Name. New York: Pantheon,
1957.

Robinson, Gregory
Ships That Have Made History. New York: Halcyon
Press, c1936.

Rockwell, Mable M.
California's Sea Frontier. Santa Barbara, Calif.:
McNally & Loftin, c1962.

Rowe, William Hutchinson
The Maritime History of Maine. New York: Norton,
c1948.

Sanchez, Nellie Van de Grift
Spanish and Indian Names of California. A. M.
Robertson, c1914.

Savage, Henry
The Santee. New York: Rinehart, c1956.

Scott, J. M.
The Great Tea Venture. New York: Dutton, 1965.

Smythe, William E.
History of San Diego, 1542-1908. v. 1. San Diego:
History Company, 1908.

Stewart, George R.
Names on the Land; An Historical Account of Place-
Names in the U.S. Boston: Houghton Mifflin, 1958.

Stoutenburgh, John L., Jr.
Dictionary of the American Indian. New York:
Philosophical Library, 1960.

Strong, Charles C.
   Story of American Sailing Ships. New York: Grosset, 1957.

U.S. Naval Institute
   The Blue Jackets' Manual. Annapolis, Md.: U.S. Naval Institute, c1963.

Vestal, Stanley
   The Missouri. New York: Farrar & Rinehart, c1945.

Wagner, Henry R.
   The First American Vessel in California: Monterey in 1796. Los Angeles: G. Dawson, 1954. (Early California travel series, 20.)

Waters, Frank
   The Colorado. New York: Rinehart, c1946.

Wildes, Harry Emerson
   The Delaware. New York: Farrar & Rinehart, c1940.

Wilson, William E.
   The Wabash. New York: Farrar & Rinehart, c1940.

Wood, James Playsted
   Colonial Massachusetts. New York: Nelson, c1969.